COIN-OPERATED
AMERICANS

CARLY A. KOCUREK

COIN-OPERATED AMERICANS

REBOOTING BOYHOOD
AT THE VIDEO GAME ARCADE

UNIVERSITY OF MINNESOTA PRESS

MINNEAPOLIS • LONDON

An earlier version of chapter 1 was published as "Coin-Drop Capitalism: Economic Lessons from the Video Game Arcade," in *Before the Crash: Early Video Game History* (Detroit: Wayne State University Press, 2012). An earlier version of chapter 3 was published as "The Agony and the Exidy: A History of Video Game Violence and the Legacy of *Death Race*," *Game Studies* 12, no. 1 (September 2012).

Published by the University of Minnesota Press
111 Third Avenue South, Suite 290
Minneapolis, MN 55401-2520
http://www.upress.umn.edu

Library of Congress Cataloging-in-Publication Data

Kocurek, Carly A.
Coin-operated Americans : rebooting boyhood at the video game arcade / Carly A. Kocurek.
Includes bibliographical references and index.
ISBN 978-0-8166-9183-8 (pb)—ISBN 978-0-8166-9182-1 (hc)
1. Video games—United States—History. 2. Video games—Social aspects—United States. 3. Coin-operated machines—United States—History. I. Title.
GV1469.3.K6 2015
794.8—dc23   2015019104

Printed in the United States of America on acid-free paper

The University of Minnesota is an equal-opportunity educator and employer.

20 19 18 17 16 15   10 9 8 7 6 5 4 3 2 1

CONTENTS

A C K ∏ O Ш L E D G ጠ E ∏ T S

ON A WEEKDAY AFTERNOON IN 2007, I took myself to the movies, alone. I wanted to take a break from work for a couple of hours, and I had the time, so I drove to the nearby movie theater, with no particular plan. I wound up watching *The King of Kong: Fistful of Quarters*, primarily because I had seen almost everything else showing, and it seemed interesting enough. I had begun to study video gaming research and news at the suggestion of one of my advisers several months earlier, but that afternoon in the theater more directly set my course. *The King of Kong* follows the efforts of Steve Wiebe to achieve the world record score for *Donkey Kong* (Nintendo, 1981). The documentary features interviews with notable gamers and traces a history of gaming world records that dates back to the video game arcade's glory days in the early 1980s.

That lineage fascinated me, especially as the documentary presented a now-iconic photograph of the best gamers in the world, taken in 1982 in Ottumwa, Iowa. I had turned to video games looking for a topic that might combine my interests in technology, gender, and popular culture, and was to some extent overwhelmed with

options. I ultimately found my subject that afternoon in the theater.
For the next few weeks, I researched everything I could about that
image (which I discuss at length in chapter 2). I then began working
on a larger history, not just of that legendary photograph but of the
cultural history of the arcade. That project became my dissertation.
This book began as a dissertation but is now the culmination of six
years of research into the early rise and fall of the video game arcade.

It is also the culmination of years of support, encouragement, and
mentoring from a number of individuals and institutions, and I'd be
remiss if I didn't try to thank at least some of them. First and foremost, I am grateful to my adviser from the Department of American
Studies at the University of Texas, Elizabeth S. D. Engelhardt (now
the John Shelton Reed Distinguished Professor of Southern Studies
at the University of North Carolina), and to the other department
faculty, especially Janet M. Davis and Mark C. Smith. Thanks also
to my peers and classmates from the University of Texas as well as
to my colleagues from the Learning Games Initiative, especially Jennifer deWinter, Chris Hanson, Ken S. McAllister, Matthew Thomas
Payne, Judd Ruggill, and Stephanie Vie. My colleagues at the Illinois
Institute of Technology have been a source of provocation, inspiration, and encouragement; special thanks to Margaret Power, who
goes above and beyond in her role as official department mentor to
junior faculty.

Financially, this book was made possible by an A. D. Hutchinson
Endowed Fellowship from the University of Texas at Austin, a
Strong Research Fellowship from the Strong Museum of Play's
Brian Sutton-Smith Library and Archives of Play, and research funding from the Illinois Institute of Technology. My thanks go to the
librarians and archivists at the Harold Washington Library Center of
the Chicago Public Library, the United States Library of Congress,
and the Brian Sutton-Smith Library and Archives of Play, who facilitated access to materials and often turned up sources I would not
have thought to look for. I am sincerely grateful to everyone who
sat down with me for an interview; each oral history is a rich archive
in and of itself. Special thanks, too, to the editors and staff at the
University of Minnesota Press and to the readers who offered review
comments throughout the process; this book is better for the work
of every person who touched it.

Thanks to my parents, Betty Kutchera and Joe Kocurek, and to my late grandmother, Elinor Kutchera, a ruthless but patient card player who first taught me to love games. They all supported me with the kind of unwavering faith that is hard to find outside family. I owe special thanks to Jill Caporale, Sean Cashbaugh, John Cline, Laurie Hahn Ganser, Melanie Haupt, Melissa Hoepfner, Adriana E. Ramirez, Xochil Rodriguez, Amanda Stilwell, and Allyson Whipple, friends who prove that sometimes you get to choose family members, too. Finally, thanks to Trent Johnson: there's nobody I'd rather go to the arcade with, and not just because he gives me all his Skee-Ball tickets.

Iptroouctiop

ON CHRISTMAS EVE 1989, my family tore into our gifts like we do every year. From the mountain of wrapping paper and tissue, I unearthed a Game Boy. It was a banner year for Christmas gifts. That Game Boy was the first new game system to enter our house, and it was a significant step up from the battered Atari 2600 we had inherited from a family friend a few years earlier. Starting that night, for roughly the next ten years, I played *Tetris* (Nintendo, 1989) constantly. I played *Tetris* after school and before bed. I played *Tetris* in the car while my mother ran errands. I played *Tetris* when I couldn't sleep and to occupy myself during family vacations. If I hadn't been so deeply committed to the proper care and keeping of the Game Boy, I probably would have played *Tetris* in the bath. During the same time, I regularly played games on the Nintendo Entertainment System and Super Nintendo Entertainment Systems at friends' houses. We played games like *The Legend of Zelda* (Nintendo, 1986) and *Super Mario Bros.* (Nintendo, 1985) with a steadfast devotion, talking strategy and eating popcorn while we waited for the games to boot. The point of this anecdote is less the importance of Nintendo for my childhood experience of gaming (although Nintendo ranks high on my personal nostalgic hit list) than the context for the fact that by the time we hit junior high, my friends and I had all more or less stopped playing video games entirely.

There are several possible explanations for this, including the rising cost of consoles in mostly working-class households and our increased focus on other hobbies like competitive horseback riding, photography, and guitar, but none fully explains the shift; after all, our male peers and our older and younger brothers often went through console after console as new models were rolled out. In retrospect, I believe that my friends and I had absorbed the message that video games were not for us. While Atari, Nintendo, and other console makers had initially advertised games as an inclusive social or family activity, game companies increasingly targeted male consumers—a practice at the time justified by research indicating most consumers were young men. In the mid-1990s, women and girls were just a fraction of game consumers; by 1998 male consumers accounted for 75 to 85 percent of video game sales.[1] My own drift away from an enthusiastic embrace of video games is not an isolated incident but reflective of a broader cultural issue.

The alienation of girls and women in video gaming has been a hot topic for several years. During the mid- to late 1990s, game designers and researchers both began looking at the absence of women and girls in video gaming culture as a significant problem. Not only did the gendering of gaming limit the marketplace for game companies' products, it also continues to have troubling implications for women's participation in an emerging digital culture. Video games can serve as early exposure to computer technology—an important factor amid ongoing concern about women's underrepresentation in technical fields. They also have emerged as a major cultural form, and the active marginalization of girls and women from such a key cultural arena is troubling.

In *From Barbie to Mortal Kombat,* Justine Cassells and Henry Jenkins present a series of essays that trouble the waters of women's and girls' positions at the margins of both gaming culture and the video game industry. These essays also explore what was, at the time, a growing interest in producing games specifically for girls and young women. The "games for girls" movement, as it came to be called, produced a slew of games of varying quality. *Chop Suey* (Magnet Interactive Studios, 1995) by Theresa Duncan gained honors as *Entertainment Weekly*'s 1995 "CD-ROM of the year." Brenda Laurel's software studio, Purple Moon, released a handful of successful titles before being bought out by the toy giant Mattel, which also had its hand in the production of games targeting girls. But even the most successful of these games, like *Chop Suey,* are little remembered, and in many cases were difficult, if not impossible, to find within months of their releases. This dismissal of "games for girls" reflects the dismissal of girls as gamers.

Researchers of gender and video gaming have often focused on women's exclusion from gaming culture. This research has drawn from efforts across disciplines and identified some of the key issues driving the ongoing difficulties in reshaping video gaming—problems that persist even as women have come to represent an increasingly dominant sector of game consumers. While I, too, am interested in the marginalization of women and girls in gaming culture, in this project I take a different approach. In this book, rather than study the *exclusion* of women and girls, I focus on the *inclusion* of men and boys. In my research, I departed from a simple question: When, and how, did video gaming come to be seen as the exclusive domain of young men?

To answer this question, I turn to the early commercial development of video gaming and the initial development of gaming culture. The gendering of gaming started long before it became a public concern in the 1990s, but there was nothing natural about this process. Rather, it resulted from a constellation of factors: the greater relative freedom of young boys to move through and participate in public culture; the alignment of computer and video game technologies with both military interests and competitive male-dominated sports; the subsequent affiliation of video gaming with violent thematic content; and the ongoing association of technological skill with masculinity. As the video gaming industry exploded in the United States during the 1970s and early 1980s, the medium became a point of articulation for anxieties surrounding broader cultural and economic changes. In particular, the medium ushered in heightened concerns about the state of American young men, who were coming of age in an era of rapid computerization and increased economic insecurity.

Discussion of video gaming and video gamers often organized around and reflected concerns about the state of young manhood in the United States. The video gamer emerged both as a type of young man in need of guidance and as a character type readily deployed in popular culture; he became a site of contentious discussion about what boyhood can and should mean in the United States.

In this book, I excavate the development of the "video gamer" as a cultural identity during video gaming's first decade. This so-called golden era of video games stretched from the successful launch of *Pong* (Atari, 1972) to the industry-wide crash that began in 1983. During the crash, the industry contracted from $3 billion in sales in late 1982 to roughly $100 million in sales in 1985. In the interim between *Pong* and the plummet in sales, video gaming became widespread and the video gamer became a figure of wide cultural fascination, as evidenced not only by popular press coverage in outlets such as *Time, Life* magazine, and *Newsweek* but by the production of Hollywood films like *TRON* and *WarGames*.

Understanding the development of gaming culture and gamer identity during this period is critical to understanding the cultural politics of contemporary gaming. While recent data indicate women now make up nearly half of all gamers, women and girls remain marginalized in gaming culture at a number of levels.[2] This marginalization—which is evidenced not only by the underrepresentation of women among game developers but by widespread sexism in gaming communities and by the hypersexualized representation of women in popular games—is not an ahistorical fact. Early games were marketed as generally appealing bar amusements as in the *Gotcha* (Atari, 1973) advertisement shown in Figure 1, and at least some games attracted women players. Atari cofounder Nolan Bushnell claims, for example, that half the coin-drop on *Pong* came from women.[3] But by the 1980s, games had become associated with boyhood and male adolescence. How and why this transition occurred is the central question of this volume.

The history presented here is a case study of how an entire emergent medium became the presumed enclave of boys and young men. It discusses the impact of popular media representations and perceptions in shaping and limiting a growing cultural phenomenon, illustrating contributing factors while making a critical intervention into

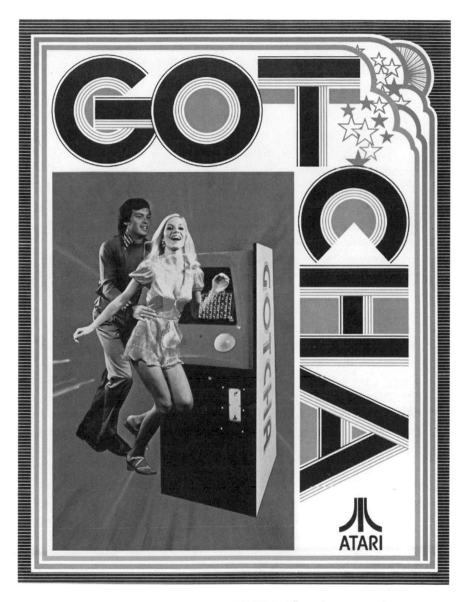

FIGURE 1. A flyer advertising *Gotcha* (Atari, 1973) highlights the game's appeal to both men and women.

an existing debate that too frequently assumes that gaming's current fraught relationship with gender is static rather than historically linked and dynamic. It uses this history as a key incident in the development of gaming, showing potential connections with and lessons for contemporary gaming culture. As the gaming industry and educational institutions work to address gender inequity in technically oriented professional fields, understanding of this critical period is essential.

This book operates at multiple levels by engaging with the historical development of the video game industry from 1972 to 1985 while focusing on the mediation and representation of gaming. It does not merely chart the rise and fall of a now booming industry but interrogates factors and incidents that contributed to the widespread view of video gaming as a medium for young men and boys. Drawing from diverse archival sources alongside popular films and television programs and original oral history interviews, the book both examines the most highly visible representations of gamers and gaming and places them in their historical context. The book shows how representations of gaming contributed to perceptions of gamers as young men and ensured that the most celebrated aspects of video gaming—individualized competition and technological competency—were those aspects most likely to be perceived as masculine.

Gender inequalities in video gaming did not develop during the industry's postcrash resurrection or with the rise of home consoles; rather, these historical inequalities emerged through public discourse and public practice that accompanied the rise of video gaming's early commercial success in the coin-op industry. The precrash period in gaming is foundational and worthy of careful consideration. Indeed, the early years of video gaming have much to teach us about the development of gaming as public culture. While this period in gaming's development has spawned numerous popular histories and several documentaries and has become a frequent site of video gaming nostalgia, there has been little academic work on the subject; the history of video gaming as a whole is an emergent field, although both a growing body of work from scholars and the recent First International Conference on the History of the Video Game, held in Montreal in 2013, demonstrate an increase in scholarly concern. As a contribution to this emerging body of historical work, this book is an inquiry into the development of the "gamer" as a figure in popular imagination and argues strongly for the significance and continued influence of this important period in video game history.

This book explores gaming culture along two major threads: the rise and fall of the early coin-op video game industry, and the consolidation of gamer identity as it came to be allied with an idealized vision of youth, masculinity, violence, and digital technology—a clustering of ideas that I refer to as the technomasculine. An understanding of this early video gaming's cultural history is essential to making sense of modern gaming culture. To demonstrate the cultural significance of this period, I examine gaming culture and the cultivation of gamer identity through popular press coverage, narrative media, trade journals, first-person accounts collected through oral histories, and even the marketing and advertising of the games themselves. These sources illuminate how early representations and discussions of video gaming shaped early gaming culture, which in turn continues to shape and restrict contemporary gaming culture.

The chapters are organized to provide a clear overview of critical moments in early gaming culture. The book starts by positioning the video game arcade—and by extension, the video game arcade gamer—in a milieu of cultural, political, and economic upheaval. This backdrop informed discussion of games and formed the foundation for many of the anxieties projected onto games and gamers. From here, the book examines specific incidents in early arcade game history, beginning with the industry's first significant moral panic and moving through other high-profile incidents and trends. The narrative propels the reader through the gradual reforming and narrowing of video gaming, from the early marketing of uprights as broadly appealing devices to the celebration and glamorization of gamers as the next generation of "bright young men" by the early 1980s, explaining how these changes corralled the potentially disruptive technology of the video game and helped forge contemporary conceptions of the gamer as cultural archetype.

THE MICROCOSMIC ARCADE

This first chapter offers a phenomenological tour of the arcade, drawn from oral history interviews, photographs, magazine and newspaper articles, and observations of arcades and individual coin-op video game machines. In reconstructing the arcade as an immersive environment, I consider the economic, competitive, and gaming behaviors embedded in the arcade machines and in the broader context of the arcade. More significantly, I consider the behaviors demanded by the arcade as a system, and the lessons embedded in the design of arcade games. The arcade itself is a key site, and this chapter establishes an essential framework for later chapters.

Throughout the chapter, I show that arcade games train players in gaming behaviors by rewarding them through points, game time, and the ability to access subsequent game levels, or by explicitly ranking them against other players on top scores lists. The economic principles of the arcade helped spark moral guardians' uneasiness with arcades in the 1970s and 1980s. This discomfort highlights how the video game arcade represented the emergence not only of the new technology of the computer but of a new credit-heavy, deindustrialized, service-based economy. While video games are frequently understood as simulations, the arcade itself can also be seen as a simulation of emergent economic values and practices that have persisted long past the eclipse of the arcade's zenith. The gamer becomes a source of anxiety because of his perceived ease in negotiation with the arcade, a space tied to disruptive, emergent cultural and economic values.

GAMING'S GOLD MEDALISTS

In chapter 2, I deconstruct the significance of the "world record culture" that permeated much media coverage of video gaming and shaped gaming practices. This chapter traces the history of the Twin Galaxies Arcade in Ottumwa, Iowa, which became the best-known keeper of gaming records. Its owner, Walter Day, attracted attention from *Life* magazine, which featured a photograph of some of the top scorers—all teen boys and young men—assembled on Main Street in Ottumwa in the 1982 "Year in Pictures" issue. As a result not only of Day's efforts but of a broader effort among coin-op industry professionals to demonstrate the respectability and value of gaming, competition became key to the dominant popular narrative of video gaming.

This development of gaming culture took place not in industrial hubs in Chicago and Silicon Valley but in local arcades spread across cities, suburbs, and even small towns like Ottumwa. The Twin Galaxies record holders featured in *Life* present a cohesive picture of gaming: young, male, technologically savvy, bright, and mischievous. Such images of gamers drew on both a long tradition celebrating the technological achievements of boys, dating at least to the early amateur radio culture of the Victorian era, and a national interest in the intellectual and physical fitness of America's youths. In both cases, members of the historically beleaguered coin-op industry benefited from and supported comparisons of young male gamers to athletes and technologists. Coin-op companies sponsored events to propagate this image, even hosting an event in which Olympic athletes competed at coin-op games.

Supported by industry and the popular press, the celebration, and even fetishization, of young male gamers helped establish an easily recognizable technomasculine archetype that is still frequently invoked in newspaper and magazine coverage of gaming. Subsequent chapters examine how this archetype of the gamer became tied to violence through popular depictions of gaming, as well as the deployment of this archetype in works of narrative fiction.

ADAPTING VIOLENCE: *DEATH RACE*

The establishment of violence as a key theme of video gaming has been integral to the construction of gaming as an arena of male cultural production and consumption, tying video gaming to other areas of culture historically dominated by men, such as military culture and sports competition. The first of two chapters on representations of video gaming as a medium linked to violence, chapter 3 examines video gaming's first moral panic, which erupted in response to Exidy's *Death Race* in 1976. The game's broader context, including the infamy of the *Death Race 2000* film, and the game's cabinet graphics, which feature drag racing ghouls wearing hoods, bolster the on-screen graphics and lend credence to the claim that the game is reveling in a smorgasbord of car-on-pedestrian violence. Moral guardians decried the game's perceived violence, and the game sparked a public debate about the propriety of video gaming for young children.

The public outcry over *Death Race* fueled sales of the game and established the Exidy brand-name. In the long run, the game set a template for future moral panics and for the process by which violent games create heavily mediated moral panics that fuel sales. This chapter identifies this particular historical incident as a critical moment when public rhetoric linked in-game violence with lived violent acts, even in the absence of evidence supporting such a connection; organizations such as the National Safety Council insisted, for example, that the game would inspire real-world actions of car violence, despite no evidence demonstrating this was or might be the case. Violence and video gaming have a persistent bond in popular perception, which means violent video games often stand in for video games more generally in public debates about the medium. By assessing the linkage of video gaming as a medium with violence, this chapter explains how popular culture can celebrate the achievements of gamers and the benefits of gaming while suggesting that gaming has a corrupting influence on culture and on players.

ANARCHY IN THE ARCADE

Numerous communities organized against arcades, fighting the opening of arcades through zoning ordinances, code enforcement, and other restrictions. Although in many cases these efforts reflect ongoing efforts to curtail the operations of the coin-op industry, which had long been associated, fairly or otherwise, with organized criminal activity, the industry saw a revival of animosity as video games increased in visibility. At the same time, the industry sought to use the appeal of video games to middle-class youth and the rise of "family fun centers" and other family-oriented outlets as a way to elevate the industry's image. The tension between these efforts provides insight into the perceived risks and values of video games as public entertainment.

Chapter 4 analyzes court cases, regional and local newspaper coverage, and coin-op industry trade journal coverage. Throughout, the chapter notes how the ills ascribed to video game arcades simultaneously reflect older anxieties about the coin-op industry and newer anxieties about technological, cultural, and economic changes happening at the national level. I argue that efforts to police video game access arise from debate about what activities should rightly be included as a part of childhood in general and boyhood in particular. Drawing from U.S. Supreme Court decisions on arcade restrictions, I argue that the arcade presents a critical moment in the configuration of youth civil rights as consumer civil rights.

PLAY SAVES THE DAY: *TRON* AND *WARGAMES*

Drawing from the discussion of technomasculine ideals and game violence from previous chapters, this chapter analyzes gaming-related Hollywood films that provide iconic examples of the deployment of technomasculinity in popular narratives: *TRON* and *WarGames*. Both films focus on the exploits of boyish gamer protagonists who display a sophisticated knowledge of computer technologies and a willingness to bend or break established rules to pursue their own ends. In both films, anxieties about video gaming and computer technologies are subsumed by celebratory narratives of sophisticated technological abilities and masculine dominance. Further, in both films, the characters' technological expertise and willingness to bend rules prevent significant disaster. The films' ongoing popularity speaks to their continued resonance, a resonance that Disney's 2010 *TRON* sequel, *TRON: Legacy,* demonstrates especially well.

The image of the technomasculine ideal had emerged early in journalistic coverage of video gaming, and these films reified the archetype while deploying it to a wide audience. Indeed, with the rise of powerful tech-business icons like Bill Gates, Steve Jobs, and Mark Zuckerberg, technomasculinity has become a dominant framework for narratives of successful tech-industry entrepreneurs. *TRON* and *WarGames* illuminate the historical context for this persistent narrative framework and the characteristics and ideologies embedded in it. In analyzing these films, I provide an important historical context for current discourse surrounding not only gamers but male technologies.

THE ARCADE IS DEAD, LONG LIVE THE ARCADE

This chapter considers how and why "classic" arcades have experienced a resurgence as an object of nostalgic desire. Classic arcade competitions reinscribe the centrality of competition in gaming culture while establishing an easily referenced canon of significant or especially beloved games. Lingering classic arcades, like Funspot in Weirs Beach in Laconia, New Hampshire, have become destinations in and of themselves. Newer businesses, like the Brooklyn-based Barcade chain of arcade-themed watering holes or Chicago's own bar-and-arcades like Emporium, rely on nostalgia for bygone arcades to attract business. I do not seek to provide a single unified explanation of the rise in arcade nostalgia but offer several potential explanations tied to the arcade's historical and cultural position.

I consider in particular the rise of nostalgia for the "golden era" arcade in the aftermath of the dot-com bubble burst of the early 2000s. The timing of this focus on the arcade boom of the past when a more recent boom in the tech industry has ended may indicate a longing for the seemingly boundless potential of an emergent economic sector. The perceived youthfulness of arcade amusements coupled with this may also indicate longings for leisure, childhood, and play. The wide diffusion of video games also raises the possibility that engagement with gaming's history through nostalgia is a way for gamers to authenticate gaming practices. Throughout this chapter, I examine potential interpretations of arcade nostalgia and consider the cultural implications of each as the arcade shifts in meaning depending on who is invoking it and why.

THE FUTURE IS NOW

In the final chapter, I consider shifts in gaming culture, including the growing prevalence of gaming in the United States. Increasingly, video gaming crosses demographic boundaries of age, race, and gender. With the emergence of the medium as a mainstream cultural form and major cultural industry, the stakes of the associated cultural politics have only risen. This chapter considers the ongoing tensions around the category of the gamer and the sometimes vitriolic debate over who rightly can claim to have a stake in gaming culture.

This chapter draws on recent events and trends, including the professionalization of competitive gaming, the persistence and resistance of women gamers who find themselves marginalized or harassed, and the increasingly visible work of video game critics. In closing, I argue that historicizing game culture is essential to understanding the current problems and potential promises of gaming as a medium. This chapter argues for the power and influence of gaming and for the importance of considering gaming not as a niche medium with an eccentric historical trajectory but as a major cultural form increasingly at the center of American culture.

By the mid-1980s the video game industry as a whole was in trouble. The market crash of 1983 significantly revamped the industry, and the move toward console systems meant that the arcade sector of the video game industry was faced with an especially acute kind of peril that was widely covered by the coin-op trade press, as indicated in Figure 2. By the late 1980s the number of video game arcades in the United States had plummeted. The end of the arcade craze was less the dismantling of video gaming than the integration of video gaming into the practices of daily life. In the aftermath of the crash, video gaming became more rather than less familiar, and even as arcades have dwindled, the rhetoric used to defend early gamers has persisted. Today, gamers are dismissed as nerds and geeks but also lauded for their technological acumen and problem-solving skills. The recent rise of the professional gaming circuit has been accompanied by increased efforts to reclaim gamers as "bright young men," as entrepreneurs, as creative thinkers, and even as athletes. This figuring of gamers through a masculinized rhetoric of success has continued and even intensified as gaming has spread across demographic boundaries.

The historical notion of gamer identity examined throughout the book continues to shape perceptions of gamers and serves as a touchstone in gaming's recent gender wars. This restrictive vision of who gaming is and should be for is used to justify the exclusion and harassment of women and other people who do not fit in, and to excuse the lack of diversity in the industry's workforce. These two arenas of homogeneity present a feedback loop. An industry of men imagines a consumer base that is like them and so makes games that reflect their own interests and experiences; with games serving as a point of entry into the industry, this production cycle helps maintain the status quo. If the industry and the culture of gaming are to change, this feedback loop must be disrupted. Changing the loop requires an understanding of how it is produced and where it originates. The mapping of origins concerns me here. Professional and industrial organizations and game program educators have a demonstrated interest in

FIGURE 2. The May 1, 1983, cover of coin-op trade publication *Play Meter* pokes fun at the decline of the video game industry and its impact on operators.

changing gaming culture, but if we are to change gaming culture to be more inclusive and less reactionary, we must understand how it developed in the first place. Historicizing popular perceptions of gamers and analyzing the cultural politics of these perceptions lay the groundwork for critical interventions into contemporary gaming culture.

The history of gaming is both a developing field and an ongoing project. It has rightfully included the efforts not only of professional historians but of preservation-minded game designers and other industry professionals, of collectors, of archivists, of players and fans. Perhaps no event has so demonstrated the broad coalition at work in building gaming history as the April 2014 "Atari Dig" in New Mexico. On April 25, 2014, I boarded a plane from Chicago bound for El Paso, Texas. There I rented a car and drove the roughly eighty-five miles to Alamogordo, New Mexico, home of the fabled Atari dump site in the desert. That evening, I met up with colleagues from the Learning Games Initiative and with Raiford Guins, an expert on e-waste and games, at a community party held in the parking lot of the local Game Stop. Hot dogs and sodas were distributed. Announcements were made. The local mayor was introduced. Children waited in line to play an authentic Atari *E.T.* (1982) cartridge. There were raffle tickets and prizes, young families and packs of teenagers. Camera crews loomed with boom mics, pulling aside various people, including, eventually, me, for short interviews. It was a small-town festival in miniature, with only one attraction. The next day, a crew would dig up the infamous dump.

Later that night, I went to the local Walmart. I bought bottled water, sunscreen, a cheap hat, and a pile of bandanas. I had been warned about the dust. I showed up early the next morning and joined a growing queue of spectators (see Figure 3). I found myself between a group of young men (college students from El Paso) and a family from a nearby New Mexico town. We chatted as we waited. The college students had brought a video camera, and the family had brought folding chairs. As the wait grew long, the parents sent their two sons to the nearby McDonald's to bring back sodas.

When we were finally admitted, we were given commemorative T-shirts and canteens and herded past the portable toilets to the designated viewing area behind an orange plastic fence. As the

FIGURE 3. Many who attended the 2014 Atari dig in Alamogordo, New Mexico, lined up more than an hour before being admitted. Photograph by the author.

day progressed, we watched and waited. There were occasional announcements, the ongoing scrabbling of excavation, and Ernest Cline, author of *Ready Player One* in a DeLorean, but most of all there was sun, there was dust, and there was garbage. I spent the day with a bandana covering my face and mouth and a hat pulled low over my eyes, but I still choked on dust like everyone there. Layers of sunscreen minimized but did not stave off sunburn. As the dig progressed, it became an endurance test. The crowds thinned before, finally, the crew began turning up buckets of Atari merchandise. This was not the mass grave of *E.T.* cartridges of legend but instead a heterogeneous mix of dozens of game titles and lots of hardware. The packaging was remarkably well preserved.

By the time the dig happened on April 26, 2014, the dump site was not a mystery, but it was still a legend. The closure of Atari's facilities in El Paso and the subsequent dumping of the near-worthless merchandise have spawned their own folklore, but this has also been the subject of Guins's careful research, which included an interview with Ricky Jones, who, as a younger man, had scavenged the Atari dump site.[4] Now, postdig, it will be the subject of more research, as the archaeologists who participated in the excavation sift through and catalog what they found.[5] As they argue, the importance of the artifacts from the Alamogordo dump is not in their value (they are not precious, and most are readily available from eBay or from used-game stores for a few dollars) but in their history and cultural context.

That cultural context is something that I have been devoted to now for the better part of seven years. As I drove back to the El Paso airport from Alamogordo, hoarse and sunburned, the trip felt like a coda to this project, an opportunity to peer into a literal unearthing that was a fitting close to years spent attempting to unearth that same cultural context through archives and interviews and hours and hours in lingering arcades. The dig at Alamogordo was something else, too: it was a moment in which the history of gaming became public spectacle and international news, and an indication of growing public interest in gaming's past. For a cultural historian, it was exciting to witness. At the dig in Alamogordo, I saw the suggestion that maybe that digging might be seen as something worth watching. The history of video gaming is a nascent field, with so much digging left to do.

THE MICROCOSMIC ARCADE

PLAYING AT THE CULTURAL VANGUARD

LIKE ALL CULTURAL FORMS, video gaming has its origin myths. One myth goes something like this: in 1972 Nolan Bushnell and his company, Atari, released *Pong,* the first commercially successful video game. Atari sold the computerized table tennis game to bars, bowling alleys, pool halls, and other amusement spaces targeting adults with money to burn and a desire for novelty. As Atari and other companies released more and more games, including perennial favorites like *Space Invaders* (Taito, 1978; see Figure 4), *Sea Wolf* (Midway, 1976), and *Centipede* (Atari, 1981), the video game cabinets began to crowd out other coin-operated entertainments in older businesses and to fill new arcades dedicated solely to these new machines. Interestingly, these arcades were frequented not by the punks in leather jackets who lurked around pool halls but by bright young boys with a penchant for technology; video games' impact on these young men was a source of moral concern, with worry over the violent content of Exidy's *Death Race* (1976) causing the first video game moral panic. Worries about youth access to the machines did little to curb enthusiasm and at times drove popular interest.

By the early 1980s, mainstream media outlets from *Life* magazine to the *New York Times* were reporting on the youth trend, and arcades had become mainstays in shopping malls, strip malls, and small-town storefronts across the United States. The coverage placed video games alongside other popular culture phenomena like the emergence of hip-hop or in the context of emerging business and technology practices like computerization, even while raising concerns about the games' cultural, psychological, or even physical effects. But the period that many consider the real glory days of the video game arcade was short-lived.

In 1983 the video game manufacturers of both home and arcade systems were confronted with their first industry crash; numerous issues, including overproduction of particular titles, poor quality control in manufacturing, and an increase in competition in the console

FIGURE 4. Two people watch as a third plays *Space Invaders* in an arcade in Santa Cruz, California. Photograph by Ira Nowinski, 1981 or 1982. Courtesy of Department of Special Collections and University Archives, Stanford University Libraries.

market, caused the crash. While the industry as a whole recovered and prospered through the growth of the home gaming market and the influence and innovation driven by international companies like Nintendo, most arcades did not. Within a few years, towns that had previously boasted numerous arcades were left with nothing more than a few grimy machines in the corner of the local Laundromat or bar: the video game as arcade machine had returned to the place of its initial success, and the arcade lined with video games seemed to be a fluke of history. Today, although video gaming itself has continued to gain cultural significance, the video game arcade as a physical space persists as an object of nostalgia, an entertainment gimmick, or a nerd mecca for the truly dedicated, even as new arcades open, making specific appeal through these forms.

The neat history I have just presented is thoroughly reductive, a popular fiction of a popular medium; debates over how the story of video gaming should be told are elaborated on and complicated in this book. Now an entertainment industry so substantial it regularly outperforms Hollywood's profits, and an arena for competition so fierce as to support an entire professional circuit, video gaming has come of age as an established industry with its own standards, professional organizations, degree programs, and lobbying groups.[1] The history of the video game as a medium offers insights into the industry's evolution, but the history of gaming as cultural form illuminates the evolution of a set of cultural beliefs now central in the digital age. As the wired generation gives way to the wireless generation, and as digital natives become the cultural elite, we are seeing the refinement of values and ideals readily observed in the arcade culture of the 1970s and 1980s.

Like the industry itself, general concepts formed prior to the crash, of what gaming and gamers can and should be, have survived and flourished, and continue to influence contemporary notions of youth, masculinity, and technology. Understanding how the formative years of gaming culture continue to influence these conceptions goes a long way toward understanding the foundations of contemporary digital culture—not only digital entertainment media but also the digitization of everyday tasks. The video game arcade, after all, exposed thousands of youths to computer technologies years before computers became commonplace in offices, classrooms, and homes across the United States. The arcade may indeed still exist in some permutations as a physical space, as a dusty relic, a nostalgic space for thirty- and fortysomethings, but more significantly, it persists as a mode not only of play but of economic decision making and cultural values.

Gameplay in arcades privileges and values individualized competition, technological fluency, and a type of consumer spending often likened to gambling; it also reinforces what have become prevailing ideas about masculinity. As the United States has shifted to a technologically driven service economy, these values have become more broadly diffused through culture. In some ways, we are still in the arcade; the values of the arcade have become the values of our daily lives, even encompassing our labor practices and financial habits. The arcade may have been an entertainment space for youth, but it was also a training ground: the first place a generation encountered computers and learned what it meant to play, to work, and to live in the age of computerization.

This chapter offers a tour of an imagined golden era arcade, drawing from histories of actual arcades (like the one at Pier 39 shown in Figure 5) and surviving arcade cabinets as well as popular press coverage of games and gamers, interviews with arcade owners and gamers, and my own experience, both as a child in a late-1980s arcade and as an adult exploring arcades across the United States over the past decade. The arcade nearest my own hometown was Aladdin's Castle, where my brother and I played until the mall's respectability took a sharp turn south, and rumors spread about a crack dealer operating out of the arcade's back corner.[2] More recently, I have frequented arcades in Austin, Texas, and Chicago, and visited arcades across the United States, particularly in California, Illinois, New Hampshire, Oregon, New York, and Washington.

Rather than analyze individual games, I treat the machines as objects—as toys with didactic implications—and explore the cultural and economic environment they existed in, both the immediate geographic environment of the arcade and the historically and nationally defined environment of the United States from the mid-1970s through the early 1980s. This tour offers context for a discussion about the meaning of the video game arcade as a place where computers became culture, boys became men, and simulation became a

THE MICROCOSMIC ARCADE   5

way of living. We travel through this imagined space not by moving from machine to machine, shedding quarters along the way, but by moving from concept to concept, individually exploring the arcade's key components: sight, sound, and play. The arcade as imagined here is both a memorial to the modern era and a map to the postmodern age we have come to know as the present—a place we have been and still are.

To journey through the arcade conceptually is to confront the digitization of culture, a process that has transformed everything from banking and education to film production and television viewing practices, and also to think critically about the role of money in daily life. The tour proceeds to a consideration of the underlying business structure of the arcade, offering historical perspective on the development of video gaming as a public commercial practice

FIGURE 5. Pier 39 in San Francisco has long included coin-op games as part of the area's attractions. This photograph of a bank of video games is from Ira Nowinski's collection of arcade photographs taken in 1981 and 1982. Courtesy of Department of Special Collections and University Archives, Stanford University Libraries.

involving not only individual gamers/consumers but also manufacturers, distributers, arcade owners, machine operators, and others
working in and around the industry. Early video gaming was a set of
consumer practices, but it also involved the production, marketing,
and distribution of the machines—all of which influenced the format
of the games and shaped the kind of consumer behavior that proved
essential to the games' early success.

While the coin-operated industry has a lengthy history, including Victorian-era amusements like the Kinetoscope and the development of vending machines and popular amusements like jukeboxes
and pinball, the overnight craze triggered by video games was unusual. Within a few years, video games came to be widely deployed
as coin-op (see Figure 6). The games' appeal to boys, who became
the most visible consumers of the entertainment form, also set the
games apart from earlier coin-op technologies. The vitriolic response
many moral guardians had to the games stems not only from the
young age of many gamers and the novelty of the medium but also
from the longer history of coin-operated amusements, which had often served as gambling machines or avenues for salacious peep shows
and frequently faced regulations and bans. Video gaming was thus
a site where old social and cultural worries about youths' access to
commercial entertainments collided with anxieties about emergent
technologies, as well as broader cultural and economic shifts. This
discussion of the arcade as a historical site requires an understanding
of the arcade as a physical site, so the tour begins with the physical
and sensory phenomena that create the arcade experience.

SIGHT

The arcade beckons visually, its name blasted in neon or cartoonish
script, the machines inside visible in flashes through the windows
or open doors. The most popular games are surrounded by clusters
of onlookers, some of whom may have added a quarter to the top
of the cabinet to hold their place in line. The fluorescent lighting is
low in much of the space to maximize the visibility of the machines'
cathode displays and allow the screens' glow to light players' faces.
The cabinets offer the flash of concert posters, screaming their names
in lurid orange and yellow, attempting to entice with images of

Van Brook is #1 World Wide

Keeping our Customers Number One has made Van Brook the Number One Leader in the Amusement & Casino Token Industry. No other supplier can offer you—

- Immediate, same day shipment on Stock Tokens and Accessory Items.
- Buy-Back Agreement 100% on Stock Tokens.
- Special-Sized Token Wrappers.
- Wide array of all necessary Signs and Stickers.
- Accessory Items in stock for immediate shipment.

  - Token Mechs (Metal & Plastic, 48 different sizes and types).
  - Cradles & Cradle Kits.
  - Push Chutes (Complete, Single-Token & Double-Token), Replacement Slides.
  - English #515 Roll-Down Acceptors.
  - English 4 x 4 Replacement Cradles & Kits.
  - Klopp Token Counters.
  - Security Cash Controller
  - Kwik Koin Token Dispensers.

- Expert Technical Advice & Assistance, based on many years of experience.
- Professional Artwork & Design Service at no charge.
- Hundreds of attractive Stock Dies.
- NOTES & QUOTES Promotion Booklet (up-dated and revised periodically).
- Exporting Expertise -- We know the Export Market, and how to solve its complex problems.
- Product Exellence -- Van Brook Standards of Precision and Quality Control are the highest in the Token Industry.

Phone or write for catalog & samples

VAN BROOK OF LEXINGTON, INC. • P.O. BOX 5044, LEX. KY. 40555
(606) 231-7100

FIGURE 6. An advertisement for tokens from 1983 evinces the wide popularity of coin-op games, including tokens from national brands like Coca-Cola, Holiday Inn, and Pizza Hut.

intergalactic robots, implausibly leggy cartoon characters, and bizarre creatures. The unoccupied games play in the attract mode, displaying top scores and titles and short bursts of simulated play. The screens tease. The giant ape takes the girl hostage and rushes to the top of the screen; aliens invade in pixilated unison, making steady progress toward the earth. The alternating images on the screens make the light in the room flash and shift in color.

If this is a particularly modern 1980s arcade, the video games may dominate the space completely; in an older one, pinball machines may line one wall or dominate one corner, or perhaps there are pool tables. If this is the case, the older patrons may be absorbed in rounds of pool or pinball wizardry, leaving the newer machines for the younger customers. Farther from the door, ticket redemption machines challenge players to Skee-Ball and Whack-A-Mole, or encourage them to try their hand at quarter pushers. Occasionally, someone hits a jackpot, and a machine spews tickets in a long ribbon, but usually tickets are dispensed in short bursts. One ticket for 200 points at Skee-Ball. Two tickets for scores over 240.

A Formica counter tops a glass case along one wall. Plastic toys, temporary tattoos, mood rings, and candy fill the case. Labels indicate ticket values. The most luxurious prizes sit on shelves and hang from hooks on the wall behind the counter. Oversized stuffed bears and dogs stare vacantly with plastic eyes. Board games, jump ropes, and classic toys seem less enticing than the RC cars and other top prizes, some of which have sat so long that there is a visible film of dust on the tops of their boxes. At the other end of the counter, there are cans of soda and bags of chips for sale. Peanuts. Funyuns. M&Ms. Even though the arcade sells sodas, employees watch with sharp eyes for anyone daring to rest one on the machines, directing transgressors to toss the half-drunk Coca-Cola or relocate to one of the desolate picnic tables.

A manager makes rounds clutching a ring with dozens of keys. He opens machines to refill ticket rolls, clear quarter jams. Occasionally, he gives up his repair efforts and tells one of the younger employees to mark the machine with a sign made from copy paper, "Out of Service" scrawled in black marker. Mall security guards pass through on their rounds. Parents duck in to retrieve their children, deposited during errands or perhaps lingering too long on their way home from school, sometimes wheedling or threatening to pry them away from especially engrossing games, sometimes giving in and handing over another pocketful of change, with a warning that mom or dad will be back in half an hour.

SOUND

Imagine entering the arcade. As the machines blink and blast, players punch and pound at them, the hard plastic buttons clacking against their casings. Change machines spill quarters in a noisy avalanche, or a teenage employee doles tokens into plastic cups. You can hear the frantic pace of play almost before you see it. There can be no quiet here; even if the place is abandoned during a midafternoon dead spell, the machines continue untended, their MIDI files playing in an infinite-loop siren song of computerized audio, the older machines chiming in with 8-bit audio boops and bleeps.[3] The pinball machines in the back corner clank mechanically, remnants of the machine age. Other machines bleed even stranger sounds, like the voices of Q*bert generated by randomized Votrax-speech synthesis. Perhaps the arcade employees are making announcements over the PA, or a cluster of children are singing "Happy Birthday" at a long table near the heart of the arcade. The voices mix with the machines; they pick up their pace. Conversations here are clipped, efficient, divided neatly into the downtime between levels.

This cacophony mingles with the mall's piped-in Muzak, which drifts in ever so faintly, a reminder of the cool serenity of the department stores farther down, of the perfume counters, shoe departments, and handbag sales. Of suits, of ties, of responsibility or adulthood or both, and security guards, reminding you, ever so helpfully, not to loiter.

PLAY

You are inside the arcade. Pick a quarter from the loose change in your pocket and choose a machine, any machine. Perhaps it is *Pac-Man* (Namco, 1980) or maybe *Centipede* (Atari, 1981) or *Galaga* (Nintendo, 1981). It does not matter which you choose. Put your quarter in the slot where the machine swallows it with a faint metallic clank before the game begins to announce itself, waking from its attract mode and switching into assault. Defend the planet from aliens, avoid the chasing ghosts, gobble cherries, dodge barrels. Make it maybe sixty seconds, or survive the first level on your first quarter on a game you have not played before, and you have proved yourself exceptional. Go again. Find yourself dead, confronted with the listing of top players—of players better than you, of players who would not blow through twelve bucks in quarters in forty-five minutes, players who know what comes next. After level one, level two, level three. Go again. More quarters. You are sweating in the refrigerated air. Go again. The last quarter burned, and you hit the machine hard enough that it stings your hand. You feel foolish, but no one notices. They are too busy watching some kid down the row who has been playing steady for an hour on one quarter. Perhaps at this point you have had enough and leave. Or maybe you stay. You feed the change machine a five dollar bill and stuff your pocket with more quarters. You challenge someone to two player. Maybe you win. Maybe you lose. Maybe it is getting late, and you realize that you have neglected your algebra homework again.

THE ECONOMY OF PLAY

Perhaps, like many gamers, you have never been to an arcade—at least not an early one—and the experience I have just described is foreign to you. Or perhaps you spent much of your childhood growing pale and tense in a place like the one I have described. Although the arcade I played in as a child did not close until the mid-1990s, the industry crash of 1983 sounded the death knell for what became a kind of protracted agony for video game arcades in the United States. No single cause triggered the crash, which resulted from a host of factors, including a general decline in the industry and rapid inflation (see Figure 7). The quarters the machines took in were increasingly devalued, which compounded the fact that there were fewer of them as more and more gamers switched from the public space of the arcade to the private space of the home, plugging in Atari 2600s, Intellivisions, and other early home gaming consoles or booting up personal computers.

Playing arcade games is expensive, and the cost is particularly pronounced for inexperienced players. When I popped a quarter into a

Galaga machine for the first time in 2008 at a movie theater in north Austin, my money bought me just 65 seconds of play. I had not previously played *Galaga* that I can remember; by the time I was old enough to be dropped off for a few unsupervised hours at the shopping mall that housed the only arcade in my home county, *Galaga* was obsolete. I was a novice player. That first game cost me 25 cents and lasted 65 seconds, and was followed by a second lasting only 55 seconds. In that round, I played a total of ten games, which varied in length from 50 seconds to 136 seconds, with an average of just under a minute and a half. Within fifteen minutes, I had blown through $2.50. Because of inflation, the true cost of those fifteen minutes in 2015 is markedly less than those same fifteen minutes would have cost in 1981 when the game was new, even if the number of quarters spent in both cases was the same.

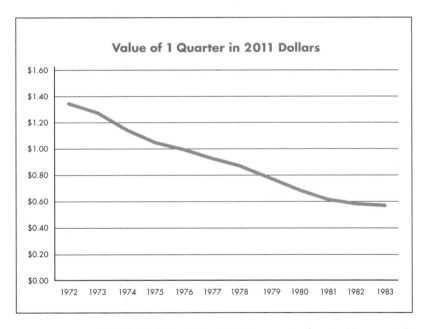

FIGURE 7. Inflation during the 1970s was a significant problem, especially for an industry that relied on standardized coin-based prices. The value of a quarter from 1972 to 1983 roughly halved. Data from the Consumer Price Index Calculator provided by the Bureau of Labor Statistics. "CPI Inflation Calculator," http://www.bls.gov/data/inflation_calculator.htm.

I mention my experience playing *Galaga* not to engage with the specifics of that particular game but to serve as an introduction to the consumer spending demanded by coin-operated arcade games. While admittedly I am not good at *Galaga,* many of the players who encountered the game early in its release would not have been either. Even working from the assumption that I am exceptionally bad at *Galaga* and that my average game time is half of what it should be, the price of gameplay is significant, with an hour of play likely running between eight and twelve dollars. Presumably arcade players increase their skill and maximize game time (even in the brief time I spent playing *Galaga* at the theater, my skill improved), but doing so requires a substantial financial investment in play. Arcade gaming requires money; arcade gaming diligently enough to improve skills and become competent requires even more money. The cost of arcade gaming, like the cost of earlier coin-operated amusements in preceding decades, made it suspect to moral guardians and also placed the games in an emerging marketplace of amusements and experiences.

I turn here to the arcade's place in this marketplace, interrogating the financial values embedded in early coin-operated video game machines and in early coin-operated video game arcades. These games prepared players to serve both as laborers in the emergent white-collar service economy, where computers would be at the center of professional activity, and as investors/players in an increasingly deregulated marketplace. They introduced a generation of young men to computers as approachable, everyday technologies, just as the workplace was entering a period of massive computerization. The move to computerization also reflected necessary shifts in ideals of masculinity. The rise of a service economy, for example, has precipitated an increased emphasis on skill as a gendered differentiator of socioeconomic class. R. W. Connelly summarizes these shifts, pointing out, too, that class exclusion combined with racism, as under apartheid, can make this system especially brutal:

> Where work is altered by deskilling and casualization, working-class men are increasingly defined as possessing force alone. . . . Middle-class men, conversely, are increasingly defined as the bearers of skill. This definition is supported by a powerful historical change in labour markets, the growth of credentialism, linked to a higher education system that selects and promotes along class lines.[4]

Under this emergent system, the potential technological skill to be derived from games made for a powerful defense, offering the possibility of socioeconomic ascendance and middle-class respectability. Perhaps the games were teaching something of value.

But this didactic function also made video games suspect, as they carried with them an emergent set of values and practices that seemed at odds with existing cultural norms and ideals: an embrace of heavily individualized, as opposed to organizationally based, competition; an acceptance of credit, most visibly consumer credit, as a part of daily economic life; the acceleration and propagation of novel amusements as a primary category of spending; and the celebration of those same technological, specifically computer associated, abilities. The competitive practices demanded by the arcade and celebrated by a broader culture of video gaming are at odds with the mid-century's "organization man" model of success, in which even the most successful individuals made their names through corporate or military outlets. In his comprehensive history of American masculinity, Michael Kimmel points to the 1970s, the early era of the video game, as a time of particular crisis. Mobilization against the Vietnam War was part of a wider generational conflict that, Kimmel argues, "was a central expression of the growing crisis of masculinity."[5] This crisis found expression in foreign relations through the divergent articulations of and anxieties about manhood expressed by three U.S. presidents: Lyndon Johnson, Richard Nixon, and Ronald Reagan. Compared with midcentury visions of manhood, competitive video gaming is a closer parallel to a postindustrial, heavily individualized labor market like that described by Connelly—one that celebrates the skills and victories of individual achievements, where workers fulfill work roles as consultants, contractors, and freelancers.

Because gameplay has ideological and didactic value and serves in creating a technological labor force, both individual games and the places they are played have become lightning rods for moral reformers whose social standards reflect existent norms rather than the emergent values of a society in transition. Arguments about the moral and economic implications of particular video games have been the bread and butter not only of public moral guardians seeking to police gaming but of numerous scholars, as evidenced by the work of researchers like Steven J. Kirsh, and Lawrence Kutner and Cheryl Olson.[6]

In writing about *The Sims,* Steven Poole says that the problematic political underpinnings of *The Sims* may be unavoidable: "Perhaps it is inevitable that, as products of decadent late capitalism, most videogames will, consciously or not, reflect the same values."[7] While Poole's argument is specific to a single game, many games work through the cultural values of late capitalism not only at the levels of gameplay and narrative but also in the kinds of economic and cultural practices they encourage. In particular, the coin-operated video games of the 1970s and 1980s were uniquely positioned to introduce the young to emergent consumer patterns and economic practices through the pay-for-play arcade environment described earlier.

This introduction to a specific set of consumer experiences and values warrants critical inquiry, especially as it offers insight into the nervous response that many moral reformers had (and continue to have) to video games.[8] While the temptation to dismiss negative responses to gaming as the hand-wringing of overly worried moralists may be strong, doing so is unfair—both to those who would have wanted to keep video games far from children and to the games themselves. To ignore would-be moral reformers is to undermine the notion that community standards are in flux and may change in ways that prove dangerous. While not everyone who participates in these kinds of discussions is right in the long run, the issues raised and rhetoric deployed throughout these cultural conflicts provide insight into the concerns of the kinds of community figures (PTA presidents, parents, ministers) who often have profound influence even when they do not garner name recognition for themselves. To argue that video games are not a legitimate source for serious social concern would be to argue against their cultural significance. As Jesper Juul points out, "Games are learning experiences, where the player improves his or her skills at learning the game."[9] I posit in this chapter that this is true both at the level of the individual game and at the level of the arcade and the surrounding cultural environment; the player improves his or skill at learning games at a content level, but also improves his or her skill at working within the values system that these games operate in. Similarly, I argue moralists' concerns about video games result from anxieties over the emergent values system— one marked by the embrace of individual success, technological skill, credit, and spending on entertainment and novelties.

Video games were not the first wave of novel amusements to become a major fad or to provoke cultural anxieties. Neither coin-operated games nor arcades are unique to the computer age; Charles Fey produced the first slot machine in 1895, and the first coin-op pinball game dates to about 1929. Both innovations are American in origin and provide a clear historical link between coin-op games and gambling. While slot machines always had gambling as a central function, by 1934, some pinball machines were designed to offer payouts.[10] Not all coin-op technologies can be linked to gambling; the oldest popular motion picture technologies in the United States include coin-op devices like Thomas Edison's Kinetoscope, released in 1894.[11] But these technologies, too, were often viewed with suspicions, and while coin-operated amusements were staples at midways and boardwalks after the turn of the century, they were also persistent targets for moral reformers.[12] Whether gambling machines or less overtly reward-based amusements, arcade machines of all kinds serve the economic purpose of accruing wealth, one coin at a time, for their owners and operators (a theme at the heart of the advertisement in Figure 8). The efficiency with which machines serve that purpose, however, depends both on factors such as machine placement and machine downtime, which are within the control of operators, and on factors external to operator control. The popularity of individual machines can be addressed through operators' adjustments in machine placement or choice, but other factors, including broader economic fluctuations like inflation, are more difficult to respond to.

Even cursory analysis of the real cost of gameplay reveals the impact that inflation had on the coin-op industry of the 1970s and 1980s. Figure 7 shows the progressive devaluation of the quarter, which had become the base monetary unit of the coin-op industry, during the video game boom. Adjusted for inflation to 2011 dollars, a single run at a quarter-operated video game would have initially cost well over a dollar, with the price dipping below the dollar mark in 1977, then steadily declining to a real cost of less than half of the 1972 value by 1981. While some game designers attempted to alleviate this issue by raising the cost of gameplay to fifty cents and machines sometimes included options by which operators could adjust costs, the effects of inflation on the coin-op industry were far-reaching and probably

We've served up more quarters for more quarters than anyone in our quarter.

Music-Vend is the company you've come to count on for fast, reliable service in amusement games, vending machines and music systems... whether you're in Washington, Alaska, northern Idaho or western Montana. And we've been doing it for nearly 35 years.

We help you get better quarterly results by always having an ample supply of the newest, hottest games in the industry.

When it comes to used equipment, our service and repair technicians give no quarter. They're all factory trained and recondition and test every used machine we sell. So you're guaranteed that it's in top working order upon

shipment from us.

Because of our location in this quarter of the country, we've become experts in exporting world-wide and can give you the edge selling overseas.

With all this going for you, it's really a piece of cake to deal with Music-Vend Distributing Company. This quarter, next quarter and every quarter thereafter.

Proudly representing: Atari, Centuri, Cinematronics, Exidy, GDI, Inc., Gottlieb, K-Tron, Lectro-Vend, Namco-America, Inc., Nintendo, Rowe Music & Vending, Sega/Gremlin, Taito America Corp., Seeburg, Stern, Valley and Williams.

Music-Vend Distributing Company. 1550 Fourth Ave. S. P.O. Box 24807, Seattle, WA 98124 (206) 682-5700 Cable: MUSIVEND East 4008 Broadway, Spokane, WA 99202 (509) 535-5757

FIGURE 8. This advertisement from 1983 for Music-Vend, a coin-op distributor, relies on a quarter pun and showcases a coin-studded cake.

hit video game operators especially hard, as the most technologically sophisticated machines usually required the highest initial investment. That the prices for games were often bound by physical limitations of the machines and their settings created difficulties in modifying older machines to accept higher prices; even on newer machines, prices could be raised only in twenty-five-cent increments or by installing new coin acceptors.

Bushnell and Ted Dabney founded Atari in 1972 explicitly as a video game company, but early manufacturers of video games were a mix of newly founded companies like Atari and Exidy that produced video games primarily or exclusively and older manufacturers like Bally and Rock-Ola, which had a history of producing other kinds of coin-operated machines, including bar games like pool and shuffleboard and jukeboxes. Video games are now indisputably their own industry, but at the outset they were largely a spin-off of other industries, including the coin-op industry, the television industry, and the computer software industry. Games developed for play on consoles and home computers now dominate the industry, but coin-operated games initially proved both financially viable and highly visible. Indeed, as coin-op video games were often produced by some of the same companies that manufactured earlier coin-operated amusements, video game machines circulated through some of the existing networks that supported distribution of earlier coin-operated machines.

Distributers purchased machines from manufacturers and then leased or sold them to operators who placed them at locations like bars, restaurants, bowling alleys, Laundromats, or arcades. The location owner and the machine operator divided the income from the machine or machines, usually on a 50/50 or 60/40 split. Factors influencing the split included the initial cost of a particular machine, its popularity, and the desirability of a particular location. These two parties would split machine revenues, with the machine operator taking responsibility for machine repair and maintenance, and the location operator absorbing the day-to-day costs of powering the machines. Arcade operators sometimes bought machines outright, which meant that they saw a higher percentage of machine revenue become profit, as they did not have to divide the income with a machine operator, but this practice was often seen as a disruption of industry operations and could push distributors and those who leased machines to operators out of the business. Regardless of industry controversy, the division of machine revenues contributed to the concentration of video games in arcades, since the clustered machines would be easier to service and maintain either by the route operator or by the arcade owner. Arcade owners who owned machines outright would have seen a higher financial return on individual machines that they operated than individuals operating machines at nonarcade locations, as arcade owners would not have had to split the machine's profits with the location.[13]

At the time that video games first emerged, other coin-op technologies such as cigarette and soda machines, jukeboxes, pinball, foosball, and pool were all in circulation. But while these were steady earners, none had the seemingly magnetic appeal for consumers that video games held; video gaming was lucrative for long-term operators and doubtless lured others into the business, as the intense media coverage made games seem like an avenue to fast riches. The opportunity to attract younger customers meant existing operators could expand their market; this appeal to youth dovetailed with industry efforts to increase respectability through family fun centers and other wholesome businesses. Video game–specific arcades emerged partly because many existing outlets for coin-op amusements like bars had unsavory connotations and were considered inappropriate environments for youth. In the arcade, video games became the primary attraction, not a secondary revenue generator as they were in most other locations. Further, the all-ages arcades enabled operators to reach a broader audience than adult venues could manage. Video games also contributed to the rise of "family fun centers" that featured coin-op amusements alongside other attractions like go-carts, batting cages, or miniature golf.

The change in venues from bars to family fun centers and arcades contributed to shifts in the audience for video games. Both adults and children would have had incidental encounters with early video games in public spaces outside arcades—trying a game out of boredom at the Laundromat, for example. Games in arcades were less encouraging of this kind of casual interaction; the arcade would have been the destination, and video games (or video game–related socializing) would have been the primary reason to enter the venue. Video game arcades attracted players who already knew they liked video games, even as they attracted casual players curious about video games and passersby, as was certainly the case for arcades in busy retail districts and shopping malls (or, as shown in Figure 9, bus stations). Contemporary representations of classic arcades frequently portray them as male-dominated spaces, but this is only partly true. Bushnell maintains that 40 percent of the coin drop on Atari's *Pong* came from women, and several individual gamers and arcade owners I interviewed stated that, while girls were a minority among arcade gamers, they still formed a significant percentage of the players.[14] About 20 percent of the competitors on the video gaming game show *Starcade* were girls and women. Studies of arcade patrons revealed a significant number of girls in the arcade both as players and as observers.[15] A 1981 Gallup youth survey found that 93 percent of teenagers played video games, with only minor differences across gender: 96 percent of boys and 90 percent of girls said they "ever

FIGURE 9. Benjamin Stone plays *Donkey Kong* at the Greyhound bus station in St. Louis, Missouri, during the 1980s. Snapshot photograph available at https://www.flickr.com/photos/benchilada/7180304860/. Licensed under Creative Commons and printed with permission.

played video games," and 11 percent of boys and 9 percent of girls admitted to playing two or more hours a week.[16]

This discrepancy in how the gender breakdown of arcade gamers is remembered may reflect changes in the audience for video games over time. Perhaps the concentration of games in dedicated arcades cut the number of women players as the games were moved into spaces that catered to teenage boys. *Pong* may have had an unusually high percentage of women players because of its initial placement in bars, not arcades. Individual arcades likely had significant differences in patronage as well. Multiple interviewees who spoke to gender divisions in the arcade guessed that girls and women made up roughly 25 percent of players.[17] There were, at the very least, some female players in the arcade. The social habits of adolescents likely also played a role in how the arcade was remembered. Much research shows that young men participate extensively in homosocial interactions; this may mean that the boys playing in the arcade interacted primarily with each other even when girls were also present.[18]

While arcades may have been more or less comfortable for various types of patrons, the cost of gameplay doubtless also affected who played the games, just as it affected who owned the games and where they were placed. The relatively high cost of individual instances of gameplay contributed to the rapid diffusion of video games, as savvy operators would have seen substantial profits. A 1977 advertorial from Amalgamated Industries' North Texas division boasted that "many machines have been known to yield in excess of $100 a week"— the modern equivalent of nearly $400.[19] The advertorial implies that video game machines could be a door to rapid wealth for the people who put games in the right locations; the suggestions for appropriate locations—cocktail lounges, finer restaurants, yacht clubs, college student centers, and golf clubhouses, among others—speak to an assumption of adult and young adult players with disposable incomes. A 1982 article placed the average yield for an arcade machine at a more conservative $90 weekly, with the investment for a new machine running roughly $2,500. Working from these numbers and the assumption that the location operator and the machine operator split profits evenly, in just over a year a machine with an average level of income would take in enough money, even after being split among the location and machine operator, for the machine operator to pay off his initial investment and begin making a profit. Of course, these promises of profits may have been exaggerated to lure buyers.

As video games clustered in arcades and developed a substantial audience among teenagers, those anxious about the potential dangers of the arcade viewed the high cost of gameplay as insidious. Numerous articles from the early 1980s document attempts by cities and counties to curb gaming, and these frequently point to the money that teens were spending on play. Several gamers I interviewed insisted that the money they spent playing video games was not given to them by their parents but earned by performing household chores, collecting bottles and cans for return deposits, or handling newspaper routes or other odd jobs.[20] While this does not necessarily suggest great affluence, it does suggest a degree of economic stability: since these players had discretionary income, they were able to fund their gaming because their earnings were not required to support the total family income. The cost of gaming imposed distinct limits on who could game and how much time and money they could spend playing. Mark Hoffman, who worked at Twin Galaxies in Ottumwa, Iowa, as a teenager, said he became interested in gaming only after his interest in computers snagged him a job at the arcade, where he enjoyed unlimited play as a perk; even as a teenager, the cost of gaming seemed wasteful to him, partly because of his family's socio-economic status.[21]

PLAYING WITH FREE SPEECH

While teenage players were doubtless aware of the money they were spending, they often viewed the income as truly disposable and did not worry about the overall cost. Adults observing these gamers' spending habits, however, saw them as a serious community problem. Many communities organized against arcades. Some towns placed high taxes or expensive licenses on machines, which discouraged operators from expanding their placements. Bans and restrictions were another frequently employed strategy, with some of these limiting the number of machines in a single location, effectively preventing arcades from opening. Legal proceedings related to efforts to curtail the spread of video games in Mesquite, Texas, demonstrate how games were seen as a threat to the appropriate use of time and money. In a February 1982 article on the U.S. Supreme Court's decision to postpone judgment in *City of Mesquite v. Aladdin's Castle, Inc.*, a *Los Angeles Times* reporter summarizes the conflict, saying that "city residents and officials complained that teen-agers were wasting time and money on the games."[22] Critics of video gaming had been quick to point to the antisocial behavior that gamers engaged in outside the arcade and suggested that gaming contributed to their delinquency. An article on efforts to curtail arcade openings in Lynbrook, New York, noted citizens' concerns:

> The residents said that the centers, which feature games that challenge the player with electronic sounds and flashing lights, had become hangouts for noisy teen-agers who drink too much beer, leave garbage around and vandalize the property of nearby residents.[23]

The games were also blamed for encouraging Lynbrook teens to "play hooky" from school, a concern echoed in other towns and communities that tried to limit the spread of arcades. In making the suggestion that arcades contributed to teenage delinquency, these communities attacked the arcades themselves. Concerns about the effect of video game arcades—that teenagers were minimally supervised, that they were spending their money on junk food and foolish games—reiterated concerns that had accompanied arcade culture for decades. John Kasson documented this anxiety about leisure and youth extensively in his writing on the history of Coney Island. The arcade's dubious history tied it to turn-of-the-century commercial amusements, among them amusement halls, movie theaters, and arcades—all of them too frequently filled with dirty pictures for the liking of many middle-class reformers, who took issue not only with the arcade's appeal to prurient interests but also with its enticement to shell out cash for frivolities away from hearth and home.[24]

The courts ruled that the Mesquite ordinance, which restricted those under seventeen years of age from playing coin-operated video games without a parent or guardian present, was unconstitutional on grounds that video games should be protected as free speech.[25] The U.S. Supreme Court maintained that the ordinance violated both the First Amendment right to free speech and the due process clause of the Fourteenth Amendment. Although some of the Mesquite residents who initially complained about the games may have thought that the games constituted some kind of incitement to violence, the Court did not show any willingness to consider them as such and has subsequently maintained a general refusal to curtail minors' access to violent materials. Further, the language frequently deployed in discussions of the Mesquite statute and similar measures taken by communities around the United States points to violence as only one factor in a more general concern about the "wasting" of valuable resources (time and money) encouraged by games. With this in mind, the intention of the original ordinance becomes clear. The restrictions on youth access to coin-operated video games were intended to force youths to use their time and money more wisely—in ways more in keeping with the values of older community members.

Although the suit ostensibly concerned the corporate entity of Aladdin's Castle, the Court was effectively siding not only with Aladdin's Castle, Inc. but also with the teenagers of Mesquite and of other cities and communities attempting to ban gamers. The court's ruling protected video games as free speech, but also protected the right of entertainment companies to sell their amusements to children and the rights of children to purchase media access without the intervention of parents or guardians. Given the generally marginal legal status of youths in the United States, this granting of rights, indirect as it may be, is still significant in its recognition of the rights of minors.

Further, the ruling nods not so subtly toward the late capitalist assertion that the freedom to consume is a fundamental civil liberty.[26] This represents a significant change from modernist conceptions of free speech, which were articulated through obscenity trials, including *Roth v. United States* in 1957, which focused on authors' rights to self-expression coupled with printers' and distributors' rights to propagate these materials, and the Berkeley-based Free Speech Movement, which insisted on students' rights to engage in political demonstrations on campus as a matter of intellectual and academic freedom.[27] While these types of speech acts persist and remain contentious in public discourse, discussions of free speech like the one in *City of Mesquite v. Aladdin's Castle, Inc.* do not focus on the issues of obscenity or intellectual or creative freedom that are at the root of these earlier, modernist arguments about the meaning of free speech. Instead, they focus on the right to sell and consume, often with little serious attention given to the materials' content. Subsequent attempts to restrict distribution of games to minors based on violence have been rejected by the courts, which have refused to intervene, arguing that the research on the effects of violent materials on minors is at best inconclusive. The earliest attempts to curtail youth access to video games through the legal system failed largely because of the effectiveness of arguments tied directly to neoliberal arguments about the free market; this departure from older justifications of free speech becomes less surprising when placed in historical context.

THROWING AWAY QUARTERS IN A LABOR CRISIS

The early period of arcade gaming, between the successful launch of *Pong* in 1972 and the video game industry crash in 1983, coincides with substantial upheavals in the U.S. economy. Larger economic trends and crises drove micro-level economic decisions made by consumers. These include the oil crisis, the end of the international gold standard, and the decline of traditional communism. The Organization of Arab Petroleum Exporting Countries (OAPEC) launched an oil embargo in October 1973, followed in 1974 by a quadrupling of petroleum prices by OPEC (Organization of Petroleum Exporting Countries). These two incidents created a shortage of gasoline and heating oil during the winter of 1973–74 and sparked a broader energy crisis.[28] The U.S. withdrawal of troops from Vietnam also happened in 1973, and the rise of communist forces in Vietnam seemed for a time to herald a significant defeat for U.S. foreign policy and for American democracy as exportable good.[29] Nixon ended the convertibility of U.S. dollars to gold in 1971, a decision made in response to a recession coupled with significant inflation in the United States and multiple countries demanding that the United States "cash out" their dollars for gold as promised. This decision ended the Bretton Woods system, which had tied the international gold standard to the value of the U.S. dollar.[30]

In particular, the elimination of the gold standard severed the tie between money and real, tangible goods, definitively abstracting capital. Consumers prove more willing and able to part with abstracted capital, a truth near universally acknowledged by anyone who has ever had a credit card. David Harvey points to two major changes in consumer culture: a "mobilization of fashion in mass (as opposed to elite) markets [which] provided a means to accelerate the pace of consumption not only in clothing, ornament, and decoration but also across a wide swath of life-styles and recreational activities (leisure and sporting habits, pop music styles, video and children's games, and the like)," and "a shift away from the consumption of goods and into the consumption of services—not only personal, business, educational, and health services, but also into entertainments, spectacles, happenings, and distractions."[31] Both trends shortened the lifetime of expenditures and accelerated spending, and enabled a move from an industrial, production-based economy to a service-based, consumer economy.

These shifts were not at all seamless; they triggered a great deal of instability affecting the day-to-day lives of workers and their families. The instability often took the shape of significant economic decline, as workers and communities that had depended on the profitability, stability, and growth of the industrial sector confronted layoffs and plant closures. The decade of the 1970s was marked by economic stagnation. The economist Ernest Mandel argues in *Late Capitalism* that the economic stagnation of the 1970s was inevitable, as the global economic boom of the preceding decades reached its limits.[32] Profitability for U.S. companies had peaked in the 1960s before entering a steady state of decline and stagnation that lasted fifteen years. National economic growth dropped significantly: after maintaining an average of more than 4 percent annually for three decades, growth reached just 2.6 percent in 1969, then plummeted to −0.3 percent the following year. Growth stood at an average of just 2.87 percent through the 1970s. Simultaneously, the national inflation rate more than doubled, climbing to 5.3 percent in 1971 after averaging 2.5 percent annually through the 1950s and 1960s.[33]

The recession hit manufacturing particularly hard, with massive layoffs in industrial plants that had previously served as the economic backbone for many communities. The postwar boom was decisively over. The labor historian Nelson Lichtenstein notes, "By the early 1980s, they [profits] were approximately one-third less than a generation before; in the manufacturing sector only about one-half." Although economic growth continued, the annual rate remained low, and real wages remained stagnant into the early 1990s. Furthermore, while wages were stagnant for most workers, young male workers faced drops in real wages of 25 percent as the workforce expanded.[34] This economic upheaval has had particular implications for men, who increasingly, as summarized by Kimmel, "experience their masculinity less as providers and protectors, and more as consumers, as 'ornaments.'"[35] The young men playing early coin-operated video games, then, were a population at a seemingly unprecedented level of economic risk, encountering decreases in their earning power and increases in unemployment while they were lured to consumption as a way to self-expression and satisfaction. The appeal of video gaming as a leisure activity may have eluded anxious moral guardians, but for many young people, particularly young men, the games presented not only an entrée into computer culture but an enticing leisure activity that offered opportunities for competition and recognition at a seeming remove from the economic realities that permeated work and family life.

The rise of the coin-operated video game industry coincided not only with a rapid increase in spending on entertainment services but also with a substantial spike in the demand for novel entertainments, which is intimately bound to the transition from modernity to postmodernity. Fredric Jameson pinpoints 1973, one year after the release of the first successful commercial video game, as the moment in which postmodernity and late capitalism emerged as dominant cultural and economic forms.[36] Based on the observations of Harvey and Jameson, gameplay's circulation as a commodity in a postmodern, deindustrializing economy makes sense. The desirability of gameplay as commodified entertainment service was stimulated by the same shifts that made the financial expenditure required seem particularly risky to older community members. Shifts in the labor market heightened anxiety about the economic practices of the young, particularly young men who were facing limited job prospects and decreased earning power. Discussion of youths' gaming practices point so frequently to the financial and time costs of the activity specifically because the economic pressures faced by many Americans would have led to increased worry about the industriousness and employability of these same youths. Video gaming may be just one among the "entertainments, spectacles, happenings, and distractions" that Harvey points to, but it would have been among the most decidedly novel, as it reflected not only the evolution of coin-op entertainment technologies but the growing visibility of computer technologies. This novelty contributed to the high visibility of video gaming and contributed to its role as a lightning rod for those concerned with the values system that the nation's youths were absorbing.

FROM PINBALL TO POSTMODERNITY

Decades earlier at the height of the modernist age, the pinball machine fulfilled a similar cultural role. Pinball games first appeared as commercial, coin-operated amusements in the early 1930s, but the "golden age" of pinball did not come until the postwar period and its robust economic growth in the United States. Real wages doubled from 1947 to 1967, allowing many Americans access to unprecedented levels of economic stability and wealth.[37] The rise of pinball coincides with the expansion of Fordist production and consumption principles in the midcentury United States. This expansion fueled growth in manufacturing jobs and incomes while providing a burgeoning array of affordable consumer goods, from automobiles and appliances to clothing and furniture. Although Henry Ford had largely developed his principles in his own manufacturing much earlier—perhaps as early as his implementation of the eight-hour, five-dollar workday in 1914—Fordism as a broader set of practices did not gain traction until after World War II.

Shifts both in class relations and in regulatory practices combined with the decentralization of the population through suburban growth to enable a sharp turn toward Fordist production and consumption practices.[38] The postwar period also saw the cultivation of adolescence as an established developmental category. It was only during the Great Depression that, because of the lack of available work, most youths, particularly young men, attended high school. Thomas Hine places the "golden age" of teenagerdom as stretching from the twenty-five years before World War II to the beginning of the Vietnam War, when teenagers faced significant reductions in their economic security and cultural visibility.[39] Teenagers in the postwar period were significant consumers; pinball was, like video gaming later, a contentious way for teens to spend their time and money.

The golden age of pinball was marked by public disputes over the value of the games and by bans of the machines in cities like

New York and Los Angeles, where the games were judged to be a threat to the moral order.[40] Warren Susman argues that pinball was an amusement uniquely suited to the period's culture:

> The pinball machine was the ideal toy of the machine age, with its spinning balls passing through a series of obstacle pins that meant points for the player if they met, although at the same time the injunction "Do Not Tilt" severely limited the player's opportunity to interfere with the chance movements of the balls.[41]

Susman's assessment of the pinball machine is that the notion of play it embodies is derivative of the age that produced it. The games played via these mechanized amusements serve a didactic purpose, instilling cultural values through physical and mental engagement with a device that is, at some fundamental level, a toy. The cultural values of the pinball machine reflect and teach the cultural values of the era during which they were most effectively produced for the broadest audience.

Playthings serve didactic purposes—classic toys like tea sets, model cars, and toy vacuum cleaners allow children to engage with the adult world, inviting them to mimic the tasks of older family members and familiarizing them with the sorts of actions that occupy adults. Most of these toys allow open-ended play. While most adults would assume that a five-year-old girl given a tea set could use the objects to stage a pretend tea service for her dolls or friends, or she could as easily stack the pieces into a tower, smash them against a wall, or otherwise play against the toy's intended purpose. Pinball machines, as Susman so distinctly describes them, do not readily allow for such play, as the games themselves limit the amount that a player may intervene in the game's outcome. The education that pinball games can provide is narrower and more tightly controlled than the learning experience that may be had with a set of crayons or a rubber ball.

Decades later, coin-operated video game machines demonstrate a similarly limited play principle at two levels—at the level of gameplay permitted by the game's programmed rules and at the level of hardware tampering possible. First, at the level of the basic rules governing play, many early arcade video games are, as suggested by Juul, games of progression rather than emergence, which means that there are real limitations on how the game may be played. Games of progression are those in which "challenges [are] presented serially by way of special-case rules."[42] These tend to have a single model of mastery, which is to say, there is a best, right way to play the game. A progressive game can usually be exhausted or beat more readily than emergent games. This is why Billy Mitchell can play a "perfect" game of *Pac-Man*. Games of emergence are those in which "rules [combine] to provide variation."

While some classic arcade games, notably *Pong*, are essentially games of emergence, they still have significant structural limitations to play variance. For example, if someone in a two-player game of *Pong* simply refused to move his paddle, the game would end almost immediately—an outcome unlikely to be mutually desirable for the players at twenty-five cents a pop. So, even in the case of more emergent coin-operated video games, the game limits the potential for playing against the game's set objectives, as many early video games will terminate if not played according to their objectives. Discussing the game *Zork* (a text-based game initially designed between 1977 and 1979 as *Zork*, then split into three games and released by Infocom in 1980; the first part is known as both *Zork I* and *Zork: The Great Underground Empire—Part I*, which was followed by *Zork II: The Wizard of Frobozz* and *Zork III: The Dungeon Master*), Terry Harpold summarizes this principle as "to behave badly is to play badly," further pointing out that the game itself will not allow types of play that run counter to the game.[43] Like pinball machines, most video games were played in public amusement spaces and were owned by businesses, not by individuals who kept them in their homes. Physical alterations or technological tampering with machines was limited by this factor, and, further, arcade machines kept in homes were prestige commodities for serious players invested in preserving the integrity of the game and, by extension, the credibility of their game scores. The "world record culture" cultivated through the efforts of individual players and media outlets that granted significant attention to the "best" players raises this issue of an individual instance of gameplay's credibility. Walter Day, the first video game referee, has said that part of the historical role of Twin Galaxies in serving as the arbitrating body of video game top scores was to develop rules of play based on notions of fairness and the perceived purpose of individual games.[44]

In total, both form and ownership limit the types of play allowable, and these limitations are further enforced by cultural factors specific to the practices of competitive gaming.

These limitations serve several practical purposes. Most relevantly, they create a player perception of fairness in competition, and they also ensure that games end at regular, usually brief intervals, thus guaranteeing that the amount of play time purchased is relatively small and that those desiring to play for extended periods will continue to spend money. Most novice players would have confronted a situation not unlike the situation I faced in taking on *Galaga* for the first time, spending a good deal of money in an attempt not necessarily to master the game but simply to gain a firm enough understanding of the rules of engagement and the game's rhythms to play for longer than a minute or two. In the economy of the arcade, the most proficient players spend the least money, as their games can last for hours. Record-breaking bouts of gameplay, referred to as marathons, often exceed twenty-four hours. The ability to extract hours of gameplay from minimal financial expenditures is exceptional and is complicated by the fact that while it enables players to "beat the house" in a sense by keeping their money, they can do this only by following the rules of the game exceptionally well—and by pursuing a goal at odds with those of most arcade managers and venue operators. Tim McVey, the first person to score a billion points on a video game at Day's Twin Galaxies, in 1984, had several marathon sessions on *Nibbler* cut off by arcade employees. A common practice among arcade staff to force marathoning players off machines they were monopolizing was to simply cut the power supply to machines. The disruption of gameplay by a factor outside the player or the game is something that game designers could not have accounted for and is outside the rules system embedded in the game.

These types of disruptions circumvent the game's design, altering play in ways that are beyond the control of game designers. Within the controlled world of the game itself, Harpold's argument that "to behave badly is to play badly" helps illuminate the point that exceptional players are exceptionally well versed in the rules. They are the best adherents to the cultural, economic, and social standards of the arcade and of the games they play. While the impulse to beat the house may have put players at odds with machine operators' perceptions of the games' economic purpose, players can beat the house in this way only by becoming exceptional gamers—usually through hours of play, many of which would have occurred before they became skilled at gaming. One principal lesson that the arcade teaches players is that there is only one way to play; even for games that can be played using various strategies, a player can sustain the game's length only by playing to the game's objectives. The better an individual plays by the rules, the more value he or she receives for his or her financial expenditure. The longer a player can play, the more points he or she can earn, and the more clout he or she has in the competitive social environment of the arcade. Superiority in game-play is, like superiority demonstrated in other arenas, an opportunity to assert dominance and gain social clout. In both video games and pinball games, this superiority is accrued by an individual, not a team or other organized group. The money fed into an arcade game's coin slot is an investment. Players assume that they will receive for their money not only a chance to play but a chance to improve, and to become noteworthy, to have the skill required to play individual games that last for hours.

The adherence to rules that is necessary for competitive video gaming suggests in some ways that video gaming is fundamentally conservative in its implications. However, if video gaming is conservative, it is conservative only in this specific way, and only in some cases. Gamers' and game developers' shared obsession with technological advance and novelty, for example, puts gaming at odds with a conservativism that would seek to preserve classical notions of childhood or to resist technological change, even as the increased interest in canonical games offers an interesting counterexample. Further, the fetishization of individualized competition as the most valuable way of gaming has not precluded the development of collaborative games, nor has it precluded the development of lively communities around video gaming. Much of video gaming in the 1970s and 1980s put gaming and young gamers at odds with the values of moral guardians, which demonstrates gaming's disruptive potential. In particular, the high individualization of video gaming competition and skills appears to look forward to the rise of freelance and contract labor as a dominant mode of work.

On a surface level, the public debates about the social and cultural value of arcade games frequently focused on anxieties about the "wasting" of money they encouraged. These arguments about the frivolous nature of entertainment spending were, as mentioned earlier, nothing new. Commercial amusements have always attracted controversy, as have media forms like the theater, the novel, and the Sony Walkman. However, the debates about arcade video gaming came at a critical transitional moment as the United States shifted from a modernist to a postmodernist economy. The teenagers who patronized arcades in the 1970s and 1980s were among the first to come of age in this new culture. They grew up in a culture not only filled with digital entertainments but shaped by a white-collar service economy, by a growing emphasis on computerization, and by the rising importance of consumer culture for self-expression and satisfaction. The discomfort that many adults felt at the prospect of teenagers spending hours and endless quarters in arcades doubtless seemed silly to the teenagers who patronized these amusement spaces. Indeed, in retrospect these concerns can often seem farcical, just another set of grumblings set off by generational differences that have caused conflict over everything from dress hems to novels to MP3 players and cell phones.

In the case of video gaming, the conflict develops at a point of massive cultural change and economic upheaval. At the back of the seemingly reactionary treatment of a new entertainment technology is a profound discomfort with radical shifts in the ordering of culture. When the Supreme Court finally ruled on the *City of Mesquite v. Aladdin's Castle, Inc.* in 1982, the Court found that the city's restrictions on arcade gaming were in violation not only of the Texas constitution but of the U.S. constitution as well.[45] Most immediately, the Court's decision hampered the ability of local and state governments to restrict gameplay by teens. More abstractly, the protection of video games as free speech and the assertion that children cannot be prevented from purchasing gameplay signals a moment in which consumption becomes protected speech. This protection of consumer practices as civil rights signals a shift to a stabilized consumer economy. Under this new model, freedom of choice often means freedom of purchase. The court decision eloquently expresses the implications of this model: individual identities come to be affixed to consumer products and practices, and disputes over the right to buy—even for children, and even when couched in terms of moral concern—seem increasingly antiquated.

If access to the arcade provides access to emergent values and practices, then the issue becomes a question of not just who had access to a relatively expensive leisure activity but also who had access to the first wave of computerization, and consequently which children would be best prepared for the labor market in which they would come of age. Researchers like James Paul Gee, Elisabeth R. Hayes, and T. L. Taylor argue that, in this vein, the gendering of video games remains a critical issue in addressing the persistent underrepresentation of women in the tech and related industries, as the games provided youths with a point of access to computer technologies.[46] Access to these earliest video games, rudimentary as they may seem now, is no less important and, in fact, may carry greater importance because of the critical role this period played in shaping not only gaming culture but public perceptions of gaming and gamers. As video gaming became a major cultural force, it received significant media coverage in the popular press, which helped solidify notions of who was gaming and why. Dismissals of gaming as a frivolous leisure activity thus undermined the real lessons being learned by gamers and effectively short-circuited early discussion about why various demographic groups were not gaming and what effect limited or no access to gaming might have on a generation of workers whose labor market would be dominated by computerization.

Likewise, teenagers feeding quarters into *Galaga* and *Pong* were not only playing but learning the cultural and economic values that would allow them to survive and thrive in a deindustrializing work environment that would have seemed as foreign to their parents as the Fordist production lines and clanking pinball machines of the midcentury must have seemed to their grandparents. At an individual level, the coin-operated video games were a didactic introduction to these new practices, allowing the young to learn by doing and preparing them for participation in a new economy—first as consumers, and ultimately as citizens and laborers. The discomfort with which many parents and moral guardians greeted the rise of the arcade stems not from knee-jerk distrust of technology but from deep anxieties about the economic and cultural changes affecting American culture as a whole.

The video game arcade as it existed in its glory days has mutated for survival: it may now take the form of the entertainment complex as represented by venues in the style of Dave & Buster's; the "classic arcade" in which vintage machines are used to lure nostalgic Gen Xers; and hangouts for those who were or wish they had been there, such as Brooklyn's Barcade. In some ways, this afterlife represents games going back to where they came from, bars, where they had been advertised as novel amusements for adult consumers. But while the appeal of the games in 1972 would have been sheer newness, any novelty in the current incarnations is really the sheen of nostalgia, the allure of the vintage bits of popular culture. The games that at the time represented the encroachment of the new now represent instead the seeming simplicity of our recent past. Arcade machines remain one of the earliest broadly diffused forms of popular computing, and the boards that enabled *Space Invaders* and its ilk were the first computers many people had access to; the machines that now look quaint once looked flashy and new.

The arcade as considered here presents a compelling moment in cultural history, tied as it is to the novelty of the computer age, the growing compulsion to spend money on novel amusements, and the reshaping of the U.S. economy and labor market. To play in the arcade was to participate in emergent cultural practices; the discomfort that many adults felt watching children feed coin after coin into the flashing machines was a reaction to tangible evidence that children were being inducted into an era that operated on different value principles. The arcade was a training ground for different models of consumption, labor, and culture, and an emergent community of young men who subscribe to the values of this new era. Many Americans are living their adult lives by the rules of engagement they first encountered in strip mall amusement halls; the video game arcade provided players with an early introduction to these values, preparing them to serve as laborers in a technologically oriented white-collar service economy and to engage as investors/players in a heavily deregulated marketplace.

The broad diffusion of video games and their focus on young men as consumers made the games uniquely threatening. Moral reformers' discomfort with the hours that teens spent playing video games reflects uneasiness with the implications of these broader cultural and economic shifts. Children were not growing up with negative moral values so much as they were being brought up as natives of the new economy; adults who had grown up in an era of company men, Fordist production, and savings accounts were watching the young grow up in an age of rapid-fire career changes, flexible accumulation, and easy credit. The intense competition of the arcade, filled with 8-bit violence and the enticement to spend this week's allowance and next week's all in one go, seemed decidedly unwholesome. The individual games of the arcade may have been simulations of sci-fi and cartoon scenarios, but the arcade itself was a simulation of those same generalized economic values we now confront as consumers, laborers, and citizens.

GAMING'S GOLD MEDALISTS

TWIN GALAXIES AND THE RUSH TO COMPETITIVE GAMING

ANXIETIES ABOUT THE ARCADE'S IMPACT on youths echoed broader anxieties about technological, economic, and cultural changes and helped fuel attacks on video gaming and on individual arcade games, like Exidy's 1976 *Death Race*. Yet the response to the emergent medium and culture was not uniformly negative. While moral guardians worried about the violence of video games and the economic imperatives of the coin-op arcade, adult early adapters and popular media looked on video gaming culture through a more favorable lens. Game designers and companies were championed for their innovation and entrepreneurial spirit, and gamers were frequently cast as technologically gifted, highly competitive young men whose more mischievous impulses only reaffirmed their intelligence and creativity. Yet these conflicting perceptions are less dueling definitive narratives of gaming than diverging interpretations.

This chapter examines how such interpretations emerged from one of the most important images in gaming history: a photograph of the top gamers in the world published in *Life* magazine's 1982 "Year in Pictures" issue (see Figure 10). After a brief history of the photograph and of the Twin Galaxies Arcade in Ottumwa, Iowa, the site of this gathering of arcade elite, the chapter analyzes several representational threads evident in the image. These include gender, technology, athleticism, youth, and American national identity and contribute to an idealization of young male gamers as representing traits desirable not only in the emerging gaming culture but in a broader cultural context—an idealization that served to counter the uneasiness over video gaming.

While the photograph ostensibly focuses on the gamers, it presents them as a social group, a pack of bright young boys and young men simultaneously at the cutting edge of a new technology and as all-American and familiar as a small-town baseball or football team. This image was the brainchild of the video game entrepreneur Walter Day, founder of the Twin Galaxies Arcade and later the Twin Galaxies Scoreboard. After weeks of selling the concept to *Life* magazine's editorial staff, Day convinced the reporter Doug Greenland that his vision—of the top video game players in the world gathered at the Twin Galaxies Arcade—was a winning way to represent video gaming in the "Year in Photographs" edition. Greenland arrived in Ottumwa with the photographer Enrico Ferorelli on assignment for *Life,* and the shoot was held in the middle of downtown. The image that resulted has become a beloved bit of cultural ephemera, appearing in arcade environments and acting as an icon conjuring up the arcade era in documentaries. The importance of the photograph to arcade culture is such that a 2005 reunion in Ottumwa, attended by Day and a number of the players featured in the original image, was arranged for the making of *Chasing Ghosts: Beyond the Arcade* (dir. Leon Ruchti; 2007), which focuses entirely on the golden era of video arcade games as depicted in the photo.

In addition to evoking the world of the arcade, however, the photograph also provides a window into how popular media imagined gaming and gamers, and how arcade owners and other members of the video game industry worked to project gaming as wholesome entertainment in the face of public distaste. With a detailed history and analysis of the photograph as an artifact from a specific moment, this chapter contextualizes the image within a cultural and political context that both amplifies and explains how competitive gaming came to be so synonymous with video gaming. Historicizing

FIGURE 10. This iconic photograph taken by Enrico Ferorelli
in Ottumwa, Iowa, appeared in *Life* magazine's 1982
"Year in Pictures" issue. Photograph copyright
Enrico Ferorelli; reprinted with permission.

this construction contributes to an understanding of the persistent
fetishization of individualized competitive achievement in gaming.
Further, it suggests that, at its perceived best, arcade gaming provided
an arena for young white men with quarters to burn to prove their
mettle. The salience of this interpretation of gaming has resulted in
a persistent cultural trope of the gamer as a young, technologically
savvy man and has also contributed to assumptions about video gaming as a culture and medium, fueling the prominence of specific types
of games.

To consider the implications of the photograph is to excavate
broad assumptions about what video gaming might mean not only to
players but to a broad public just becoming aware of video gaming
as an emergent, and potentially threatening, culture. The producers of the image, including Day, Greenland, Ferorelli, and of course
the young gamers, do much work to make gaming appear normal.

In the final result, video gaming is represented using the existing codes of young male identity provided by the cultures of sports and technology, presenting the brave new world of video gaming as simply another arena for America's young men to demonstrate their excellence.

THE PHOTOGRAPH

The arrangements between Day and gamers began months in advance; since many of the players were still in high school, their parents were hesitant to allow them to travel hundreds or thousands of miles away from home for the arranged photo shoot. *Life* ultimately allowed Day to hand out Greenland's direct number to skeptical parents, and Day not only promised to pay for the hotel rooms of the majority of the players and some of their parents but signed affidavits assuring parents that he would be responsible for chaperoning their sons.[1] After weeks of arrangements, Ferorelli photographed sixteen players in the middle of Ottumwa's Main Street in November 1982.[2] In the photograph, the players perch behind a bank of arcade games dragged into the middle of the street just for the occasion. In front of the games, members of the Ottumwa High School cheerleading squad strike a spirited pose. The street, lined with businesses, is largely desolate, with a few cars in the remote distance. Movie marquees and business signs are visible down the block. The scene presents a strange postcard of middle America. Upon further inspection, the image becomes only stranger, a montage of pop culture, technology, and nubile, youthful femininity specially arranged to support the ideological construction of the young men at the center.[3]

INTERPRETING GAMING

The gamers as photographed by Ferorelli fit into the framework of the most desirable gaming type: bright, clean-cut boys and young men from small towns, suburbs, and other regular places who were, at their very worst, a bit mischievous or a hair too competitive. This image of video gamers was one that those working in the coin-op business had a strong investment in, as it served as a counter to moral guardians' insistence that arcades were hotbeds of delinquency. The worst qualities on display in the *Life* photograph were qualities easily redeemed through comparison with earlier boy technologists or to athletes: at their worst, the boys were harmless troublemakers; at their best, they were entrepreneurs and innovators on the rise. Other aspects of the photograph help render the gamers familiar, from the setting in Ottumwa's neatly kept Main Street to the poses taken by the players.

To glamorize the top gamers was, inherently, to glamorize a competitive posture highlighted again and again in representations of the boys and men selected as the ambassadors of this new techno-cultural vanguard. Again, however, the new is shown tied to the old. The arrangement of the players and their games in neat rows is much like group portraits of sports teams—an impression driven home by the presence of the cheerleaders. In the individual shots that accompany the group photograph, most of the gamers stand with their arms crossed, a posture that visually references the poses struck by athletes in numerous portraits taken over the preceding century and reflects gendered standards of portraiture.[4] This tie to sports was a cultural connection that many made in the ensuing decades. It is also a connection that anchors competitive gaming to a culture of sex-segregated organized sport in which, as Michael A. Messner argues, " 'gendered cultures' come to seem natural."[5]

Only two of the young men photographed, Ned Troide and Billy Mitchell, deviate from the otherwise standardized athletic postures. Troide, who stands with one hand on his hip, gained notoriety for playing *Defender* for 62.5 consecutive hours on one quarter. Mitchell, who in the group portrait is holding a stuffed gorilla, was featured prominently in the 2007 documentary *The King of Kong: Fistful of Quarters* (dir. Seth Gordon) and remains one of the most famous classic arcade gamers in the world. In the *Life* portrait, the teenage Mitchell stands with his shoulders squared and his fists on his hips, wearing a gray sweatshirt with his high score for *Centipede*—a substantial twenty-five million points—printed on it in heat-seal letters. Both Troide's more lax pose and Mitchell's posture still echo the poses struck by varsity athletes, even if Mitchell's does seem to gesture toward the overstated macho of professional wrestling. The dominance of sport as male proving ground was widespread through the 1960s, and the visual reference here to the cultural institutions that had bolstered the development of young boys, that had been believed to "make men," is significant in what it implies about the role of gaming in the players' lives.[6] This implication is especially interesting, since, as T. L. Taylor notes in her exploration of more recent competitive gamers, geek masculinity and athletic masculinity are often presented as irreconcilable or conflicting.[7]

The individual visual nods toward modernist masculinity present in the image are furthered by other components in the group photograph. Heterosexual male desire is everywhere and nowhere in the photograph, revealed in background elements and in the cheerleaders who serve almost as props in the image. The movie theater is playing *Night Shift,* billed on the marquee as the "comedy sleeper of the year." In *Night Shift,* Bill Blazejowski (Michael Keaton) convinces straitlaced Chuck Lumley (Henry Winkler) that they should run a brothel out of the city morgue, where they work the deadly dull night shift. The film is a patriarchal fantasy of dead-end employment—take the job, make solid money running a sexy, illicit side business dependent on masculine authority because you want to "help" women stuck working for abusive pimps, then find and fall in love with your very own hooker with a heart of gold. Further, of the six arcade games featured—*Tempest* (Atari, 1981), *Defender* (Williams Electronics, 1980), *Ms. Pac-Man* (Midway Manufacturing, 1982), *Tutankham* (Stern, 1982), *Centipede* (Atari, 1981), and *Donkey Kong* (Nintendo, 1981)—only five are from the Twin Galaxies Arcade. The *Ms. Pac-Man* machine in the photograph was obtained after phone calls to other businesses in town, including rival arcades. The only *Ms. Pac-Man* that could be located was, in fact, in a topless nightclub located just yards away from Twin Galaxies.[8] The machines in the photograph were intended to match one-to-one with the players, meaning one of the players in town for the shoot had made his name with a top score at *Ms. Pac-Man.* Neither the marquee advertising *Night Shift* nor the topless nightclub are central to the photograph, but they are there on the edges like flying buttresses in support of the image of the young men at the center. The presence of these elements does not directly counter the presumed wholesomeness of the setting; doubtless, most viewers likely overlooked these details. However, their subtle, matter-of-fact presence demonstrates the extent to which such neutral territory was heavily marked by masculine identity and power.

Of course, the presence of the cheerleaders is inescapable. They drive home not only the attempt to frame the gamers in the rhetoric of wholesome athletic competition but also the attempt to locate them within a familiar framework of young manhood. The five young women are white, thin, and fresh-faced, wearing the pleated skirts and saddle shoes typical of cheerleading uniforms. They are also anonymous; nowhere on the pages that feature the photograph are they named, nor have they been sought after by documentary makers invested in producing "where are they now?" pieces about the players—although one appeared in a 2014 re-creation of the image circulated by *RePlay* via the magazine's e-mail newsletter. In the original image, the cheerleaders are, for better or worse, props to bolster the visual impact of the men displayed behind them, despite being separated from them by the looming arcade machines. The young woman in the center, who is wearing a different uniform shirt and appears to be the captain, is holding pom-poms over her lap, a pose that not only adds a further touch of varsity glamour to the image but also reduces the risk of unintentionally providing an upskirt view to the camera's prying eye. The other four cheerleaders each have an arm raised at an angle, a flat-palmed hand pointing toward the center of the bank of games. The cheerleaders here are blank slates, stand-ins for a specific kind of American feminine beauty presented so often as the rightful spoils of other kinds of American champions, normally reserved for football captains and other hometown heroes.

In many ways, the sixteen gamers in the photograph look much like other such heroes—one player near the center is even wearing a facsimile of a letterman's jacket featuring a patch advertising the Reflexions Fun Centre with a crude Pac Man logo. The setting, aside from the arcade games, is almost right. If they were baseball players or football players, they would be featured on the modernist pastoral scene of the sports field or, if basketball players or other indoor athletes, in the gym, that shrine of turn-of-the-century physical fitness. But these young men are a new kind of competitor and so are shown in a new kind of setting. The scene seems to revel in the developed, civilized background. There are neon signs and movie marquees, neat storefronts and street signs—one of which designates a certain stretch of curb "for taxis only." In this setting, the cheerleaders may seem a little bizarre, their manicured fingers reaching skyward, their knees pressed to the filthy blacktop, but their presence makes an ideological sense that is apparent in the other aspects of the photo; if these players are champions, then the cheerleaders are necessary, a marker of success.

According to Day, the crew from *Life* had initially wanted to haul the machines into a cornfield, but had decided against the idea after visiting a cornfield and getting a better handle on the logistics involved in such a stunt. The idea had been to emphasize the quasi-rural, agricultural character of Ottumwa, to highlight the unlikelihood of the seemingly sleepy midwestern town becoming the video game capital of the world.[9] But, even having settled on the less technically challenging tactic of placing the machines in Main Street, the arrangement remains visibly precarious. At least two of the young men in the photograph have their eyes closed. Several of the players grip the arcade machines or clench their fists with white knuckles. The two cheerleaders farthest from the center are delicately balanced and are also clinging to the machines to keep themselves from toppling. The struggle, then, to render these individuals intelligible to the audience manifests itself in the image where each human subject struggles to maintain composure long enough for the camera's shutter to close. The hurry implied by the failure to capture a photograph in which all group members are looking at the camera and the uneasiness evidenced by the tense knuckles highlight the tensions in the image itself and suggest similar tensions in the cultural context that produced it.

CRAFTING A DESTINATION FOR GAMERS

Just as the *Life* photograph happened at least partly because of Day's dogged insistence, the Twin Galaxies Arcade, the justification for the convergence of top gamers in Ottumwa, rose to prominence as a result of Day's entrepreneurial efforts. Even before he and Jon Bloch opened the arcade in November 1981, Day had begun maintaining a database of top scores for video games, largely out of personal fascination, by jotting down top scores from machines across the country as he traveled the country selling historical newspapers—Day had acquired a large collection of newspapers and was selling papers with notable historical headlines. As Day traveled from town to town attempting to make sales, he would stop in arcades:

> Where I'd go, I'd stop and play video games, so I was in a hun— more than hundred arcades just in the summer of 1981 alone. And, in fact in Salt Lake City I remember in particular that a TV, two TV stations were going to interview me, and I arranged for each one of them to show up at the local arcade that I insisted on meeting them at so I could play video games waiting for them and then play video games after they leave.[10]

Returning to Fairfield, Day aspired to open an arcade of his own. His friend Roger Silber, who co-owned arcades in Fort Madison and Dubuque, Iowa, helped Day form connections with route operators, and Day set up an arcade in Kirksville, Missouri, and one in Ottumwa, Iowa, with Bloch, who helped fund necessary renovations.[11] In February 1982 Day decided to make his score records public information as the Twin Galaxies National Scoreboard, an effort doubtless intended to draw more attention to his two arcades. As knowledge of the scoreboard spread, the Twin Galaxies Arcade and Walter Day (shown in Figure 11) both gained in fame.[12] Day launched the scoreboard by calling seven video game manufacturers—Exidy, Midway, Nintendo, Williams, Stern, Atari, and Universal—and the two trade publications, *RePlay* and *Play Meter*. On the first day, players referred by the manufacturers began calling the arcade to report their scores. Within three weeks, the arcade employees were fielding interview requests almost daily. By April, players from outside the United States began calling to report scores, and Day rechristened the board the Twin Galaxies International Scoreboard.[13] By maintaining the scoreboard, Day and Twin Galaxies contributed to the standardization of gaming practices. By celebrating achievements like highest scores, longest games, and even perfect games, the scoreboard created a kind of rubric for quantifiable gaming success, much as the similar celebration of player statistics has helped quantify sports like baseball, football, and basketball.

The rise of Twin Galaxies as international scorekeeping entity made the small-town arcades nationally and internationally significant

FIGURE 11. Walter Day, photographed in his home office in 2009, wearing his iconic referee's uniform. Photograph by the author.

(at least for those who had most fully immersed themselves in video game arcade culture and for those tasked with reporting on the cultural phenomenon), and Day's promise to *Life* that he would round up the top players in North America was far from idle. The players Day convened had all reported scores, verified by letters of proof from arcade managers, to Twin Galaxies. In submitting scores to Twin Galaxies, players and arcade staff members involved themselves in what was becoming a national and international network of players, with Twin Galaxies as a significant hub. While the business of video game design and manufacture may have been run by either old-line pinball manufacturers like Chicago Coin and Midway headquartered in Chicago or by more tech-focused upstarts like Atari and Exidy, based in California, the places where coin-operated gaming became a set of public practices were scattered across the United States. Unlike the manufacturers, which often relied on existing technology hubs as a pool of resources and talent, route operators and video arcade owners needed only a space accessible to young people with pocket change to spend. Indeed, operators and arcade owners often sought spaces without others in their business to offer competition. Route operators benefited from finding new types of locations for coin-op machines and from seeking under-used locations while maintaining their existing routes. The model of business expansion for a route operator was one that encouraged geographic expansion, as an operator would have no other option for growth after saturating the immediate area.

PRESENTING TWIN GALAXIES

When Day began working to arrange the *Life* photo session, he ini-tially had the arcade in Kirksville in mind as the setting. The arcade itself was larger, and Kirksville had a significant student population. But, as Day began planning for the event, he realized the arcade would need some renovations:

> So, I started working furiously getting ready for them coming when they said we're going to come. And I suddenly realized, I think I even asked the landlord, "Hey, will you give me some credit, or will you give me some loan, some money if I renovate your place to get ready for *Life Magazine* to come?" And I think that they said no, that they couldn't afford that, and so I realized that Ottumwa would be easier to renovate. So even though there was a huge following at Kirksville, Ottumwa became the video game capital of the world, by a stroke of fate. No one really knows the story because I've not really told this out. Ottumwa became the video game capital of the world because that's where *Life Magazine* came, and that's where everything—they had to come there, because it was easier to reno-vate Ottumwa to get ready for such a prestigious event, than it was to do it in Kirksville.[14]

The decision to invite *Life* to the arcade in Ottumwa instead of the arcade in Kirksville may have been a twist of fate, but for *Life* to send reporters out into the Midwest to cover "video games" for the 1982 "Year in Pictures" issue made perfect sense. Day's enthusiasm not only sold *Life* magazine but gained the support of the Ottumwa community. Before the renovations to the Ottumwa arcade were completed, including the addition of an actual display of top gamers (the scores had previously been maintained as a listing but not publicly displayed), the "world record headquarters" of gaming may have, in name, been Twin Galaxies, but it was in practice Day himself. After all, it was Day who had begun recording the scores and Day who persisted in recording them; in announcing the scoreboard publicly and giving out Twin Galaxies' phone number as the place to report scores, he involved the arcade employees, but without a location—a place where the scores were given physical form of some kind—the scoreboard remained an abstraction. With the renovations, the Twin Galaxies Scoreboard became a real place, and that place was Ottumwa.

With the renovations completed, Twin Galaxies became not only the place that journalists called for quick comments to fill out articles on the arcade phenomenon but the place where rivalries were born and carried out, and where competitive players were crowned the best, even if temporarily. The Ottumwa arcade was unique not only for Walter Day's ambitions but for the amount of community support and national attention it attracted. However, despite these areas of exceptionalism, Twin Galaxies demonstrates several important aspects of early arcade culture, and indeed, the ways in which Twin Galaxies seems to have been anomalous are still reflective of broader cultural trends.

For example, the competitive gaming culture so associated with and fostered at Twin Galaxies depended on the participation of thousands of gamers and arcade operators across the United States and abroad. So, while Twin Galaxies was the arcade with the most name recognition as a home for competitive gaming, it could exist as such only because competitive gaming was well established at many other arcades and in many areas. The scoreboard persisted because thousands of gamers had ambitions of high scores; many games had built-in scoreboards that recorded the highest scores attained on specific machines and allowed players to enter their initials when they scored high enough to make the list.

Competitive scoring was a key component of gaming and would have been even for players who had never heard of Twin Galaxies and whose ambitions did not exceed the desire to rank on the *Galaga* or *Centipede* machine in their local arcade. The arcade games themselves developed in urban and industrial hubs, but the development of arcade culture was much more diffuse, drawing on the experience of innumerable game players in thousands of arcades. Twin Galaxies' status as an "exceptional" arcade positions it perfectly to provide insight into aspects of gaming that were then common across the United States. Twin Galaxies was not a newfangled family entertainment center or megaplex, nor was it part of a boardwalk, amusement park, or other larger tourist destination. It did not offer the competing amusements, such as carnival rides or mini golf, that characterized many of these other sites. The Twin Galaxies Arcade, even as it became established as scoreboard and gained attention outside Iowa, was first and foremost an arcade. Further, it was an arcade frequently held up as embodying the broader arcade culture through media attention.

When *Life* decided to buy into Day's vision of how to best represent "video gaming," the magazine's editors were committing not only to Twin Galaxies Arcade in Ottumwa as the setting but to the arcade as the true location of video game culture. Further, they were committing to represent a gaming culture tied in profound ways to individualized competition, technological proficiency, youth, and masculinity. So while the account of how and why *Life* magazine chose to photograph a group of young men gathered behind arcade machines in the middle of downtown Ottumwa may be a story about a photograph, it is also a story about the way cultural and economic anxieties affect the articulation of youth, about the construction of masculinity and cultural power, and about the deployment of nostalgia in the construction of the future—or what we believe will be the future.

COMPUTER CULTURE AT PLAY

Arcade cabinets occupy both the literal and metaphorical center of the image. They are the cultural artifact most readily identified with the nascent gaming culture and therefore occupy an important ideological position in the image, but they are also placed directly in the center, backdrop for the beaming cheerleaders and foreground for the gamers posed behind. In 1982 the arcade cabinets that to us look quaint would have looked new—perhaps, in the context of Main Street, Ottumwa, even shockingly new. In significant ways, the type of masculinity on display in conjunction with the arcade games was also new. Rochelle Slovin, founding director of the Museum of the Moving Image in Astoria, New York, argues that the proliferation of video games as popular entertainment represented a significant shift in Americans' understanding of what computers might mean for the average person. Drawing from Sherry Turkle's description of the movement "from a modernist culture of calculation toward a post-modernist culture of simulation," Slovin says it was "the moment when we stopped using computers as tools and started using them as culture."[15] The "computer" technologies on display in the *Life* photograph doubtless fall into the arena of computers as mass culture, the video games providing a relatively approachable form of computerization, accessible to anyone who happened on a machine and had some spare change in his or her pocket. The photograph both shows computers as culture and shows what the culture of computerization and video gaming might look like.

But what can we make of this moment of computers as culture? The questions over who would have access to this culture and what that access might mean present several troubling quandaries. Writing about the implications of computer use for the workplace, Shoshana Zuboff warned that the machines would bring with them shifts in the very nature of work:

> Computer-based technologies are not neutral; they embody essential characteristics that are bound to alter the nature of work within our factories and offices, and among workers, professionals, and managers.[16]

A similar point can be made about computers as mass culture. The essential characteristics that Zuboff sees have implications not only for work but for leisure and play, which is not to suggest that these arenas are easily separable. As statistics continue to demonstrate inequities of access not only to computer technologies but also to the socioeconomic mobility they can bring, the fact that the wunderkinds presented in this moment of shift from computers as tools to computers as culture are wonder*boys* takes on added significance, as does the seeming racial homogeneity and the fact that these "world"-renowned players were overwhelmingly American.

In 2008, when women made up 38 percent of video game players, they were just 12 percent of those working in the video game industry, a gender inequality reflected in other tech-related fields as well.[17] Further, research has consistently shown that access to computer technologies and the Internet is not universal, even in affluent nations like the United States, and more pronounced inequalities of technological access in the developing world have become a serious policy concern as Internet access has become essential to many industries, and a lack of access usually exacerbates limits on educational and economic opportunity.[18] A broad overview of Internet access in the United States in 2000, for example, revealed that even while there was gender parity in the online population, women lagged behind men in participation. Further, while 50 percent of whites had Internet access, only 36 percent of blacks and 44 percent of Hispanics had access. Household income directly affects who has access. In the 2000 report, less than one-third of those in households earning less than $30,000 yearly were online. Those in rural areas also had less access.[19] Young, white, American men were and are among those most likely to have access to emerging technologies.

The seemingly homogeneous racial composition of video game players as represented not only in the *Life* photograph but through many of the other representations discussed in later chapters bears noting. That the top gamers themselves appear to be all or mostly white may reflect socioeconomic inequality along racial lines, since white teens are more likely to have the kind of disposable income necessary to pursue competitive gaming. But this explanation is not wholly satisfactory, particularly when considering this racial exclusion as part of a larger trend in representations of gamers from this period. Certainly there were video games in neighborhoods that were predominantly African American and Latino. Day noted in an interview that operators had told him that some machines were more profitable in black neighborhoods, while others would make more money in white neighborhoods.[20] This evidence is anecdotal, but does suggest that coin-op video games were placed in minority neighborhoods with some regularity. If this is true, then the choice of which games to include in the photograph may have affected the racial diversity of the gamers included. Additionally, the group of gamers who competed on *Starcade* reveals some racial diversity, which suggests that competitive gaming as well was likely not entirely homogeneous.[21] The representation of gaming, and of video gamers, is bound to certain ideals of white middle-class male identity through the exclusion of diverse narratives of gaming and through the exclusion of gamers who do not fit assumed notions of race and gender.

GOOD TECHNOLOGY, GOOD (ENOUGH) KIDS

The approach to computer technology represented by the group portrait in *Life* may, as Turkle and Slovin suggest, been new, but it was simultaneously backward looking, participating in an existing—and persistent—discourse of manhood and technology. The identities invoked by the young people in the photograph also exist at this intersection of the new and the established. The novelty of video games had been preceded by decades of technological novelty packaged through narratives of progress and prowess. The "new" man, buttressed by his affinity for and close association with cutting-edge technologies, had also been preceded by a long history of narratives of masculinity.

Susan Douglas writes about the celebrity of William J. Willenborg, an amateur radio experimenter who, at the age of twenty-six in 1907, was featured prominently on the front page of the *New York Times Magazine*. His technological achievements were constructed as feats of manly prowess—the writer took pains to point out that Willenborg could "destroy" messages from other operators and that he had built his radio station himself. Later articles claimed that Willenborg, though boyish and well-mannered, spoke like "a man of science."[22] Willenborg and his peers were examples of nascent modernist masculinity—they were boy geniuses expected to become good organization men and, most likely, experts in science or technology who would channel their boyish curiosity and passion into acts of invention that would benefit society.

Boys' culture in the postwar period further supported the centrality of scientific and technological pursuits. While boys' culture stressed "physical competition, construction, and rough-and-tumble play," the period also saw an intensified focus on science, math, and foreign language as public school subjects. This focus resulted from a perceived crisis in education triggered by the Soviet Union's successful launch of Sputnik, the first satellite.[23] While girls often received much of the same science instruction at school as their male peers, professional limitations for women in the postwar period proved to be significant barriers to women's entry to these fields.

During this period, scientists and engineers emerged as valuable fighters in the U.S.–Soviet "space race," and educational reforms reflected this focus. The success of the Manhattan Project cemented the national interest in scientists, and popular narratives of atomic science cast scientists as potential heroes. Several films of the 1950s showed scientists as world-saving protagonists.[24] Astronauts gained a kind of celebrity status during this period. Both astronauts and the engineers and technicians who made space travel possible also embodied idealized concepts of masculine identity, as summarized by Roger D. Launius, curator of Planetary Exploration Programs at the Smithsonian Institution's National Air and Space Museum:

> The Apollo astronauts all had an image of hard-working, fun-loving, virile representations of masculinity. The expression of public comfort with the white male establishment is palpable throughout the recounting of the story of Apollo. The quintessential company man worked for NASA during Apollo. The engineering "geeks" of Mission Control, with their short-sleeved white shirts, narrow black ties, slide rules hung on their belts like sidearms, and their pocket protectors complete with compass and ruler and myriad pens and mechanical pencils all personified a conservative America that many look back on with fondness and nostalgia.[25]

Popular perceptions of astronauts and Mission Control engineers as summarized by Launius demonstrate an ongoing investment in and fascination with technologically skilled men. Launius's identification of these types of masculinity as objects of nostalgia also suggests how these ideals have shifted or been effaced over time.

Henry Jenkins argues that video games are an extension of the gendered play spaces developed in nineteenth-century boy culture. Gaming comes as a progression in a set of cultural tropes that have deep roots in nineteenth-century boy culture and that were sustained well into the postwar period. For Jenkins, boy culture helped young men cultivate social bonds that trained them for participation in social organizations like clubs and fraternities while also helping initiate them into a male business culture.[26] Coverage of early video games contained echoes of the coverage of Willenborg and his peers, and similarly celebrated technological skill throughout coverage of the space race and through midcentury educational reforms. However, coverage of gamers also demonstrated a break with this legacy that speaks to significant shifts in labor and economic expectations of young men.

While writers at the turn of the century worked to assure readers that amateur radio operators would be good organization men, as the end of the century drew near, the necessity of such appeals had dwindled. In a post-Watergate, post-Vietnam era, many were skeptical, if not downright suspicious, of the ethics of the organization mentality that had so marked the modernist culture of the midcentury United States. And the stagnation in economies nationally and globally had contributed to an increased sense of instability among U.S. workers in the face of a restructuring of labor, which had implications for masculine ideals. Moreover, the viability of such claims was limited. Gamers were often engaged in illegal or semilegal activity, including phreaking practices, using audio frequencies to manipulate the phone system to score free long-distance and conference calls. Phreaking is, of course, tied culturally to hacking.

Although Day wrote later, "They were all super brilliant, computer proficient, clean-cut kids," he referred to the group in the same piece of writing as "bored, mischievous pranksters." None of the players to his knowledge smoked, drank, or used drugs, but he still had to handle the headaches of them being thrown out of two hotels in Ottumwa, and two of the players slept through the photo session, missing it entirely.[27] In an interview in 2008, Day again reiterated that the champion gamers were intelligent, mostly well-behaved teens:

> Essentially the champions would be 16, 17, or 18 usually. Very rarely older. And they were all smart, they were all like genius type people, and they hard—and none of them ever drank. They weren't like drinkers, they didn't smoke cigarettes, and they didn't take drugs. They were very much like athletes. Very clear, bright, creative young kids. Didn't drink, who didn't smoke, who didn't take drugs. It was an interesting phenomenon.

He further suggested that some of the same characteristics that made these young men exceptionally good gamers may have inclined them to mischief:

> I think that what it is, is that they have so much creative energy. The creative force that gives them the understanding to uh understand how to solve a game, that creative force also just wanna bust out, it's just like a, just too much dynamism, too much energy, too

much creativity, so they just become just driven to do more things. I think, I think that they didn't like restrictions and that's why they were so mischievous, because they just had so much creative force going on. I think that's the only way I can describe it. They were just too talented and they didn't like structure or restrictions or limitations, so they misbehaved a bunch in the hotel and found ways to creatively express themselves in mischievous ways, so I think that sort of sums it up.[28]

Day frames the players' troublemaking as a positive indicator of creativity and intelligence.

The late twentieth-century romanticization of "thinking outside the box" and "innovation" has made it easy to redeem these behaviors as markers of intellectual and entrepreneurial inclination. Examples abound of the way that a specific kind of technologically oriented boyishness has become a desirable quality for entrepreneurs. This propensity toward troublemaking, or at least giving the appearance of troublemaking, may have as its totem the Jolly Roger flag that flew above Macintosh headquarters in the 1980s.[29] But in the face of a widespread uneasiness with video gaming's influence on youth, such behavior may have been more difficult to reframe as positives.

In thinking about the framing of mischievousness as a desirable quality, the differences in perception of this quality based on the race, class, and gender of individual actors is important to bear in mind. For example, studies have shown that the same actions deemed "youthful hijinks" when carried out by white boys are often considered signs of delinquency if carried out by African American boys. In a similar way, socioeconomic class has a strong impact on the consequences that juveniles face for drug- and alcohol-related infractions. Girls often face more rigid limitations on social behaviors than boys, a cultural reality succinctly summarized in the phrase "boys will be boys." This saying implies that mischief is integral to boyishness and therefore excusable or even admirable, as boyishness is a positive quality in an androcentric culture. I am not implying that these inequalities are comparable or that they are the only inequalities that affect the cultural construction of mischief; rather, I am offering them as a few examples of how the kind of "mischievousness" that Day highlights as an easily redeemable quality is limited by categories of identity.

All of this is to suggest that the troublemaking of the young men and boys in the *Life* photograph could be recast as symptoms of socially desirable qualities such as intelligence and creativity because of their sociocultural position. This interpretation of the limitations of *mischief* is bolstered by the word's etymological origins. The root *chief* in the term refer to head or rule, and is the same root as the modern *chef* who serves as head of the kitchen.[30] Mischief, then, is a poor exercise of power or authority, a meaning that carries the implication that only the powerful can engage in mischief. These implications explain why "mischievousness" as a neutral or even endearing characteristic is ascribed only to the most enfranchised of youths. While youths lack the level of authority that adults wield, the discrepancies in relative power and privilege among youth populations reflect more general hierarchies of power based on race, class, and gender. Young white men are allowed to be "mischievous," while other youths are deviant or delinquent.

GAMERS AS ATHLETES

In addition to framing the boys' mischievous behavior, Day also makes explicit the connection between athletic competition and gaming competition that is suggested, visually, in the photograph by the cheerleaders. This connection between athletic competition and gaming competition predates Twin Galaxies and has persisted as a trope as competitive video gaming has been professionalized (although, as Taylor notes, Twin Galaxies never quite successfully crossed over into the professionalized, or at least semiprofessionalized, world of e-sports).[31] The notion of gaming as "all-American pastime" and competition was salient enough that in 1977 Coca-Cola ran a television advertisement set in an arcade. In the advertisement, a group of teen girls challenges a group of teen boys to a video game. The main actors, one boy and one girl, are both wearing a shirt emblazoned "Champ." The two compete at *Pong,* with the girl winning the match. The girl then offers the boy a Coke and a kiss. The writer who summarized the advertisement in *RePlay* considered it a conscious nod to Billie Jean King and Bobby Riggs.[32] The engagement with gaming as athletic competition here is overt. The ad also exists in a moment of high visibility for feminism and seems to offer a postfeminist reassurance that competitive women can still be attractive to and attracted to men.

Route operators and others in the video game industry cultivated the ties between gaming and athleticism. At the 1980 Winter Olympics in Lake Placid, New York, athletes could also choose to compete in the Olympic Arcade Tricathlon in the Olympic Village. The event had been proposed by Jack LaHart of Lake Placid, a coin operator who worked with Irving Kaye, Bally, and Midway to secure a collection of pinball machines, video games, and foosball tables.[33] The winners of the Arcade Tricathlon included the Canadian ski jump team member Steve Collins (see Figure 12), Alex

FIGURE 12. Steve Collins, a member of the Canadian ski jump team, won the Olympic Arcade Tricathlon held in 1980. Photograph from *RePlay* magazine; reprinted with permission.

Michaelides of Cyprus, and British biathlete Paul Gibbons. Collins, aged fifteen, scored impressively on the pinball game *Harlem Globetrotters* and Midway's video game hit *Space Invaders,* performing well enough to take the top title despite winning no foosball games. In coverage of the event, *RePlay* cites Collins as saying that pinball and skiing require similar levels of talent, discipline, and reflexes.[34] In a perhaps unwitting historical echo of this promotional event, the Global Gaming League made efforts to bring video gaming to the 2008 games as a demonstration sport.[35]

Efforts to tie video gaming to the perceived wholesomeness of athletic competition were a calculated effort to raise the visibility of video games and produce a positive image of gamers and gaming. These efforts drew on a long history of sport as a way to deter young men from criminal activities and prepare them to participate appropriately in civic, familial, and corporate life—in short, to make them into men. As early as the 1890s, "Muscular Christianity," an ideology that combined Christian activism and athleticism and is perhaps most directly associated with the Young Men's Christian Association (YMCA), and athletic organizations were seen as essential to maintaining order as the American frontier closed.[36] While the YMCA and other organizations served working-class men, colleges and universities had begun fielding organized teams in sports including football, tennis, golf, and rowing in the nineteenth century. According to the sports historian Harvey Green, participation in these sports was intended to prepare young men for the workforce:

> The growth of collegiate athletics was itself a result of the efforts of physical education instructors, coaches, and eager alumni who in one way or another envisioned "manly sport" as a way to develop the strength of mind and body that would aid American men as they endeavored to meet the challenges of a new corporate industrial order.[37]

Framing of video gaming as athletic competition tied gaming to this legacy of sport as a way to socialize young men for adult pursuits. By presenting video gaming as a new type of sport, industry advocates argued that video gaming should be embraced as a new way to socialize young men.

ARCADES AS TEENAGE WASTELAND

The aggressive response to the video game arcade was part of a more general attack on the public culture of adolescence, which had a long history but a great deal of momentum in the 1980s. Youth mall culture died out partly because of private restrictions on loitering and on minor access to businesses without adult chaperones. By the late 1970s, communities had begun taking measures to prevent video arcades from proliferating, and zoning ordinances and other hurdles helped slow the pace of arcade openings and machine placements. By December 1976, the coin-op trade magazine *RePlay* was warning that zoning measures were posing an acute threat to the industry. Certainly such efforts were not new, but the craze for video games seemed to inspire fresh vigor. An unsigned editorial in *RePlay* warned operators of the dangers these regulations posed:

> How many of you realize that arcades are being zoned out of existence, regardless of the type of equipment placed in them; TV games, or flippers, or rifles, it makes no difference. Once classified as an arcade, they are not permitted. . . . Let us determine the places where we are being hampered the most. Let us examine the psychological reasons for the prejudices that still linger against us as a business community. Let us not be afraid to defend ourselves against unfair attacks.[38]

Play Meter ran its own coverage of efforts to regulate arcades; in "Fighting City Hall," the writer Gene Beley referred to the efforts to regulate coin-op games through fees and licenses as "economic discrimination."[39] Arcade owners and route operators saw these provisions as efforts to clip the wings of the industry based on an unfair assumption that the businesses contributed to delinquency or were themselves tied to organized crime. To be fair, the coin-operated industry had in the past served as an easy money laundering racket, but by the mid-1970s, the U.S. Department of Justice claimed that this was no longer the case.[40] Associations lingered despite the Department of Justice's assurances. The newness of video games may have helped sever associations between the coin-op industry and criminal elements as they presented a new yet unsullied type of coin-op game.

At least one *RePlay* editorial claimed that video games raised the overall profile of the industry, helping coin operators place machines in formerly unlikely locations like hotels, airports, and department stores.[41] However, the same proliferation likely helped curtail the spread of video games and arcades gain traction.

These efforts may have reflected an anti–coin-op bias, but they also reflected efforts to limit the proliferation of crowds of young people in public places. The number of 1970s and 1980s horror films that feature children and adolescents as monsters suggests how acute discomfort with youths had become. This fear of children was contrasted with a fear *for* children. The 1981 kidnapping and murder of six-year-old Adam Walsh and subsequent made-for-TV movie sparked a public frenzy, which was further fueled by a hotly contested Department of Health and Human Services estimate that put the number of children kidnapped annually at 1.5 million.[42] Regardless of the questionable accuracy of these statistics, the scare they caused was pervasive and a very real part of the daily lives of most children and caretakers in the 1980s. Terrorized parents were inundated with milk carton pleas for the safe return of sweet-cheeked children and news reports warning against satanic rituals, unmarked white vans, and strangers with candy. The full-fledged paranoia over child-snatching creeps only furthered the uncertainty many adults felt about the wholesomeness of arcades, shopping malls, and other youth spaces.

In addition to the more long-standing unease surrounding arcades, and the period's general uneasiness with public youth culture, authority figures raised specific concerns about the effect that video games might have on young people's physical health. U.S. surgeon general C. Everett Koop and other health experts warned of the dangers of injuries like "video elbow" and "arcade arthritis," ailments similar to carpal tunnel syndrome that were caused by the repetitive motion required for effective game play. "Video elbow" is a reference to and pun on the well-known sports injury commonly referred to as "tennis elbow" and may be another example of the linkage between sports and video gaming. Both of these creatively named ailments, however, make the point that video gaming may be physically dangerous to young people.

These ailments are also an interesting link between the seeming leisure of video game play and the labor of the computerized work-place. The association of physical injury with specific occupations has a long history; carpal tunnel syndrome (CTS) was previously known by the specific occupations that seemed to cause it, as in "telegraphist's cramp" and "tailor's cramp." CTS gained attention as an occupational injury in the 1980s largely because strikes at meatpacking plants highlighted the prevalence of repetitive motion strain injuries among workers. For meat packers, repetitive motion injuries became another of the many physical risks faced by factory laborers. However, for white-collar jobs, the rising number of CTS cases seemed to reveal the potential dangers of jobs frequently assumed to be less risky to physical health.

In the aftermath of this increase in public awareness, the number of worker's compensation claims related to CTS increased over 500 percent between 1986 and 1992, despite increased awareness of risk and improvements to work environments.[43] With computerization, the risk of repetitive motion injuries including CTS among white-collar workers has risen; today, CTS is most associated with those whose work involves a high volume of typing. Repetitive motion injuries have become so common in the computerized workplace that companies like Hewlett Packard have ergonomic specialists on staff to help address the physical safety of their white-collar staff.

Leisure-related injuries like arcade arthritis and video elbow may have been an early warning of emerging occupational hazards for a wide range of white-collar workers. That young people were suffering ailments associated with the old or overworked as a result of leisure activities made these activities suspect. Youths were playing video games too much, they were taking the games too seriously, and both problems demonstrated the bigger problem that video gaming was bad for children. These young people, however, were suffering the same kinds of injuries that would confront them after they entered the workforce, and in this way, the physical rigors of video gaming can be seen as a precursor to the physical rigors of occupations such as, for example, computer programming.

In addition to the physical hazards the games posed, the games were suspected of presenting an array of psychological or mental dangers. An August 1980 *New York Times* article raised the possibility

that video gaming could trigger compulsive or even addictive behavior. Although the experts cited in the article were ambivalent,
several suggested that they or their organizations had been contacted
by parents concerned about their children's gaming habits.[44] Koop
was quoted in the copy that accompanied the photograph in *Life* saying, "There is nothing constructive in the games." The statement's
implication, of course, was that video gaming was at best a waste of
time that would be better spent on more meaningful pursuits. Koop's
assertion is relatively mild in contrast to more forceful criticism from
journalists and the National Safety Council, which held that many
games were outright destructive, promoting war through simulated
warfare, or reveling in violence.[45]

The persistence and variety of the attacks on the video game
arcade make a clear case for why arcade owners, route operators,
and others invested in the coin-op video game industry felt a need
to defend the industry and so actively campaigned to create a more
positive impression of arcades and gamers. Human interest pieces
about exceptional gamers; the opening of clean, modern, family-
oriented arcades; or industrial entrepreneurs all helped create a strong
counternarrative. The gamers were not delinquents; they were bright
young men. The arcades were not for teenage troublemakers; they
were for families. The game designers were not opportunists send-
ing out violent games without a care for their consequences; they
were brilliant engineers and businessmen. The effort to help craft
this alternate vision of video gaming is evident in the work of LaHart
and Day to draw attention to arcade games and shape the image
of gamers.

In addition to these physical maladies, and aside from the debatable effects of video game violence, which had been a topic for
intense scrutiny since the video game version of *Death Race 2000* set
off a national moral panic in 1976, the games demonstrably fostered a
culture of intense individual competition.[46] The players on hand for
the *Life* magazine photo session spent most of their time in Ottumwa
challenging each other on various games, during which Steven San-
ders was revealed to have reported a false score for *Donkey Kong*—he
proved incapable of replicating his reported high score or a score
even close to it, and several of the other players easily beat him at the
game.[47] He remained in the photo, regardless.

LIFE MAGAZINE'S ANTHROPOLOGICAL EYE

The presentation of video gaming in *Life* may have looked to gaming through Day's vision of gamers as bright young athletes or budding technologists, but it also looked to gaming as an only semi-explicable youth phenomenon, a topic to be viewed and interpreted by a detached observer. In many ways, *Life* magazine took on the type of outsider-looking-in posture that had become common with ethnographic films and writings at the turn of the century, and this perspective had long formed the magazine's bread and butter. *Life* applied this perspective rather broadly, deploying it with equal skill in articles about Australian aborigines and in articles about teenage rock and roll fans and mods. By the time the 1982 "Year in Pictures" issue hit the stands in January 1983, *Life* had a long history of translating youth culture for those whose lives kept them at a distance from the practices of teens. As James Gilbert suggests, the magazine had, by the 1950s, become one of the primary interpreters of American youths, running story after story about the seemingly bizarre cultural practices of juveniles:

> *Life* . . . assumed the role of responsible guide for social change. It mixed equal measures of warning and reassurance into a recipe followed closely by almost every other periodical of the decade [1950s] writing about teenage culture.[48]

In these explorations, the magazine frequently alternated postures, simultaneously stimulating fears of delinquency and bad behavior while assuring adults that the kids were basically all right. In the pages of *Life,* youths were always exotic and in need of explanation to adults who worried about these strange creatures wandering the streets of the suburbs and participating in unfamiliar cultural rituals. *Life* approached the foreignness of American youths with an anthropological eye much like the one that *National Geographic* used to peer at the peoples and cultures of developing nations. In this role, *Life* alerted adult readers to youth trends and guided them toward conclusions about these trends. The mix of warning and reassurance generally took the form of trying to convince adults that the new was somehow old, that the shocking was easily understood, and that any upheavals at work would certainly right themselves soon enough.

Placed in this context, the coverage of arcade gaming was in some ways unexceptional; indeed, the "Year in Pictures" issue also included articles on other youth trends and current events. There was a piece on "rap" and another exploring the cuteness craze as represented by the Smurfs, Strawberry Shortcake, and other "kids' stuff." More serious coverage of national and international affairs appears alongside these pieces on pop culture. Articles addressed the national unemployment crisis, the Palestine Liberation Organization, and the conflict in the Falkland Islands. One piece features Nancy Reagan's breathless recounting of her trip to Europe. A particularly jarring photograph shows young women at the Illinois statehouse, fasting to show their support of the Equal Rights Amendment.

Throughout the magazine, the insider–outsider age dichotomy dovetailed and worked with similar divides like rural–urban, male–female, and old–new. Arcade gaming was located at an intersection of many of these dichotomies. Some adults, like Day, quickly latched on to the new entertainment technologies. But they were relatively few, forming a small but significant group of "early adapters" who did not represent the reactions of the general public. Many small towns had arcades for at least a few years, and many arcades existed in the suburban sprawl where they were easily accessible for teens. Even urban arcades were quickly marked as spaces for youth, and doubtless many adults would have found the darkness, flashing lights, and constant noise an effective deterrent. *Life*'s coverage of youth cultures worked toward several goals: interpreting and translating youth culture for adult readers, simultaneously soothing and stimulating fears raised by the otherness of the young and by the threat of urban decay.

As an act of interpretation, an attempt to make sense of an emergent culture, *Life*'s photograph is a key image of the golden age of arcade gaming. It reveals the ease with which the maleness of gaming was assumed and naturalized through popular representations and highlights how active key individuals like Walter Day were in fighting for particular presentations of video gaming and video gamers. The photograph exists at a moment of cultural, economic, and technological uneasiness. Even as the image overtly engages with new technologies, it presents compelling evidence that the "new" technologies and the attendant cultural changes need not be threatening. In fact, the details of the image suggest that these changes will not be so dramatic; the emerging technological culture will still be the domain of white, heterosexual men. The prodigies of this emerging technological order may be young, but their youth will enable them to adapt to the changing demands of the economy and the work-place. Their very youth, their boyishness, will help them to succeed, and the youthful qualities that seem to distinguish them, when placed in coverage of earlier boy geniuses like early radio operators, are not so novel. As *Life* magazine presented them, then, the young men of the early 1980s arcade were different from their predecessors in their technological fluencies and their cultural obsessions, but were other-wise familiar. Ultimately, the vision of gaming displayed in *Life* was a somewhat defensive measure intended to show the wholesomeness and familiarity of the young men who found success and recognition in the arcade; it is a significant and highly circulated attempt to inter-pret video gaming as culture and render it intelligible and familiar to an audience who may never have set foot in an arcade.

In the *Life* photograph, we are viewing the struggles between familiar forms of industrial modern masculinity and emergent forms of postindustrial, postmodern masculinity. The machines' newness is contrasted with the cheerleaders' traditional uniforms and the play-ers' athletic posturing. The photo presents a complex exploration of what it might mean to be an American man in an era long after the deployment of Theodore Roosevelt's rugged masculinity, in a historical moment just as the space race was giving way to Star Wars, when headlines were warning again and again that Japan and other Asian economies were outpacing the United States and threatening the nation's role as a world power and technological innovator. The *Life* photograph attempts to frame the gamers—the best in the world and overwhelmingly from the United States—as all-American, draw-ing on the ethos of athletic display and of boy genius narratives. In entering into this negotiation between the old and the new, the pro-ducers of the image, including Walter Day, Enrico Ferorelli, Doug Greenland, and the young men and women in the photograph, at-tempt to render themselves and this new mass culture intelligible and familiar, suggesting that the new medium of the video game and, by extension, the newly domesticated technology of the computer were nothing to worry about: they were merely further arenas for Ameri-can men to prove their masculinity and superiority.

ADAPTING
VIOLENCE

DEATH RACE
AND THE HISTORY OF
GAMING MORAL PANIC

IN JULY 2011 the U.S. Supreme Court ruled in *Brown v. Entertainment Merchants Association* that video games qualify for the same free speech protections that cover other forms of expression; in their ruling, the justices cite a rich history of prior free speech cases.[1] These cases include landmark decisions that helped deregulate film screenings and cable television broadcasting, and the Court's 2010 decision in *United States v. Stevens*, 559 U.S. 130 S.Ct. 1577, which "held that new categories of unprotected speech may not be added to the list by a legislature that concludes certain speech is too harmful to be tolerated."[2] At stake in *Brown v. EMA* was not the fate of a single game but instead the circulation of games in the state of California; the contested statute barred the sale or rental of "violent" games to minors without the consent of a parent or guardian. In the majority opinion in *Brown v. EMA,* the justices note that "this country has no tradition of specially restricting children's access to depictions of violence" and hold that "California's claim that 'interactive' video games present special problems, in that the player participates in the violent action on screen and determines its outcome, is unpersuasive."[3] In the

United States, debate over the alleged social ills of video gaming has a lengthy and colorful history.

The fetishization of novel media technologies in industrial and public narratives of video gaming helps obscure the medium's long cultural history. Debates about video game violence seem perpetually new, as the specific technologies used to depict violent acts are endlessly retooled with an eye toward interactivity, immersion, and realism. Each installation in the *Grand Theft Auto* franchise, for example, has stirred new outrage based partly on the games' increasingly sophisticated graphics. The seeming freshness of outrage masks a history of moral panics about video game violence stretching almost as long as the history of the industry itself, beginning with Exidy's *Death Race* in 1976. The game, based on the 1975 film *Death Race 2000,* made waves far beyond the confines of the coin-op industry and helped establish the Exidy brand nationally. For moral guardians suspicious of or hostile to the budding culture of video gaming, *Death Race* became the most prominent example of video games' depravity and corrupting influence.

OF SILVER SCREENS AND DEATH SCREAMS

In the film *Death Race 2000* (see Figure 13), set in the year 2000, the United States has collapsed because of a financial crisis and a military takeover. In the wake of the upheavals, the United States has been reconceived as the United Provinces. The Bipartisan Party has subsumed all political parties, creating a one-party system. The Bipartisan Party also serves as the nation's religious leadership, as church and state have unified. The nation's figurehead is the charismatic Mr. President (Sandy McCallum), who alternates between soothing assurances and fiery incitements like the most skilled cult leader. The citizens of the United Provinces remain placated through the spectacle of ultraviolent sports. The most popular is the Annual Transcontinental Road Race. The race, considered an important symbol of the nation's values (which include "the American tradition of no holds barred"), is a cross-country road race in which motorists run down pedestrians for points. Elderly victims are worth a whopping 70 points, while women are worth 10 more points than men in all age brackets, teenagers are worth 40 points, and so on. For efficiency's

In the year 2000 hit and run driving is no longer a crime. It's the NATIONAL SPORT!

DAVID CARRADINE

DEATH RACE 2000

DAVID CARRADINE "DEATH RACE 2000" SIMONE GRIFFETH SYLVESTER STALLONE
SCREENPLAY BY ROBERT THOM AND CHARLES B. GRIFFITH · ORIGINAL STORY BY IB MELCHIOR · PRODUCED BY ROGER CORMAN · DIRECTED BY PAUL BARTEL · RELEASED BY focus film distributors

FIGURE 13. A poster for *Death Race 2000* (1975) features David Carradine's Frankenstein character and letters oozing blood.

sake, the race coincides with the ever-popular Euthanasia Day, so motorists can contribute to the public good by mowing down pensioners whose wheelchairs and hospital beds have been rolled out for the occasion.

The film is intended as dystopic social satire. Despite a sense of general malaise, the citizens of the United Provinces are not universally content. A resistance group called "the Army of the Resistance," led by Thomas Paine's descendant Thomasina Paine (Harriet Medin), works to assassinate the racer Frankenstein (David Carradine) and replace him with a double. The resistance believes Frankenstein is a personal friend of Mr. President, and the leader will end the race in exchange for Frankenstein's safe return. Annie (Simone Griffeth) is Thomasina's granddaughter and Frankenstein's navigator; she plans to lure Frankenstein into an ambush. She learns, however, that Frankenstein wants to win the race so he can blow up Mr. President with a grenade disguised in his prosthetic hand. Frankenstein becomes the winner—and only survivor—of the race, but his hand grenade plan is derailed by an injury. Annie dresses in his costume and plans to stab Mr. President, but is shot and wounded by her grandmother in a case of mistaken identity. Mr. President is ultimately mowed down by Frankenstein in his race car. In the film's epilogue, Frankenstein and Annie are married, and Frankenstein has become the new president. He overhauls the United Provinces legal system and includes among his reforms the abolition of the Transcontinental Road Race.

The film seems to skip glibly between outrageous deaths and car stunts. The cars' spiked fronts equip them as killing machines. A worker performing road maintenance is gored, and his freshly minted widow is later interviewed on national television and informed that as the widow of the race's first victim, she has won an apartment in Acapulco and a fifty-inch three-dimensional television. A fan who has won the opportunity to meet Frankenstein insists "scoring isn't killing . . . it's part of the race." Another racer chases a fisherman down a creek and flattens him. These and other scenes of violence present a deliberate excess, which goes far beyond any attempt at realism and slips into the camp presentation so common among B-movies.

While reveling in violence, the film also engages the United States' real midcentury car culture, including the horsepower wars that peaked in the early 1970s before ending in the wake of the oil crisis and a bevy of car-obsessed films and television series released during the same period. *Death Race 2000* takes the visuals of car culture to an often comical extreme, but these same visuals provide a key aesthetic and thematic point of reference. U.S. car culture, particularly muscle car culture, is tied to expressions of masculine identity and technological power and mastery, a configuration of associations that parallels video gaming's then emerging social and cultural position. Car culture reflects both R. W. Connell's identification of skill as the marker of middle-class masculinity and her identification of force as the marker of blue-collar or working-class masculinity; further, car culture can be seen as an example of the growing masculine consumer culture identified by Michael Kimmel.[4] Cars have long been a highly visible example of U.S. consumer culture and middle-class stability or aspirations, and by broadcasting class identity, cars become an extension of their drivers' identities, as evidenced in the use of phrases like "I'm a Ford man, myself." The cars in *Death Race 2000* are similarly extensions of their drivers' abilities and personalities, as indicated by the drivers' outlandish themed costumes and the cars' often impractical visual styling.

Critics were divided over whether the film was scathingly funny or simply a crass bloodbath delighting too easily in the same culture of violence it ostensibly critiques. Writing for the *New York Times,* Lawrence Van Gelder dismissed the film by suggesting it had failed as satire:

> In the end, it [*Death Race 2000*] reveals itself to have nothing to say beyond the superficial about government or rebellion. And in the absence of such a statement, it becomes what it seems to have mocked—a spectacle glorifying the car as an instrument of violence.[5]

Roger Ebert, writing for the *Chicago Sun-Times,* awarded the film zero stars and did not engage with the film much in his review, choosing instead to meditate on his experience seeing an audience full of children watch the movie with glee.[6] Negative critical response to the film was not universal. In the *Los Angeles Times,* Kevin Thomas said that the film "demonstrates that imagination can overcome the tightest budget." In addition to praising several actors' performances, he dismissed criticisms of the film's violence, saying, "there's much slaughter in 'Death Race 2000,' but it's presented so swiftly that the film avoids an unduly hypocritical exploitation of that which it means to condemn."[7]

As in the case of many other cult films, critical distaste did not mark the film as a failure. The outrage evident in reviews like Ebert's and Van Gelder's may have served the contrary purpose of driving viewers *to* the theaters. I know the film's infamy, and the difficulty of finding a VHS or DVD copy during the years when it was out of print only added to my adolescent desire to see it. When I finally did find a copy to watch, in a moment marked by the emergence of the horror films derisively dubbed "torture porn," I found it more comical than unnerving. Exploitation films had—and still have—an audience of devotees who came to them for bare breasts, violence, and scandalous subject matter.[8] The movie was a low-budget piece produced by Roger "King of the B-Movies" Corman. Intended to compete with *Rollerball, Death Race 2000* performed well, despite having a budget of only $300,000.[9] Rental revenues totaling $4.8 million fleshed out the film's box office profits.[10] The same visual orgy of visceral pleasure that delighted many audience members—some of them quite young—also outraged moral guardians. As Ebert had noted, the film's R rating did not seem to be an adequate barrier between the film and the minds of impressionable youngsters.[11] Despite the film's modest budget and relatively low box office take, it gained a high profile. Reviews in the *New York Times,* the *Los Angeles Times,* and the *Chicago Sun-Times* would have reached a large audience.

In addition to fitting within the historical production category of the exploitation film, *Death Race 2000* was released simultaneously with an emergent mainstream cinema more prone to displays of violence and overt sexuality. The U.S. Supreme Court's decision in *Memoirs v. Massachusetts* in 1966 held that only materials which could be shown to be both "patently offensive" and "utterly without redeeming social value" did not qualify for First Amendment protections.[12] Two years later, the Hayes Code, which had restricted cinema production, was replaced by the more permissive voluntary Motion Picture Association of America ratings system. In 1973 the U.S. Supreme Court further extended free speech protections in the decision in *Miller v. California,* permitting obscene materials as long as they were not distributed to minors or to third parties who had not specifically requested these materials.[13] Looser definitions of obscenity led to a proliferation of violent and risqué films in the United States that would not have passed muster under the previous regulatory standards. Many like *Death Race 2000* or even pornographic films like *The Devil in Miss Jones* (1973) and *Deep Throat* (1972) gained cult status that sustained their popularity long enough to make them early video rental favorites later that decade.

The relaxing of governmental and industry regulation of film production meant that films like *Death Race 2000* could make some claim to cultural legitimacy and were less likely to face outright banning or suppression. *Death Race 2000* may have been a low-budget film, but it had a cast of legitimate actors and a production team with enough clout to garner reviews in major papers. The film was a recognizable name and became a cult hit; film listings for the *Dallas Morning News* indicate that theaters in the area were still screening the film with some regularity in 1978, three years after its release, with screenings also in 1979 and 1980, often alongside domestic and international horror/action films like *Death Rage, Master of the Flying Guillotine, Schoolgirls in Chains,* and *Chain Gang Women.*[14] Despite Ebert's concerns about the film reaching a young audience, *Death Race 2000* fit in well at drive-ins and late-night screenings catering to devotees of oddball cinema, an outlet where it persisted long enough to become a recognizable brand, and where, at least in the case of the drive-in, viewing context may have added to the effect of watching cars mowing down hapless pedestrians.

The cultural context into which Exidy launched *Death Race* as an arcade upright in 1976 was shaped not only by the film that inspired the game but also by a broader debate about media and amusement regulation and youth access in the United States. Coin-op amusements had long been regarded with suspicion in the United States, and moral reformers had successfully influenced the regulation of film and comic books, among other media. The Comics Code, in particular, resulted from efforts to curb the spread of materials deemed inappropriate for young readers. While U.S. video game manufacturers may have early thought of their machines as bar amusements intended for adult consumers, the appeal to and popularity among younger players fueled moral guardians' anxieties about video games. Arcade video games had no ratings system to indicate the intended or appropriate audience for particular machines. Even the MPAA film ratings system was quite young at the time, and, as Ebert notes in his review of *Death Race 2000,* that rating system was not entirely effective at keeping younger viewers away from adult materials. In the absence of a clear definition of appropriate audience for *Death Race,* moral guardians seem to have assumed that the game's accessibility to children meant that it was intended for them, and newspaper coverage of the game, featuring photographs of young players, helped promote this idea. The photograph from the *Sacramento Bee* featured in Figure 14 is one example of such images circulated.

MARKETING CONTROVERSY

In 1976 when Exidy selected the name *Death Race* for a new chase-and-crash game, the game company was attempting to cash in on the film's infamy, a strategy that guaranteed the game a certain level of name recognition and invited controversy. Exidy was not alone in attempting this strategy; a year earlier, Atari had released *Shark Jaws* (see Figure 15) as an unlicensed tie-in to the highly successful *Jaws* (1975) film. Like *Shark Jaws, Death Race* was not licensed, and the film's copyright holders were not consulted, but consumers readily made the connection between the game's pixilated graphics and the film's orgy of automotive violence. This connection precipitated what became video gaming's first significant moral panic. Atari's *Gotcha* (1973) had caused a kerfuffle several years earlier over its pair of round pink rubber controllers, which looked a bit too much like breasts for the comfort of some critics—especially since the controllers had to be squeezed to operate the game. Employees at Atari reportedly referred to *Gotcha* as "the boob game." Overall, *Gotcha* fared poorly in the market even after the pink globes were replaced with standard joysticks.[15] But the mild controversy over *Gotcha* was nothing compared to the deluge of media attention and moral outrage that met *Death Race*.

FIGURE 14. This photograph from the *Sacramento Bee* in 1976 shows two young children engaged in a game of *Death Race*. Courtesy *Sacramento Bee*.

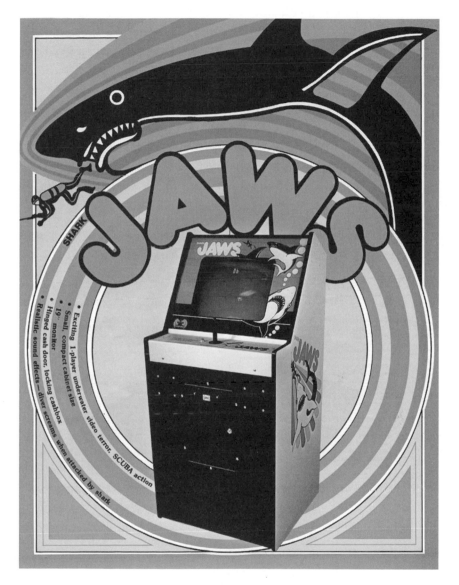

FIGURE 15. The flyer for Atari's *Shark Jaws* (1975) emphasized the game's shark theme while drastically minimizing the word "shark" in the title; the game title is easily misread as simply "Jaws."

Death Race followed on the success of Exidy's *Destruction Derby* (1975), which had sold well. However, while *Destruction Derby* was one of at least three car crash games on the market, *Death Race* was presented as something innovative and exciting.[16] The first of a series of advertisements for the game to appear in trade journals boasts of the game's unique design and links it to various historical car- and motorcycle-loving bad guys (see Figure 16):

Death Race 98
It's indescribable. So different. It's in a class by itself!
Death Race 98 is what the player wants it to be
mobsters in the 30's
commandos in the 40's
dragsters in the 50's
hells angels in the 60's
street racers in the 70's
The first game to require the player to "get involved."
If you liked Destruction Derby . . .
   Double your profits with Death Race 98.[17]

The advertisement features the marquee picture from the game cabinet complete with muscle-car racing ghouls. The statement that the player will have to " 'get involved' in whatever way he wants" suggests a male audience, but more important, it suggests that the game will provide an immersive, engrossing environment.

The advertisements in *RePlay* do not target players directly, just the route operators who purchase and place coin-op machines in public places. The goal is not to convince individuals to play the game but to convince operators that the game will hook a general audience and prove a moneymaking investment. Exidy considered the cabinet graphics to be a major selling point for *Death Race,* and so the flashy marquee graphic dominates the advertisement. Individual coin-op machines represented significant investments for route operators, and the move to video games increased the investment required for each machine. Operators could be hard to sell on new games, especially when they could instead purchase and place more copies of games already successful at their existing locations. The reference to *Destruction Derby* links the game to Exidy's past success, while the text as a whole suggests, none too subtly, that the game is different enough to

EXIDY introduces:

DEATH RACE 98

* IT'S INDESCRIBABLE * SO DIFFERENT, IT'S IN A CLASS BY ITSELF *

DEATH RACE 98 is what the player wants it to be

> mobsters in the 30's
> commandos in the 40's
> dragsters in the 50's
> hells angels in the 60's
> street racers in the 70's

The first game to require the player to "get involved" in whatever way he wants.

If you liked Destruction Derby . . . . double your profits with DEATH RACE 98 — It's a chase and crash game with a twist.

1 or 2 player — 25¢ per player — adjustable playing time

for more information contact your nearest distributor or Exidy, Inc., 166 San Lazaro Street, Sunnyvale, California 94086 (408) 733-1104

FIGURE 16. This early advertisement for *Death Race* (1976) emphasizes its connection to Exidy's earlier successes while suggesting the game's action is broadly appealing.

hook a larger audience of players, whether they are interested in '50s dragsters, '30s mobsters, or '70s street racers, while ensuring that it will be as good an investment as *Destruction Derby*.[18]

A second advertisement for *Death Race* features simple typography with a photographic image of the game cabinet. Exidy's marketing and sales manager Linda Robertson suggests that the graphics were at least as important to the game as the gameplay: "The artwork alone on this game . . . showing the skeletons, gremlins and graveyard . . . is certain to invite immediate player interest. The play of the game is so much fun they'll come back again and again."[19] More obviously appealing to operators, the ad includes promises of high profits and excellent technical service:

> Step Aside!
>   Here comes the leader of the pack!
>   Death Race by Exidy
>   A chase and crash game
>   With a twist

This text is followed by a bulleted listing of the game's technical specifications, such as setting options and screen size. The advertisement ends by stressing the game's profit potential, claiming that gamers will want to replay the game:

> Double your profits with Death Race
>   It's Indescribable!
>   So different, it's in a class by itself!
>   Captures your eye when you see it
>   Captures your fancy when you play it
>   And brings 'em back for more[20]

The advertisement appeals to profit motives at several points, promising double profits, repeat customers, and readily available service to save operators from profit-sucking downtime. In a third advertisement, elements of the cabinet graphics make up most of the ad, with a photographic image of a cabinet shown as well. The ad shows the Exidy name several times, but the main text reads simply: "New! Death Race. It's fascinating! It's fun chasing monsters" (see Figure 17).[21] Although controversy did not begin brewing until the spring buying season had ended and operators began placing machines, the

FIGURE 17. The slogan "It's fun chasing monsters" serves to distance *Death Race* from accusations that it celebrated vehicular homicide.

ad makes explicit that players are chasing "monsters," not to be confused with people.

The advertising copy and the featured artwork on all the advertisements for *Death Race* tie the game to a male-dominated car culture and suggest, both implicitly and explicitly, that the intended player will be male. Even in the first advertisement, which attempts to tie in with an array of cultural references, these references are heavily skewed toward an appeal to male players. These references also, perhaps more subtly, tie the game to earlier male-identified technologies, from the motorcycle and the drag racer to machine guns and other military weaponry.

The gameplay of *Death Race* is similar to more recent games like *Carmageddon* (Stainless Games, 1997) and *Grand Theft Auto* (Rock Star North, 1997), which allow players to drive over human or humanoid figures in the game world. *Death Race* can be played as a one- or two-player game. The operator could adjust the game to give players between 80 and 135 seconds of playtime per purchased game with games costing 25 cents for a single-player game and 50 cents for a two-player game. Each player operates one of two on-screen cars using a steering wheel, pedal, and a shift lever. The objective is to hit as many "gremlins" as possible. Each struck gremlin leaves behind a cross-shaped tombstone, which becomes an in-game obstacle for the duration of the game; because of this, each possible iteration of the game has a unique playing field depending on how many gremlins were struck and where they were struck.[22]

Gremlins can be struck only when they are in the central "legitimate playing field." In two-player mode, players are competing against each other for the most kills. A player therefore might choose to deliberately crash into the other player to prevent him or her from striking a gremlin. The game ranks players depending on the number of points they score. These rankings—skeleton chaser for 1–3 points, bone cracker for 4–10 points, gremlin hunter for 11–20, and expert driver for scores greater than 21—further the horror-inspired theme of the game.[23]

As opposed to the lush cabinet graphics, the on-screen graphics in *Death Race* are rudimentary. The "gremlins" are stick figures and the cars are simple blocks with wheels. The game's "violence," then, is very dependent on context. But to perceive pixilated black-

and-white graphics as simple as those in *Death Race* as violent gore is not fantasy. Context contributed to the certainty that reformers felt when criticizing the game. The film *Death Race 2000* had already become a notable example of violent cinema, familiar even to those who had not seen the thing. Despite the film's limited circulation, reviews like Ebert's primed the public to assign outrage to any media affiliated with the film. Because the game's title deliberately associated it with the movie, the film's story became the game's narrative world. No matter how many times Exidy executives claimed that the figures were "gremlins" or how many advertisements stressed that the object of the game was to chase "monsters," severing the association with the film's pedestrian targets was an impossible feat. Within a few months of its release, *Death Race* was attracting national scandal and earning coverage in major news outlets, including the *New York Times* and *60 Minutes*. Interviews with Exidy executives made clear that the company found the controversy a combination of annoyance and good source of publicity.

VIOLENT NARRATIVES AT PLAY

One peculiar aspect of the controversy is the larger context of other coin-op video games available in 1976. While the lively used market certainly expanded the number of games available for purchase at any given time, I focus here on the new machines sold through distributors. Even a cursory glance at listings of new machines makes clear that *Death Race* was not the only violent game on the market. Atari's offerings in 1976 included five games that could be categorized as violent: the rather self-explanatory *Cops 'N' Robbers*; the chase and crash *Crash 'N' Score*; the Wild West–themed gunfighting game *OUTLAW*; *Jetfighter*, which featured simulated jet dogfighting; and *TANK 8*, an eight-player tank warfare game. Chicago Coin, of course, had its chase and crash, *Demolition Derby*, available. Electra's offerings included *AVENGER*, a scrolling shooter game in which the player piloted a fighter plane. Digital offered a jet-fighting game with the rather self-explanatory name *AIR COMBAT*. Meadows was manufacturing *Bombs Away*, in which players piloted bomber planes and sunk ships, and Fun Games had a seek-and-destroy aircraft game named *BiPlane*.

Death Race was not an isolated incident of violent gaming; it existed in a field packed with competitor games with equally violent premises. Despite the overt violence in these games, they did not attract the scrutiny that greeted *Death Race*'s entry into public consciousness. The public response indicates that the game's monster chasing was considered more horrifying than the human-on-human violence featured prominently in many other games at the same time. Several factors may have contributed to the specificity of the response to *Death Race*. At a basic level, the game's flashy cabinet graphics set it apart from other games in the arcade. The game's on-screen graphics, rudimentary as they look in retrospect, were unusual in featuring humanoid figures as general targets. Other games, like *OUTLAW* and *TANK 8,* that featured human-on-human violence fit within broadly accepted cultural and historical narratives of violence. Military games, in particular, would not have disrupted the accepted governmental monopoly on violence. War is commonly justified, or even glorified, as a defensive practice at the very least, as well as a way to preserve certain ideals or even prove national vigor. The vigilante justice of the Wild West is often romanticized as a critical step in the "civilizing" of the region. The violent fantasies of the other games listed here would have fit within accepted violent realities.

The violence of many of these games may have been overlooked because it was not considered violence against human actors; although tanks, airplanes, and submarines are presumably operated by people, these human actors never appear on-screen and are rarely, if ever, alluded to. Nolan Bushnell implied as much:

> We were really unhappy with that game [*Death Race*]. We [Atari] had an internal rule that we wouldn't allow violence against people. You could blow up a tank or you could blow up a flying saucer, but you couldn't blow up people. We felt that that was not good form, and we adhered to that all during my tenure.[24]

Of course, Atari's *OUTLAW* directly violates this purported policy. Regardless of where the line was drawn about human actors, the violent realities depicted by Atari and other companies were like games in being governed by specific rules of engagement. The quickdraw contest starts reliably at ten paces, and limited warfare of any kind is predicated on rules of engagement. In this way, as James Campbell suggests, once it has been reduced to a historical narrative draped in nostalgia, even the proverbial hell of war can operate ludologically, which is to say, as a game.[25] Video games based on war and gun duels, then, may not have offended because they are based on realities already experienced as games at some level. *Death Race* did not fit within these violent realities, instead presenting a fictional landscape that most closely echoed the reality of the pedestrian hit-and-run accident. The reality presented is too unregimented, too suggestive of violent chaos. The objection, then, may not be the violence per se but the lawlessness of that violence and the suggestion it carries of violence outside the accepted social order.

MEDIATING THE MAYHEM

By 1976 there were several dozen video games on the market, and route operators were clamoring to place the most successful machines in prime locations. When *RePlay* reported on the top-performing games in October 1975, just three years after video games became the hot new thing in the coin-op industry, video games already made up a significant percentage of route collections. The estimated weekly gross for video games was $43 per machine, outpacing every other type of machine except pool tables, which inched ahead with a weekly gross of $44 per machine. In bars and taverns, video games were tied with shuffle alleys as the third most popular type of game after pool tables and pinball machines. In less explicitly adult venues, they fared even better: in restaurants and other food-serving businesses, they ranked second after pinball games.[26] Efforts to curtail the spread of video games, through zoning, code restrictions, and other local measures, speak to a more general discomfort with the games and an assumption that the games were reaching and potentially damaging young players. The violent actions depicted in *Death Race* became a lightning rod for a broader uneasiness about games, particularly with regard to youth access. Several of the factors outlined above likely contributed to the reaction to the game, and different factors may have helped mobilize different people.

Once identified as a controversy, *Death Race* attracted high-profile media attention. Even coverage that appeared as news helped perpetuate the controversy by legitimizing concerns and raising awareness of the issue. An article in the *New York Times* in December 1976 indicated that the game had attracted the attention not only of local authorities but of the National Safety Council. In the article, the author refers to the game's stick figure targets as "symbolic pedestrians" and quotes extensively from the manager of the NSC's research department, the behavioral psychologist Gerald Driessen. Driessen notes that nearly nine thousand pedestrians were killed in the past year, presumably in driving accidents, and argues that video game violence is categorically different from television violence:

> On TV, violence is passive. . . . In this game a player takes the first step to creating violence. The player is no longer just a spectator. He's an actor in the process. . . . I'm sure most people playing this game do not jump in their car and drive at pedestrians. . . . But one in a thousand? One in a million? And I shudder to think what will come next if this is encouraged. It'll be pretty gory.[27]

In the article, Exidy's response, delivered by way of General Manager Phil Brooks, is that the game is not actually depicting graphic violence: "If we wanted to have cars running over pedestrians, we could have done it to curl your hair." He goes on to comment that the sound that accompanies the gremlins' destruction is a "beep," not a scream or shriek: "We could have had screeching of tires, moans and screams for eight bucks extra. . . . But . . . we wouldn't build a game like that. We're human beings, too." At the time of the *New York Times* article, Exidy had already built and sold nine hundred *Death Race* units (like those shown in Figures 18 and 19), and Brooks explicitly said that coverage of the game, no matter how negative, had driven sales.[28]

A *New York Times* article published in August 1977 again summarizes the game and quotes Driessen, but here the tone is different. Titled "Postscript: Controversial 'Death Race' Game Reaches 'Finish' Line," the article presents itself as a close to a controversy that had made headlines for the better part of a year. Exidy had ceased manufacturing *Death Race* earlier in 1977, and though the remaining machines might be problematic, the game seems less of a clear and present danger. The article does recount a scene from Westwood Electronic Amusement Center in Los Angeles, where the reporter

FIGURE 18. The *Death Race* cabinet featured horror-inspired graphics and twin controls. Photograph by Rob Boudon; cropped by the author; licensed under Creative Commons 2.0 (https://creativecommons.org/licenses/by/2.0/).

FIGURE 19. Exidy staffers gathered around a
Death Race cabinet in 1976. Reprinted
with permission of *Play Meter* magazine.

saw a young girl score six hits on the machine while under the supervision of her father, who encouraged her by saying, "You sure were
chasing them." The article closes by quoting a thirteen-year-old fan
of the game who responds to the suggestion that the game may make
him violent: "That's stupid, and besides I don't even know how to
drive."[29] The issue is presented as somehow resolved, no longer a
serious threat, even though children are still playing the offending
game.

When Exidy first began manufacturing *Death Race,* the company
had not considered the game one of its more important designs. According to Paul Jacobs, who served as executive vice president for
Exidy in the 1980s, the game was "originally viewed by the company
as nothing more than an intermediary piece with a limited run."[30]
The game had performed well, but had not attracted much attention
and did not seem slated to become a hit when an Associated Press
reporter based in Seattle wrote a story raising questions about how
child-appropriate the game was. The story captured public interest
and triggered coverage in other outlets. In defending the game, Exidy

rarely addresses the game's intended audience; instead, the company seeks to minimize the game's violence and stresses that the publicity has been beneficial. Jacobs repeated the belief that the publicity had been good for the company's image, had driven sales of the game, and had raised the image of the video game industry:

> We're not at all ashamed to talk about "Death Race." . . . The net result was that we handled the whole thing very well and the publicity was good for the industry. . . . As for the game, the media attention made it more popular than we ever imagined it would be. . . . We built over ten times the number of machines in the original release.[31]

As media outlets cast attention, even negative attention, on the Exidy brand and interviewed Exidy executives, they raised the profile of the company among operators choosing games for purchase. A short *Play Meter* article covering the game's success claims that Jacobs was "badly misquoted" in the initial AP story and quotes an "elated" Jacobs: "*Death Race*'s obvious acceptance by the general public is evidenced by looking in the cash box. It's always full of quarters!"[32] The infamy of the *Death Race* game not only drove sales of the original game but prodded Exidy to release a sequel, *Super Death Chase*, in 1977.[33] In a *RePlay* article giving a ten-year retrospective on Exidy's early success, Kathy Brainard says that *Death Race* received "more media attention than any other game prior to 'Pac-Man.'"[34] Brainard's hyperbole makes an important point about *Death Race*'s infamy and what that infamy afforded. In addition to helping establish Exidy as an industrial player to watch, *Death Race* helped drive Exidy's sales and helped secure the company's financial position.

LINGERING IMPACT

Death Race helped establish not only the Exidy brand but a pattern for future moral panics over video games. *Death Race* may have been the first of these, but controversy greeted various subsequent games, many of which, like *Death Race,* enjoyed a spike in sales because of the publicity. While for the remainder of the 1970s and the early part of the 1980s the public debate on video games moved from concerns over specific games to worries about the arcades themselves, the issue of violence simmered in the background, boiling over at the release of certain games or in the face of particularly horrifying acts of violence perpetuated by youths. Two particularly infamous game franchises, *Carmageddon* and *Grand Theft Auto*, draw inspiration directly from *Death Race 2000* and the legacy of the *Death Race* game.

When the British company Stainless Games released *Carmageddon* in 1997, the public response bore striking similarities to the response to *Death Race*. *Carmageddon* is a racing game with vehicular combat in which players gain extra time by damaging other vehicles, collecting bonuses, or striking pedestrians. Like *Death Race*, the game featured vehicular violence that existed well outside established and accepted narratives of violence. In the United States, the Entertainment Software Ratings Board gave the game an "M," the board's second-most restrictive rating, intended to indicate that the game is suitable only for players who are at least seventeen years of age. The game was censored in other countries, including the United Kingdom, where censors insisted pedestrian victims' blood be changed from red to green to give credence to the claim that the victims were not human.[35] As with *Death Race*, the controversy did not stifle sales and instead drove them. According to lead programmer and company cofounder Patrick Buckland: "We weren't known, the brand wasn't known. . . . The game had to stand on its own two feet, and it might not have done that without the violence—though it did get fantastic reviews."[36]

Positive reviews or not, *Carmageddon* would not have drawn much attention outside publications intended for gamers had it not been for the surrounding controversy. As a small studio, Stainless Games did not have the resources to mount large-scale advertising or publicity campaigns. As Buckland points out, the game may not have sold well had it not been for the violence. Even with its positive reviews, *Carmageddon* would not have reached an audience outside the population of dedicated game consumers if it had not received attention from mainstream media outlets, which it did only as a result of the game's controversial content.

Another twist on the gleefully violent car game is Rockstar Games' *Grand Theft Auto* franchise, which appeared in the same year as the first *Carmageddon*. In the *Grand Theft Auto* games, the protagonist is an aspiring criminal who climbs the organized crime ladder by completing assigned tasks; the game features nudity, gun violence, drunk driving, drug dealing, and vehicular violence including pedestrian hit-and-run collisions. Notably, all the games in the franchise have male protagonists in their core narratives; when criticized, Dan Houser, vice president of creativity, defended the choice to have all playable characters be men, claiming that "the concept of being masculine was so key to this story."[37]

The franchise has proved so controversial that the *Guinness Book of World Records* named it the most controversial video game series in history.[38] Again, like *Death Race* and *Carmageddon, GTA* focuses on violence outside the established social order. This is not the violence of war or the Wild West or even the police procedural, which are often framed as necessary to maintaining order, but instead a violence that is reckless and at times seemingly joyful. Additionally, high-profile cases in which the games were blamed for acts of violence have fueled the controversy. In 2003 William Buckner, age sixteen, and his stepbrother Joshua Buckner, fourteen, killed one person and seriously wounded another by shooting at their cars. The boys told authorities that they had decided to shoot at vehicles with rifles because of *Grand Theft Auto III*.[39] In another suit, plaintiffs blamed *Grand Theft Auto* for the shooting deaths of two police officers and a dispatcher at the hands of a seventeen-year-old.[40]

The increasing sophistication of graphics, sound, and other design components of titles like *Carmageddon* and *GTA* helps animate debate over these games. The novel media technologies employed contribute to the sense that the games pose a new, unique threat and help differentiate them from earlier games in public discourse. While *Death Race* and the controversy that surrounded it may in retrospect appear quaint given today's media context, they occupy a critical role in the development of public perceptions of video gaming and public debates about the appropriate and intended audiences for video games. As evidenced not only by *Death Race* but by these more recent franchises, controversy does not stifle the production of violent video games; in fact, public discourse about violence only helps reiterate that video games are violent, not only by making the connection between video games and violence over and over again but also by raising the profile of particularly violent games.

Sales figures further suggest that controversy drives sales. In 2010 the Entertainment Software Ratings Board reported that only 5 percent of the games rated by the board received an M, or "Mature" rating, but five of the ten top-selling games that year were rated M.[41] All five of these M-rated top sellers—*Call of Duty: Black Ops, Halo: Reach, Red Dead Redemption, Call of Duty: Modern Warfare 2,* and *Assassin's Creed: Brotherhood*—received their M rating largely for violence. That several of these games depict militarized violence, as in the case of the *Call of Duty* titles, or Wild West violence, as in the case of *Red Dead Redemption,* is worth noting, as these games continue to adhere to acceptable discussions of violence and are by degrees less controversial than the transgressive violence depicted in *Death Race, Carmageddon,* and the *GTA* franchise. Regardless, however, these games prominently feature violence and are frequently cited as examples of violent games while garnering spots on top-seller lists. Violent games become the most popular partly because they draw the most attention, which further normalizes them. There is much more discussion about a game like *Death Race* or *Grand Theft Auto* or *Call of Duty,* and this discussion, in reaching people who would not necessarily be playing games, renders this violence an integral part of video games *as a medium.* From 1976 to the present, violent games have become so common, if not at the level of manufacture then at least at the level of play and of public discourse, that it is impossible to separate violent video games from the broader category of video games. The focus on male protagonists and the thematic ties between these games and historically male domains like car culture and the military have also helped present gaming as a masculine pursuit.

The case of *Death Race* makes provocative suggestions about the way that moral panics drive the production and distribution of violent games and help normalize violent content across the medium. In the history of video game violence specifically and the history of moral panics about media culture and youth more generally, the role that public controversy plays in shaping industrial production and distribution of certain types of games is a point worthy of further research and consideration.

4

AΠARCHY IΠ THE ARCADE

REGULATING COIN-OP VIDEO GAMES

ALTHOUGH THE REACTION against *Death Race* in 1976 may be the earliest moral panic about video gaming, it was far from the last. Coin-operated video games remained a source of contention through the mid-1970s and into the early 1980s. During the same period that video games proliferated and were celebrated as a sign of technological progress, numerous communities organized against arcades through zoning ordinances, code enforcement, and other restrictions. While many of these efforts reflect an ongoing push to curtail the operations of the coin-op industry, which had long been associated, fairly or otherwise, with organized criminal activity, the industry saw a revival of animosity as video games increased in visibility. Community leaders often explicitly cited video games in their campaigns to regulate the coin-op business. And, even where efforts to regulate the coin-op business appear to take a more general approach, the timing of these efforts is revealing, coinciding with the moment during which video gaming is the most widespread.

Ronnie Lamm of Brookhaven, Long Island, became nationally visible because of her fight to regulate video games in her community. In a 1982 article in the *New York Times,* she summarized the push against video games in her town:

> Our community was becoming like Las Vegas with one-armed bandits in every store. We asked the town of Brookhaven to call a moratorium on granting permits for any more arcades.[1]

Lamm and other advocates in Brookhaven were not alone. The Board of Trustees in Irvington, New York, imposed a moratorium on the opening of arcades, and a debate in Lynbrook, New York, on a potential prohibition of coin-op video game access for minors caught national attention.[2] The efforts were not limited to small towns or suburbs, and major cities like Boston, San Francisco, and even coin-op industry hub Chicago seriously considered or enacted regulations. Communities across the United States engaged in pushback against the spread of video games through new regulations or through fresh enforcement of existing, often neglected, policies. While these efforts were often localized, they were part of a larger, national conversation about the values and dangers of video games and their appropriateness for youths.

Moral guardians and would-be regulators often conflicted directly with the coin-op industry, particularly route operators, who fought back through public relations efforts aimed at framing games as wholesome and beneficial. Industry boosters like Walter Day were aided in their celebration of video gamers' desirable qualities by popular media including major Hollywood films like *TRON* and *WarGames* and positive articles in reputable newspapers and magazines, but even the most glowing accounts of video gaming often revealed some tensions. Day admits, for example, that the champion gamers who converged in Ottumwa got kicked out of a hotel, and although audiences are led to sympathize with and celebrate the protagonists of *TRON* and *WarGames,* these same protagonists evidence some tendencies that set them against established social order. Even when celebrated, then, video games are seen as enabling or encouraging boys' disruptive behavior. Not everyone was seduced by the argument that video games would instill such potentially positive values as technological literacy, problem solving, or even hand-eye coordination. While many advocates for gaming brushed aside these disruptions under the trite adage that "boys will be boys"—as gamers were, already, frequently assumed to be boys—those invested in curtailing access often cited the same types of problems in pushing for regulation, arguing that the games were corrupting a generation of boys.

In this chapter, I detail efforts throughout the late 1970s and early 1980s to regulate and restrict the spread of coin-operated video games and arcades. I connect these efforts to existing regulatory regimens intended to curtail access to coin-operated games more generally, including earlier regulations addressing both pinball and gambling machines, but argue that the emergent technology of video gaming and the games' seemingly direct appeal to youths revitalized these efforts in many communities. Throughout, this chapter notes how the ills ascribed to video game arcades simultaneously reflect older anxieties about youth delinquency and the coin-op industry alongside newer anxieties about technological, cultural, and economic changes happening nationally. Throughout, I argue that efforts to police video game access arise largely from debate about what activities should rightly be included as a part of childhood in general and boyhood in particular. Drawing from U.S. Supreme Court decisions on arcade restrictions, I argue that the arcade presents a critical moment in the configuration of youth civil rights as consumer civil rights.

COIN-OP'S DUBIOUS HISTORY

Efforts to regulate coin-op video gaming were geographically widespread, and they also drew on long-standing suspicions of the coin-op industry. Existing regulations in several communities facilitated the ongoing or increased regulation of a wide array of coin-op machines as did existing stereotypes and history. The coin-op industry suffered for its associations—fair or otherwise—with money laundering and organized criminal activity, its long-standing cultural and historical ties with gambling, and a more general distaste for amusement devices as a frivolous use of leisure time. All three of these reputational problems facing the industry drew on long-standing historical precedent and presented significant challenges to respectability. They also, perhaps more importantly, create a context in which video games may be readily judged morally suspect through even vague association.

Assumptions of criminality have long plagued the coin-op industry. There is evidence tying the operation of machines to various types of illicit activity, most notably money laundering, as the machines present an easy way to account for an influx of cash. Al Capone famously used a chain of Chicago coin-operated laundromats to figuratively launder the profits from his illegal prostitution, gambling, and racketeering business. The *Chicago Sun* estimated in 1946 that the Chicago Syndicate accounted for about 75 percent of the city's coin music business and that some five thousand pinball machines were being operated illegally in the city.[3] A 1967 report issued by the Chicago Crime Commission exposed organized criminal activity in the coin-operated vending machine business.[4] While Chicago may provide particularly lurid examples of the coin-op industry's association with criminal activity, such connections were widely assumed. Ties to organized crime plagued the industry until well into the 1970s. Some ordinances, such as the Mesquite, Texas, ordinance at question in *City of Mesquite v. Aladdin's Castle, Inc.* responded to these associations. Under the Mesquite ordinance, those applying for a license to operate a coin-operated amusement machine would be assessed by the chief of police, who would make a recommendation based on whether they had any "connections with criminal elements."[5] In 1983 in Marshfield, Massachusetts, Thomas Jackson, "a former Massachusetts narcotics officer and head of the Marshfield Vandalism Committee," proposed a complete ban on coin-op video games because, he claimed, the local arcade sites were businesses suspected of drug trafficking and the local industry was run by "hoods." Said Jackson, "I don't want my children supervised by those kind of people."[6] (The Marshfield ban was enacted and remained in place until 2014.) Like many ordinances, these were presented as efforts to prevent criminal activity in a more general way while targeting specific coin-op practices and reveal anti-industry bias driven by the assumption of criminal ties.

Connections between coin-operated gambling specifically and the coin-operated industry as a whole further added to the unsavory connotations of coin-operated machines. While in the case of connections between the coin-op industry and organized crime, the industry could argue for respectability, gambling presents a thornier issue. After all, many coin-op manufacturers had a hand in the manufacture of slot machines or other gambling devices, including controversial "gray area" games, and gambling has remained the bread and butter of many manufacturers. WMS Industries, Inc., for example, has long removed itself from the coin-op pinball and video game industries it was once known for as Williams Electronics and has focused on slot machines and other gambling devices since the 1990s. Many other coin-op manufacturers have moved in and out of the production of various types of machines, including gambling machines. Questions over which machines, exactly, are gambling devices and which are games of skill have long animated coin-op policy arguments, and the slippage between these two categories means that it is easy for the suggestion of gambling to cling to coin-op machines even when they are markedly removed from gambling practices.

Coin-op gambling machines and other coin-op games often also resemble each other in physical form, perhaps owing to manufacturing and design processes. The similarities of these machines can be suggestive and contributes to the association of all coin-op games with coin-op gambling. Pinball particularly suffered from these associations, as regulations and debates on pinball distribution and access lasted well into the 1970s because the earliest forms of the game could be construed as gambling devices. The associations between coin-operated gambling and coin-operated games more generally contributed to the unsavory connotations of the coin-op industry because of long-standing prohibitions on gambling. Efforts to curtail coin-operated game access often stress these connections, arguing either that the games in question are a de facto type of gambling or that the games will encourage gambling even if they are not themselves gambling devices.

The third long-standing issue affecting the coin-op industry is a more general effort to steer leisure toward constructive or respectable pursuits. When late nineteenth-century reformers in the United States turned their attention toward the recreational pursuits of the working class, coin-operated and midway amusements, in particular, emerged as morally suspect. Debates about proper, edifying uses of off-work hours drove much of late 1800s landscape and urban design and was on particular display in the White City of the Columbia exposition, where despite organizers' efforts, the midway emerged as the most popular attraction.[7] Cheap entertainments were seen as frivolous or wasteful and could be framed as evidence of the working class's poor management of financial resources or of the corrupting influence of such entertainments. The impact of reformers' attacks on coin-operated amusements, midway games, and other entertainments have been long-standing.

POLICING PINBALL

Pinball provides the clearest policy precedent for the debates over coin-operated video games. Pinball machines and coin-op video games were produced by the same industry and distributed along the same channels. Pinball, as coin-op video gaming later would be, became associated with juvenile delinquency—an association that drove regulatory efforts. Pinball also suffered for the coin-op industry's associations with gambling and illicit criminal activity; attacks on pinball as a game of chance, in particular, drove regulatory efforts. Importantly, bans on pinball persisted through the mid-twentieth century and, in rare cases, into the twenty-first. For all these reasons, pinball regulations and bans set a key precedent, both regulatory and rhetorical, for the reception and treatment of coin-operated video games.

The player-operated flipper now ubiquitous in pinball games was not introduced until 1947, which meant early machines relied on chance rather than player skill. Early pinball machines sometimes offered cash or other prizes and were often made by the same companies that produced slot machines. Bally, for example, which emerged as one of the most prominent manufacturers of pinball machines, had begun as a producer of slot machines. The combination of cash prizes, or free plays that could be redeemed for cash, with the connection to gambling device manufacturing and the unsavory reputation of the coin-op industry provided a compelling case against the machines. Community leaders leveraged these factors into the regulation of pinball; for decades, even after the introduction of the flipper, the games were subject to regulation and were frequently treated as gambling devices.

While the regulation of pinball machines in the 1940s often emphasized their role as gambling devices, reformers also emphasized the appeal of the machines to young players, a concern echoed by the courts. In 1941 Justice Joseph L. Bodine of the New Jersey State Supreme Court denounced pinball:

> You don't have to argue that this is a gambling device. I have talked with my associates and they agree it is a gambling device. Men and boys are not going to stand around sticking nickels in a wall without getting money back. In this day and generation it may be that youth has so deteriorated that it has become a practice, but if so, some doctor should place them in an insane asylum and have their heads examined.[8]

Worth highlighting is the judge's reference to the players as "men and boys." The worry that pinball either reflects or will cause the degradation of youths, particularly boys and men, is worth noting and is echoed elsewhere in the historical record. In a successful campaign against pinball, New York City mayor Fiorello La Guardia claimed the machines were fleecing schoolchildren of lunch money; in related court proceedings, a sixteen-year-old boy testified that he had skipped school and spent his lunch money on pinball.[9] The same regulations intended to prevent youths from cutting class or spending lunch money on pinball games also stigmatized the games, connecting pinball in public discourse with youth delinquency and antisocial behaviors.

The connection between delinquency and pinball and the related implication that pinball somehow caused delinquent behavior among young players continued even as pinball bans were lifted in the 1970s and became a touchstone in American film and television. The greaser character in *Happy Days,* Arthur Fonzarelli, better known as "The Fonz," is shown playing pinball, and in the 1979 film *Tilt,* a young Brooke Shields plays the title character, a grade-school-age runaway and pinball hustler. Amid the Hollywood romanticization of pinball as youth rebellion, those officials setting policy remained concerned about the games' real-world impact. When a Los Angeles ban on pinball was overturned by the California Supreme Court in 1974, Justice Louis Burke expressed worry about youths in his dissent: "These games are particularly tempting to children and reasonably may be viewed as a notorious waste of both time and money, encouraging loitering, gambling and other unproductive habits."[10]

Burke's concern in 1974 comes after the early success of video games and to some extent forecasts growing uneasiness with coin-op video games. The end of the New York City ban is another bit of colorful city history. Roger Sharpe, a journalist and pinball player, gave a live demonstration of his pinball skills at a city council hearing to reassess the long-standing ban in 1976.[11]

By 1974 *Pong* was a familiar sight for most Americans, the explosion in video game manufacturing had begun, and the transition of coin-op video games from bar amusement to widely available craze was well under way. The golden age of pinball over, the machines no longer presented a pressing concern, but the decades of public debate and regulation over pinball games had set important precedents for treatment of coin-op video gaming, a newer technology that was, at that moment, entering its own golden age. As I have argued throughout this book, video games arrive at a moment of cultural change. The lifting of bans on pinball in several major U.S. cities is one of these changes. During the mid-1970s, moral guardians turned their attention from coin-op pinball to coin-op video games, seeing the new games as causing many of the same problems as pinball and new problems specific to the video game's novel technology. Meanwhile, the coin-op industry saw in video gaming an opportunity to address long-standing public relations problems and to push for increased respectability. Throughout the 1970s and well into the 1980s, the coin-op industry worked to leverage the connections between video gaming and youth to present a more favorable image even as communities pushed to regulate youth access.

THE FUTURE'S IN PIXELS

Despite the unsavory connotations of the coin-op industry in preceding decades, by the 1970s, those in the industry were working toward professionalization and acceptance as a legitimate business. The two major trade journals serving the coin-op industry, *RePlay Magazine* and *Play Meter,* were both founded in the mid-1970s. *Play Meter* began publication in 1974, and *RePlay* was launched in 1975. Offering profiles of industry professionals, updates on industry news, and business advice including reports on the state of the industry and earnings rankings for individual coin-op machines, both magazines are focused on professionalization. *RePlay* presents certain types of establishments, such as family fun centers, as appropriate types of operations, and editor's notes frequently call out bad individual behavior within the industry as undermining the legitimacy of the entire business. *Play Meter* includes similar content and ran a lengthy series titled "PR Problems/PR Solutions" reprinted from a pamphlet, "A Community Relations Manual for the Coin-Operated Amusement Games Industry," which was jointly produced by the Amusement and Music Operators Association, Amusement Games Manufacturers Association, and the Amusement and Vending Machine Association.[12] In both *Play Meter* and *RePlay*, the sense is that the industry's respectability is tenuous, hard fought, and in need of constant reassertion.

While video gaming proved contentious, it also brought positive attention as a major technological innovation. Those invested in the coin-op industry's respectability embraced video gaming not only for its profitability but also for an opportunity to reposition the industry as a provider of wholesome, mainstream entertainments. The same appeal to youths that made coin-op video games seem insidious to some community leaders was, for the industry, a positive, a demonstration of the games' cultural significance and respectability. Industry reportage featured the innate value of the games themselves, highlighting the level of hand-eye coordination and skill required for competitive players and the games' accessible deployment of cutting-edge computer technologies. Skill, of course, had long been an important defense of coin-op games against regulation as gambling devices, and so was an obvious strategy. Technical skill also, drawing from R. W. Connell, linked the games to increasingly recognizable and desirable forms of middle-class masculinity.[13]

Additionally, comparisons of video games to sports relied on this focus of skill and attempted to place the games in an existing cultural context of legitimated masculine pursuit that was readily intelligible. The connection to sports is one that industry boosters and media coverage both deployed as a way to explain video games. This comparison is one now widely familiar because of the organization of professional "e-sports" leagues for competitive gaming, but the positioning of video games as sports has a long history because the coin-op actively suggested and courted these comparisons.

In 1983 *RePlay* reported President Ronald Reagan's cautious endorsement of video games in a talk to a group of students with exceptional math and science scores at Walt Disney World's Epcot Center:

> Many young people have developed incredible hand, eye and brain coordination in playing these games. The air force believes these kids will be outstanding pilots should they fly our jets. . . . Watch a 12-year-old take evasive action and score multiple hits while playing "Space Invaders" and you will appreciate the skills of tomorrow's pilot. . . . Now don't get me wrong. I don't want the youth of this country to run home and tell their parents that the President of the United States says it's all right for them to go ahead and play video games all the time. Homework, sports and friends still come first.

While Reagan separates video games from sports and argues that sports should "come first," the article ends by comparing coin-op games to sports:

> Very true, Mr. President. But the amusement machine industry is truly pleased that you have considered our "sport" as a positive force in the leisure/educational activities of tomorrow's leaders.[14]

In linking video gaming skill to potential military capabilities, Reagan places games in a context of nationalism, masculinity, and techno-logical sophistication, a framing of the amusement devices that serves the industry's desire for mainstream respectability while suggesting that gamers may be a distinctive, but valuable, subset of American youth.

Reagan's framing of gamers, like the industry's emphasis on skill, athleticism, and technological competency or *Life* magazine's report-age on record-breaking players, all work toward making sense of games and gamers as beneficial cultural developments. Video games were part of a moment of significant cultural, economic, and tech-nological change, and the effort to frame games positively is, to some extent, an effort to make sense of these broader changes. The effort to regulate games, too, is aimed at these changes. Fredric Jameson, David Harvey, and other critics of late capitalism have pointed out how a move toward spending on novel amusements and experi-ences is a major symptom of economic changes occurring through the late twentieth century; it is also, as Michael Kimmel points out, one that affects the formation of identity in young men.[15] Coin-op video games are one of the types of amusements highlighted by Jameson and Harvey.

They are also one of the first computer technologies that many Americans would have had ready access to while appearing in a moment of rapid computerization of work processes. Moral guardians bristled at these changes and pushed back against them through efforts to regulate the coin-op industry, even as they looked to existing regulatory regimens for pinball and other coin-op amusements for strategies and precedents. Meanwhile, the industry itself attempted to fit video games into a narrative of technological progress and personal development, arguing for the value of video games in preparing youths for new professional and economic realities and presenting gamers as a community of bright, young men who were practically athletes. Industry respectability and the respectability of young gamers both were oft-cited as a counter to regulatory efforts. At stake in the discussion is a debate over appropriate pursuits for youths—more specifically for boys and young men—and over the interpretation of cultural and economic changes that would have been far beyond the reach of small-town city councils to control.

Despite the coin-op industry's efforts to position itself as a group of professional businessmen, both the popular press and the trade press list numerous community efforts to regulate the spread of video games. Some of these efforts involved the enforcement of existing coin-op regulations; in others, the regulation represented a fresh targeting of coin-op video games. The focus of these regulations is revealing, demonstrating that while these efforts were localized, they were part of a broader, national discussion in which video games figured as an emerging crisis. While the reaction to *Death Race* in 1976 is distinct in focusing on a specific game, the concern that youths would learn undesirable behavior from games continued through regulatory efforts aimed at coin-op video games. Even as the industry organized against regulation and fought for acceptance, many communities continued to view video games as an encroaching threat to civic order and a potential crisis in youth culture. These attempts at regulation point at mounting tensions about video games and provide insight into popular perceptions of both the coin-op industry and the emerging cadre of video gamers.

Efforts to regulate video games relied on various tactics. Few resorted to the types of outright bans that had curtailed pinball access—although Marshfield is an interesting exception—but licensing and taxation were common, and many towns considered age-based restrictions. The concerns voiced are nearly identical to those that drove pinball regulation. In a 1981 *New York Times* article on potential regulation of video games in Irvington, New York, the author ends by summarizing community concerns: "Many parents had complained that the machines cost children lunch money and caused some of them to be late for classes."[16] Lamm, nationally visible in her campaign against coin-op video games in Brookhaven, was interviewed on PBS's *MacNeil/Lehrer NewsHour*, where she said that the rise of video games in her community had resulted in an increase in children showing up to the local grade school without lunch money.[17]

In another article on the push for regulation in Irvington, Ruth DeVivo, who presented a petition supporting the restriction of gameplay to "after-school hours during the school week," is said to have compared the games to gambling: "Mrs. DeVivo said that the free games offered by machines to high scorers amounted to 'gambling' and that the games encouraged 'behavior modification' among youths."[18] In advocating regulations in Lynbrook, New York, Susan Ruchman, a "past president of the Central Council of Lynbrook's Parent-Teacher Association," noted similar community problems: "These game centers are a bad influence. What's more, during the school year they are open during school hours, and they induce a number of students to play hookey."[19] A ban that restricted children under eighteen from playing coin-op pinball or video games after 10 p.m. or during the school day in Marlboro, Massachusetts, was justified by drug trafficking fears, and an ordinance in Bradley, Illinois, forbids youths under sixteen from playing video games at "shopping mall arcades." The mayor of Bradley also stated that the games were enticing children to squander their lunch and book money.[20] The assertion that video games were a form of gambling and could be linked to youth delinquency was a continuation of the rationale used to justify the regulation and banning of pinball.

Many communities focused on limiting the spread of parlors, as in the case of Lynbrook, or restricting youth access, as was discussed, but ultimately dropped, in Irvington. Licensing of machines, as in both communities, or limiting the number of machines that could be located in a single business, as in Irvington, was also common. The frequency with which access was restricted by age underscores the extent to which coin-op video gaming was viewed as a youth problem. As the most famous of these local regulatory efforts—the ordinance passed in Mesquite, Texas, which would have limited youth access and submitted those wishing to license machines or open arcades to review by the chief of police to evaluate connections to criminal elements—was winding its way through the court system in a widely covered and discussed series of lawsuits, communities continued to push for regulation. The youth bans in both Bradley and Marlboro, for example, were enacted between a federal appeals court ruling that struck down the Mesquite statute and the final ruling by the U.S. Supreme Court. Regulations emerged and, to some extent, differed from town to town, but both the discussion calling for regulations in communities across the United States and the regulations themselves demonstrated shared assumptions and concerns about the effects of coin-op video games.

The push toward professionalization in the coin-op industry was newly possible during the 1970s because of the successful policing of organized crime. In 1975 the U.S. Department of Justice went so far as to say that the newer games had not attracted the involvement of organized crime.[21] The founding of *RePlay* and *Play Meter* during the same period demonstrated growth in the industry, fueled largely by the success of coin-operated video games, and also suggested the appeal of industry-wide pushes for professionalism and respectability. In covering bans and other efforts to regulate coin-operated games, the trade press built a sense of shared concern among operators working in far-flung towns. Just as the popular press presented towns' efforts to regulate gaming as part of a national conversation, so the trade press presented local drives for regulation as part of a broader-reaching attack on the industry. By addressing coin-op route operators as members of a professional class facing national pressure, the trade journals encouraged broader allegiance among the industry's rank and file and often directed readers in proper business behavior and effective lobbying. In one issue, *Play Meter* even provided a reproducible sign (see Figure 20).

Professional associations were another key arena for cultivating coalitions among route operators and others in the industry. Trade journals and professional associations both posited professionalization, networking, and public relations efforts as potential weapons against regulation. Regional professional associations in many states also provided an important source of information and support for those route operators confronted by anti–video game campaigns and often presented a public, respectable face for the industry. For example, Millie McCarthy, president of the New York State Coin Association, spoke to the *New York Times* about increased regulation facing operators in the state.[22] At the national level, Glenn Braswell, executive director for the Amusement Game Manufacturers Association, was able to push back against Surgeon General C. Everett Koop's condemnation of video games as harmful to children. In the article "Video Game

FIGURE 20. In 1982 *Play Meter* offered this reproducible sign for arcade owners to post in their businesses warning youths that the machines were off-limits during school hours.

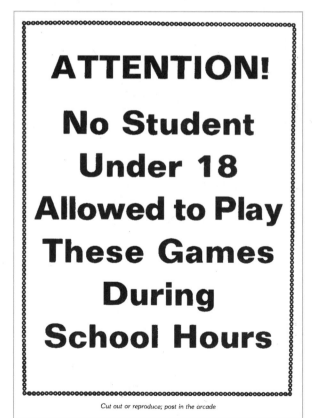

ATTENTION!

No Student Under 18 Allowed to Play These Games During School Hours

Cut out or reproduce; post in the arcade

Makers Rap Surgeon General," part of Braswell's response to Koop is quoted: "Respectfully we must remind you that your only official mandate and authority is to develop scientific evidence. Your casual comments do violence to the integrity of your high office and do enormous potential damage to major segments of American industry."[23] Given the wide broadcast of Koop's condemnation of video games, which even Koop himself admitted were based more on personal impressions of gaming than any scientific grounding, a response like Braswell's, reported in the *New York Times,* was a boon to local operators fighting for respectability and even survival in the face of regulatory efforts.

That moral guardians argued so effectively for regulations as a way to protect youths speaks to the strength of the association between them and video games. The industry's resistance to these regulations points to the importance of young consumers for industry operations. The conflict between community leaders' desire to "protect" children from the pernicious influence of video games and coin-op professionals' desires to maintain their customer base of young players animated much discussion within and about the industry. The industry responded to this conflict through the push toward professionalization and respectability. This push, however, also included the identification and rejection of undesirable behaviors. In *RePlay,* arcade owners are praised for their clean, family-friendly businesses, and family fun centers are hailed as an exciting development for the industry. The success of these types of businesses and their close ties to the industry are evident in the success of Chuck E. Cheese's Pizza Time Theatre, a chain of family fun centers founded by Nolan Bushnell. While successful family fun centers provided visible evidence of the industry's wholesome nature and were celebrated in the trade journals as such, editorials in the same publications sometimes scolded other arcade operators for poor customer service, dirty or poorly maintained storefronts, and other transgressions. Trade journals attempted to guilt route operators and arcade owners into conforming to the industry's broader aspirations while also providing positive examples. A *Play Meter* feature on the Chicago Game Company game room, provocatively titled "Cleaning Up an Arcade: Out with the Hoods, In with the Families," talks about the increased earnings achieved by Erick "Ricky" Rothner. Rothner took over the arcade from its previous owner and worked to increase business. He did so by changing the arcade's floor plan to make it easier to supervise and by working with local law enforcement. The article reports that five young patrons were arrested over three nights. After that, the "delinquent problem" was solved. The increase in the game room's business is held out as further proof of the value of Rothner's strategies.[24]

Video gaming made the coin-op industry more visible, which increased both business and scrutiny. Speaking to the *New York Times* in 1982, Ed Adlum, publisher of *RePlay*, said that the industry had exploded in the preceding decade: "Ten years ago we were a nice quiet business. Today people complain that they fall over video machines in every store they go to, except a funeral parlor."[25] That decade of increased visibility and the rapid spread of coin-op games corresponds with the boom in video game production begun with the release of *Pong* in 1972, a boom that offered exciting opportunities for expansion to coin-op professionals. In pushing for legitimacy, and in celebrating the growth of family-friendly entertainment centers featuring coin-operated games, the coin-op industry was also pushing for ongoing access to young players. Simultaneously, the industry was using the attraction of games to young players to argue for mainstream acceptability.

The same boom that tantalized coin-op industry insiders meant that coin-op video games spread rapidly in communities across the United States. The sudden appearance of video games in gas stations, delis, and bowling alleys across the country provoked serious concern about what impact these games might have on young players and their communities. The conflict between the coin-op industry and community leaders in dozens of towns across the United States highlights this specific issue but also points to the long-standing reputation of the coin-op industry and its associations with organized crime and juvenile delinquency. As the industry worked to leverage video gaming into an era of respectability, moral guardians attempted to tie video games to pinball and other predecessors while expressing concern about the new technology that video games presented. The industry, aided by popular presentations of gamers as bright young men, fought to present video gaming as a positive activity. In covering competitions and other events like, for example, the Texas Video

FIGURE 21. *RePlay* featured the winners of the Texas Video Championships, held in 1982, highlighting the positive community of the event and the smiling faces of the young victors. Photograph by Lee Langum; courtesy of *RePlay*.

Championships sponsored by 7–11 and shown in Figure 21, the trade press highlighted the family atmosphere and the ties to established businesses and charitable organizations.

Despite efforts by the industry, would-be regulators continued to express mounting anxieties about American boys—about their access to and use of technology, their appropriate use of leisure time, and their abilities to appropriately embody ideals of masculinity—through attacks on coin-operated video games. These anxieties found clear expression in the city ordinances that were passed and in court cases debating these ordinances. Legal considerations of coin-operated video games provide insight both into the specific ills ascribed to video games and the ways in which reformers sought to curtail their spread. In addition to demonstrating the anxieties attendant upon video games as an emergent technology, court cases also present an emergent understanding of youth rights as consumers.

FIGURE 22. *Vidiot* magazine was intended for players but was advertised to operators as merchandise to be sold on consignment. The August–September 1983 issue is shown here.

Those fighting for the rights of young players to access coin-operated video games are effectively fighting for players' rights to purchase gaming as a consumer good. Ultimately, under the U.S. Supreme Court ruling in *City of Mesquite,* the courts side with this articulation of youth rights, arguing that games are protected as free speech and therefore cannot be restricted. This case, like other cases related to the spread of video gaming during the 1970s and 1980s, demonstrates that video games served as a point of articulation for the conflicting values of community leaders, youths, and the coin-op industry.

Many policies focused on concerns about juvenile delinquency, sometimes claiming that the games caused bad behavior or served as a cover for such. In claiming that the games attracted specific youth or precipitated certain youth behaviors, these policies imply that the emerging fan base for video games—now called gamers, then, sometimes "vidiots," as in the title of a short-lived magazine (see Figure 22)—are a distinct group of youth with their own social codes and values. In some ways, gamers in the late 1970s and early 1980s were treated like prior youth subcultures; the association, for example, with greasers and other deviants had helped sustain pinball regulation through the midcentury. But the video games were perceived as new, or at least new enough to cause fresh concern, and so the youths who flocked to them, too, were treated as new. In some ways, they were. Growing up as the postwar economic boom fizzled, in an era of computerization, as industrial growth seized up like rusted gears, the youths of the 1970s and 1980s faced distinct cultural and economic challenges. They also faced, and sometimes embraced, computerization. Video games were one of the most visible symbols of this technological shift.

COIN-OPERATED LEGAL BATTLES

Across the United States, arcade owners and others working in the coin-op industry fought regulation, arguing for the value of the games and the wholesomeness of the youth who played them. These lobbying and public relations efforts were not always effective. Ordinances were passed in numerous communities, and in at least some of these communities, local business owners fought back through the legal system, filing lawsuits to prevent the enforcement of bans or limits on the operation of coin-op video games. These cases are revealing, both for the frequent claims that video games should rightfully be protected as free speech and for the information they provide about the specifics of town ordinances and the rationale used to justify them. The cases also, at times, seem to have been potentially embarrassing. Even when coin-op industry advocates lost—and they frequently did—the cases provide a catalog of both the resistance to and the fight for coin-op video games as mainstream culture. They also, again, demonstrate that the conflict over video games was a national conversation carried out through local legislation and community-driven debate, and show why Ottumwa's embrace of video gaming as community identity attracted so much attention.

Like other communities, Buffalo, in New York, relied on existing coin-op regulation for its initial regulation of video gaming. The Buffalo ordinance, enacted in 1952 to address the spread of pinball, forbade the licensing of "gambling devices." In 1980 sixteen distributors, denied licenses for coin-operated video games, petitioned the court for licenses. The plaintiffs had been denied licenses for six specific titles—*Space Invaders, Galaxian, Double Play, Lunar Rescue, Asteroids,* and *Cosmic Guerilla*—even though in some cases identical games had been granted licenses.

Justice Samuel L. Green of the New York State Supreme Court ruled in favor of the distributors, stressing that the games involved were games of skill and that Buffalo's enforcement of the ordinance in question was demonstrably arbitrary. Green, also, ended on a celebratory note that likely pleased both the plaintiffs and other distributors:

> Today, coin-operated video games are distributed to shopping malls, movie theatres, bowling alleys, roller rinks, pizzerias, and neighborhood grocery stores. Video games, originally introduced in Japan several years ago and mass-marketed in this country for the last 18 months, have recently been adapted for use on television screens for home entertainment. A recent Space Invaders competition in New York City, sponsored by a reputable manufacturer and distributor of video games, attracted over 4,000 entrants and awarded as the grand prize, not surprisingly, a $2,000 Asteroids table top video game. (*New York Times,* Nov. 9, 1980, p. 24.) Thus, the contemporary context in which video games are manufactured, distributed, and operated bears little resemblance to the Buffalo atmosphere in 1952.

The time has come for the City of Buffalo to join its neighbor-
ing communities and to enter the electronic age of coin-operated
amusement.[26]

In placing games in a context of everyday amusement spaces and the
competition "sponsored by a reputable manufacturer and distributor," Green stresses the games' legitimacy and positions them as a
welcome part of the state's public culture.

Green's enthusiasm for the games, however, was not necessarily
held by his colleagues. Two years after Green encouraged the city of
Buffalo to update its coin-op ordinance to better reflect cultural and
technological changes, prospective arcade owners in New York City
were still fighting zoning and licensing laws. A 1982 federal district
court case addressed the efforts of America's Best Family Showplace
Corporation to open a video game–themed restaurant in Queens.
The city denied the restaurant, which would have featured a video
game embedded in each of its proposed forty tables, a license to
operate the machines based on an ordinance limiting the number
of coin-op devices in an establishment to no more than four. While
special arcade permits were available for some businesses wishing
to obtain more than four coin-op machines, America's Best Family
Showplace had not been able to obtain one.

In petitioning the court, the plaintiffs tried to argue for the artistic
merit of video games, comparing them to film as " 'visual and aural
presentations on a screen involving a fantasy experience in which
the player participates.' "[27] Unfortunately, the court found neither
this comparison nor the plaintiff's argument concerning a U.S. Supreme Court case that had previously ruled coin-operated viewing
of live-action peep shows a type of protected speech compelling. In
ruling against the notion of video games as free speech, McLaughlin
is rather tight-lipped on the games themselves. He compares them,
briefly, with other types of games including pinball, baseball, and
chess, to highlight the notion that they are "pure entertainment with
no informational element." Ironically, a comparison to sport that
might have pleased industry advocates is here used to justify the continued regulation of games.

Neither Green's nor Laughlin's rulings are isolated. Cases covering similar issues and presenting similar findings emerge from courts
across the United States. In 1983 the Massachusetts Supreme Court,

for example, upheld a ruling against the owners of 1001 Plays, Inc., who filed suit after being refused a license to open an arcade in Boston.[28] When denied a license to operate fifty "video machine devices," the Malden Amusement Company of Malden, Massachusetts, also took to the courts, losing the case in a 1983 federal district court ruling.[29] The owners of two separate pizza parlors sued the city of New York to try to keep their video game licenses after it was found that the businesses were less than two hundred feet from a local school; a Department of Consumer Affairs regulation required that "common show devices," including video games, be more than two hundred feet from the school. The plaintiffs lost.[30] The prohibition of games near schools, like age-based restrictions, suggests the extent to which worry about games was worry about *youths* playing games more than a generalized concern.

The two best-known cases involving video game ordinances were both appealed to the U.S. Supreme Court, although the court declined to hear one of them. In that case, business owners in Marshfield, Massachusetts, sought to have an outright ban on coin-operated games declared unconstitutional. The state's Supreme Judicial Court upheld the ban, and it took effect in December 1983. Some seventy machines had been in operation in the community of roughly twenty thousand, and profits had already declined significantly from their peak levels of 1981 and 1982. While Marshfield was unusual in banning games outright, the rationale used to justify the measure was not.

The initial proposal by the board of selectmen would have limited the number and placement of games, but the town rejected it, voting instead 191 to 19 to ban mechanical and electronic amusement games entirely. As in other communities, both the initial proposal and the one later adopted were aimed at limiting youth access to video games, and concerns about drugs and organized crime fueled support.[31] The Massachusetts Supreme Court, in reviewing the case, was not convinced by claims that video games qualify for freedom of expression—going so far as to call them "in essence, only technologically advanced pinball machines"—nor were they convinced by claims that the ban was inconsistent with state law and in violation of due process and equal protection under the state and federal constitution.[32]

The U.S. Supreme Court did hear a second video game–related case. In *Aladdin's Castle, Inc. v. City of Mesquite,* the Court ruled against an age-based regulation that would have prevented those under the age of seventeen from entering an arcade unaccompanied by an adult. While the Court referred part of the ordinance back to a lower court for clarification, the final ruling in the case invalidated the ordinance. The Court ruled that the age-based restriction was without a rational basis because video games, or at least youth access to the games, should be protected under the right to free speech and assembly. The majority opinion also maintained that the ordinance would have violated minors' rights under the due process clause, going so far as to say that "it is impossible to conclude that a coin-operated amusement device presents a physical, mental, or moral threat under which 'the State is entitled to adjust its legal system to account for children's vulnerability and their needs for "concern, . . . sympathy, and . . . paternal attention." ' "[33]

While the outcomes of the Marshfield and Mesquite cases differ significantly, it is interesting that both have endured. Voters upheld the ban in Marshfield in 2011.[34] It lasted thirty-two years and was finally revoked in 2014.[35] Video games have remained contentious in a number of communities, but concern has shifted to the console and computer games that are now much more common. Marshfield and Mesquite both share a concern for the impact of games on young players and the proper place of those games in a community context. Although the Marshfield ban may have stood, at least for a few decades, it both began as and remained an anomaly, an instance in which "Marshfield took a lonely step beyond."[36] The Mesquite ordinance is more in line with efforts in other communities, and it is, over time, that ordinance—or at least, that ordinance's failure—that has most shaped the place of video games in youth culture.

The Supreme Court ruling in Mesquite set a precedent by accepting games as free speech, but it also set a precedent by protecting youths' access to commercial entertainment. In preserving youth access to video games, the Court's ruling also draws from a growing sense of consumer rights, derived from the landmark free speech cases of the preceding decades. Several things are at stake in the public debate about youth access to video games during this period: the propriety of commercial, coin-operated amusements for young players, and the respectability of those games in general; the position of video games in an emerging computer culture, and whether those games can be considered expression or speech; and the ability of communities, rather than parents, to regulate the behavior of young people.

But, woven throughout the regulation of video games and the legal cases addressing those regulations is a mounting anxiety about American youth—an anxiety frequently expressed as an anxiety about boys and young men. Both when communities push to regulate games and when the industry mounts resistance to these regulations, the gamers are either explicitly named as or coded as boys. There is a host of reasons for this, including the dominance of boys in many forms of public youth culture and the relatively lax supervision of boys as compared with girls. Regardless, the debate over video games effectively framed gamers as boys and young men—both in the negative, as delinquents playing hooky, squandering their lunch money, or even resorting to theft to support their gaming habit, and in the positive, as technologically savvy, bright, creative, competitive boys participating in a new American pastime.

As numerous cases moved through America's courtrooms, video games were entering the mainstream and solidifying as a cultural form; at stake in these cases was not whether games will be but what they will be, not whether there will be gamers but whether those gamers can be rightly construed as something other than miscreants. In *Aladdin's Castle v. City of Mesquite*, the U.S. Supreme Court effectively took the side of youths, defending their easy access to the games as a new type of constitutional right to purchase and to play.

5

PLAY SAVES THE DAY

TRON, WARGAMES, AND THE GAMER AS PROTAGONIST

THE EARLY DEPICTION OF GAMERS as unlikely heroes in Hollywood narrative cinema drew heavily on tropes already deployed in popular media coverage as well as on the existing cinematic codes of the action and science fiction genres. The long tradition of movies addressing cultural uneasiness with emerging "smart" machines readily incorporated the emergent culture of video gaming and hacking; in the case of *TRON* and *WarGames,* the two films discussed at length here, that culture is targeted as the province of boys, insinuating that the boy technologist/gamer (see Figure 23) is the solution to the problem of smart machines, an essential line of defense against the dangers of computer technologies run amuck.

By the 1960s the potential of emerging computer technologies proved to be a ripe topic for filmmakers, especially those working in the action and science fiction genres. As in their literary dystopian predecessors, cinematic considerations of the new machines often revealed significant uneasiness with the machines' potential power. Stanley Kubrick found computerization a particularly troubling topic, exploring it through the computer network–operated

FIGURE 23. The first time that viewers see David in *WarGames* (1983) he is in the middle of a high-scoring game of *Galaga*.

Doomsday Device in *Dr. Strangelove or: How I Learned to Stop Worrying and Love the Bomb* (1964) and in his landmark science fiction work *2001: A Space Odyssey* (1968), in which the HAL 9000 computer malfunctions and terminates much of the Discovery One crew. As computers entered consumer markets in the 1970s and 1980s, both through personal computing and the proliferation of computer technologies in products ranging from sophisticated calculators to coin-op games, anxiety over computerization increased.

Video games proved to be a uniquely vexing form of computerization, alarming moral guardians who worried in particular about the games' impact on youths. However, troubling or not, these games also provided one of the most widely accessible and approachable computer technologies.[1] The games gained in popularity because they provided this access to emergent computer technologies. *Life* magazine's feature of video games in the 1982 "Year in Pictures" issue encapsulates the arcade as an established cultural craze; films about video gaming from that time manifest the degree to which the arcade had captured the popular imagination, not only building fictional narratives around gaming but also exploring the possibilities and risks of gaming culture.

The popularity and financial success of video games in the United States made them an appealing topic for commercial filmmakers looking to cash in on the games' existing visibility. The best known of these early video game films, *TRON* (dir. Steven Lisberger; 1982) and *WarGames* (dir. John Badham; 1983), were released shortly before the 1983 U.S. video game industry crash. In both films, a boyish protagonist is pitted against a dangerous computerized entity fostered by reckless adult use of computer technologies. While both films end happily ever after, with humans prevailing over the digital risks facing them, the films' major narrative tension lies in presumed public uneasiness with these rapidly proliferating technologies, their social role, and their potential power. Drawing from a cinematic tradition set by films like the two Kubrick films mentioned, *TRON* and *WarGames* are benchmarks in the consolidation of perceived ties between masculinity, violence, and youth in the new digital landscape.

While the films work with divergent visual aesthetics, both rely heavily on the generic conventions of action movies and target a young, presumably male audience. Each follows the exploits of male leads and highlights engagement with both video gaming and hacking as practices that these films often conflate. Significantly, computers have the sheen of novelty in both films; given the obsession with emergence that drives the market for computer technologies, this sense of novelty reconfigured a trope readily deployed now in media addressing crime, espionage, and even medicine.[2]

In *TRON* and *WarGames* specifically, and in other films addressing computerization more generally, mastery of computer technologies is the domain of the technocultural young male elite. Older characters often fail to fully understand the machines or the machines' nature, demonstrating the unwarranted trepidation or blind allegiance that can result from an unplastic mind. In this vein, the two films examined here flirt with the implications of virtuality, engaging more open-minded characters in situations that teeter at the edge of "the real" and, in the case of *TRON,* pulling the characters into a disembodied "virtual" world. But to confront computer technologies is to enter into direct confrontation with significant real-world implications; the "virtual" world as presented in these films is no safe haven for play but instead a foreign landscape that routinely threatens the safety of the "real" world outside the machines. Throughout, young

men—a group popularly, if erroneously, considered the most adapt-
able members of society—are depicted as the most capable explorers
of this unfamiliar and hostile landscape.

These digital landscapes, rife with violence, are the domain of
highly sophisticated programs—programs so advanced, in fact, that
their artificial intelligence threatens to outpace the organic/natural
intelligence of the humans who have designed them. This threat
of human obsolescence is coupled with fear of human eradication
or enslavement, the possibility of an inversion where the human
masters are reduced to serving the machines they manufactured.
As Tom Engelhardt notes in *The End of Victory Culture,* filmmakers
in the early 1980s began to dwell on the extent to which war had
become mechanized and computerized. These changes in warfare
also meant that war films and conflict narratives could be targeted
directly to youth. As Engelhardt puts it, "Future war would be a
machine-versus-machine affair, a bloodless matter of special effects,
in the revamped war story designed for childhood consumption."[3]
The reliance on technology to estrange society from the physical
violence of war drove several Reagan-era research efforts, including
the Strategic Defense Initiative, intended to provide an antimissile
shield to protect Americans from attack.[4] The virtuality of modern
warfare likewise manifested in the use of video games as military recruiting tools, most notably with *America's Army* (2002), an ongoing
video game series released as a public relations and recruiting tool for
the U.S. military.[5]

The computer–human conflict narratives of *TRON* and *WarGames*
are part of this cinematic interest in technologized warfare. Engelhardt notes that *WarGames* is also part of a culture of growing anti-
nuclear sentiment of the early 1980s.[6] While other action films from
the period such as *First Blood* (1982) or *Red Dawn* (1984) present
their conflict as between human actors who live and die to defend
their nationalist beliefs, in *TRON, WarGames,* and later similar films
like *The Terminator* and *The Matrix* franchises, the conflict is between
computers/machines and humans.[7] The lengthy run of *The Matrix*
and *The Terminator* franchises and their success as transmedia narratives stretching across media forms underscore the wide appeal of
human–computer conflict narratives.[8]

The most desirable quality for the protagonists in these films, then,

is not the brute strength of *First Blood*'s John Rambo but the intellectual acumen to take on a hyperintelligent machine. Indeed, when
comparing *WarGames* with "hero revival films" like *Rocky IV,* the action films of Chuck Norris, and the *Rambo* franchise, Michael Ryan
and Douglas Kellner note that the movie is relatively liberal, carrying
a criticism of militarism—and perhaps, therefore, of brute and bloody
conceptions of masculinity.[9] Centered as the films are on the conflict
between man (women in the two films play auxiliary, quasi-romantic
roles exclusively) and machine, both films suggest intimate ties between masculinity and computerization. They reflect the growing
association of middle-class masculinity and present an appealing defense of geek masculinity; the films' protagonists are not *less* than their
more hegemonically masculine peers but simply *different* from them.[10]

The anxiety over machines' competition with human laborers and
thinkers is a topic that long predates cinema. Concern over machines
replacing men rushed in at the very earliest signs of modernity. The
folk hero John Henry, who famously battled a steam-powered ham-
mer to save his job and the jobs of his crew members, is likely based
on a real nineteenth-century railroad worker; the myth of the larger-
than-life character who supposedly died of exhaustion after winning
the contest has long outlasted the era of railroads.[11] That early Hollywood films—themselves a product of modernity—address these kinds
of anxieties is unsurprising. In *Modern Times* (1936), Charlie Chaplin
is terrorized by a hyperefficient assembly line that attempts to mold
him into an ideal worker; while the situation is played to comedic effect, the film speaks to real anxieties over efforts to rationalize
and mechanize the motions of human workers in modern factories.
In "Job Switching," a 1952 episode of *I Love Lucy,* Lucy and her
friend Ethel confront a situation similar to that faced by the Tramp;
they take jobs at a candy factory only to find themselves struggling
to handle the pace set by the conveyer belt and ultimately stuffing
the excess chocolates into their mouths (as shown in Figure 24).

Computerization added a new dimension to these anxieties, lac-
ing them with the threat not just of mechanical competition with
human laborers for jobs but of competition for decision-making
powers and authority. Kubrick's *2001: A Space Odyssey* presents this
usurping of human agency as the ship's intelligent computer turns
from a benevolent assistant/caretaker into a goal-obsessed egomaniac

FIGURE 24. Lucy and Ethel stuff their faces with chocolates in a desperate attempt to keep up with the relentless speed of the conveyor belt in the 1952 episode of *I Love Lucy* titled "Job Switching."

unconcerned with the safety of the ship's human crew. But sometimes computerized or robotic intelligence is portrayed as friendly, even nurturing. In a 1962 episode of *The Twilight Zone* written by Ray Bradbury and based on his short story "I Sing the Body Electric," a family adapts to life with an electric grandmother; she cares for the family with the same love as a traditional grandmother but comes free of the impending threat of mortality and will likely outlast her young charges. In the *Star Wars* franchise begun in 1977, the droid character C-3PO is a quirky cultural expert intended to help humans with language, etiquette, and customs; his counterpart, R2-D2, communicates in musical tones and seems sympathetic to the humans he serves. While used for comedic effect throughout the *Star Wars* franchise, C-3PO and R2-D2's characterizations blur the line between the human and the computerized or robotic; this fuzzy demarcation is explored much more deeply in the science-fiction neo-noir *Blade Runner* (dir. Ridley Scott; 1982), which follows the hunting and destroying of renegade androids called replicants.

TRON and *WarGames* occupy an important place in the cinema of human–machine conflict; uniquely among related science fiction and action films, the conflict is experienced through computerized gaming. This focus on human–machine conflict also distances the two movies from other teen films of the same period, including those that include more superficial aspects of gaming culture. In particular, the arcade-focused *Joysticks* (dir. Greydon Clark; 1983) takes its cues not from *TRON* but instead from *Porky's* (dir. Bob Clark; 1982), as evidenced by the poster shown in Figure 25. The arcade in *Joysticks* serves primarily as a conveniently teencentric setting for generational conflict, invoking the discomfort of moral guardians with arcade-focused youth culture but ignoring the games and process of gaming. While the conflict between young and old plays a part in *WarGames* and *TRON,* implying that youthfulness is a characteristic necessary for the respective protagonists' successes, the motivating conflict remains that between humans and computers.

Other films of the period used and addressed video gaming. *The Last Starfighter* (dir. Nick Castle; 1984) follows the template of a young gamer being drawn into conflicts larger than himself, but sets it within the context of a coming-of-age film. The film's protagonist, Alex Rogen (shown on the poster in Figure 26), is not presented as a technologist or even as unusually bright; he is instead a talented gamer with ambitions driven by his desire to leave his isolated hometown and see the world. Although unable to get a student loan to move away for college, Alex is recruited as a gunner (or starfighter) by an intergalactic defense force after defeating *The Last Starfighter* game. His recruitment as a starfighter is based on his gaming ability, and by the end of the film Alex finds his way out of his hometown by committing to long-term intergalactic military service. Working-class Alex, skilled but not brilliant, can be trained and recruited through computer technologies, but he is not portrayed as a master of them.

Alex's experience, while touching on the ties between masculinity, video gaming, and the military, plays out as fantastical, paralleling in meaningful ways the experience of many Americans who join the military in order to fund higher education or find work opportunities that will take them away from their home communities. This context, Alex's position as a working-class youth, puts him at a considerable remove from the lead characters of *TRON* and *WarGames,* as does his

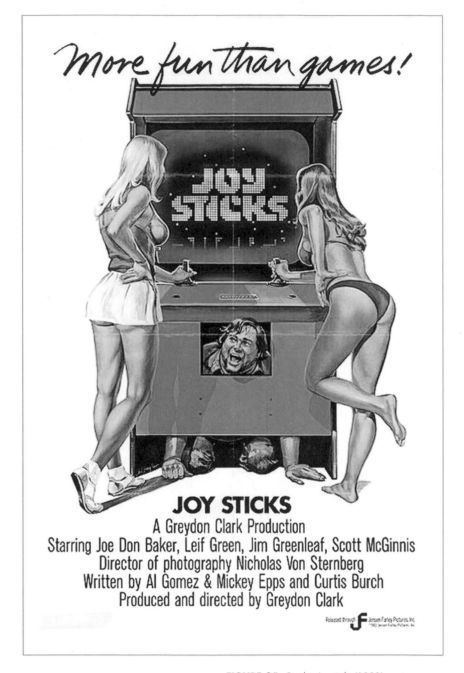

FIGURE 25. On the *Joysticks* (1983) poster, a man leers at two women from inside an arcade cabinet.

lack of specific technical ability. Likewise, his presentation as part of a social group of peers suggests a character far removed from the socially awkward David of *WarGames* and *TRON*'s romantically aloof Flynn. So, while *The Last Starfighter* is certainly worthy of lengthy consideration—particularly in light of the U.S. military's long interest in and recruitment through video games—the overlap of Alex with Flynn and David is limited to age and gaming ability.

Given the Cold War rhetoric of technological achievement and knowledge as arenas for international competition, the consolidation of masculinity, youth, and violence is a point of continuation and not departure; what makes the moment noteworthy is the explicit attachment of youthful masculinity to a nascent entertainment medium and the configuration of that medium to address and simulate violence. Over time, the ties among masculinity, violence, technological literacy, and gaming have become so tight and so persistent as to be naturalized. Abstract ideas of what manhood might mean in the era of computerization have been reified through popular depictions of gamers that have helped entrench these ties and limit the possibilities of video gaming as a medium. This process has significantly shaped the development of the video game industry, as it has influenced notions about both what kinds of people play games and what kinds of games should be made. The establishment of gaming as a specifically male pursuit has doubtless contributed to the obscurity of women gamers, as they are believed to be atypical and therefore less interesting to those intent on making money in a commercial marketplace where the customers are assumed to be male. This process is one that occurs across media. Whether gaming is framed as beneficial and admirable, as in the world record coverage, or as detrimental and dangerous, as in the coverage of *Death Race,* that gaming is primarily the domain of young men and boys is taken as a given. While the print and television coverage discussed earlier certainly intersects with the kind of gamer identity presented in *TRON* and *WarGames,* the two Hollywood films represent a unique moment. In the films, video gaming and video gamers are characterized and narrativized, then presented to national audiences. Released from the boundaries imposed on documentary and journalistic coverage of gaming, these fictional gamers demonstrate what video gaming looks like through the lens of popular imagination.

FIGURE 26. The poster for *The Last Starfighter* (1984) features young Alex Rogen on the verge of intergalactic adventure and heroism.

In narrating 1980s computerization, *TRON* and *WarGames* not only anchor these technologies to masculinity but also articulate emergent forms of manhood and stress a strong bond among computer technologies, militarization, and real-world violence. This bond emerges from the historical origins of computers, video games, the Internet, and related technologies as military technologies intended to aid in war and defense efforts. But the understanding of the risks, values, and capabilities of the digital landscape demonstrated in *TRON* and *WarGames* is not simply military in nature. It persists, its key tenets affixed not only to the now long-established character type of the gamer but also to contemporary ideas of entrepreneurship, technological development, and success. By consolidating the ties among masculinity, technology, and violence as they pertain to gaming, these films have served as establishing texts in constructing a distinctive, late twentieth-century form of masculine identity that has had profound implications for the development of video gaming and of the tech industry more broadly. To further explore these themes, the connections between the two films, and their historical implications, a summary of the two films is necessary.

TRON SYNOPSIS

TRON follows Flynn (Jeff Bridges), a brilliant programmer and adept gamer (Figure 27). While working at a tech firm, ENCOM, Flynn designed five games, including the smash hit *Space Paranoids*. His colleague Ed Dillinger (David Warner) took credit for these games, leveraging their success into corporate ascent before firing Flynn. Flynn goes on to open a successful arcade named Flynn's, but he continues to obsess over taking down Dillinger by proving the authorship of *Space Paranoids* and the other games. The fired programmer has received no financial benefit from his games' success, aside from the quarters taken in by the machines in Flynn's—an insufficient reward for his brilliance.

At night, Flynn accesses ENCOM's computer system, looking for evidence to use against Dillinger. Flynn's hacking triggers Dillinger to temporarily limit access to the ENCOM system, which closes out Alan Bradley (Bruce Boxleitner), an ENCOM programmer who has been developing TRON, a program that will detect and prevent

FIGURE 27. Flynn (Jeff Bridges) is shown in screen's-eye view as a crowd, consisting primarily of young women, watches his feats of gaming prowess in *TRON* (1982).

unauthorized actions in ENCOM's system. Alan and his girlfriend, Lora (Cindy Morgan), who is Flynn's ex-girlfriend, seek out Flynn, as they believe he is the hacker whose actions triggered the shutdown.

Flynn, Lora, and Alan return to ENCOM after-hours, and Lora logs Flynn into her workstation. As Flynn confronts the Master Control Program and the MCP's minion Sark (both played by David Warner), Alan and Lora log in to terminals elsewhere in the building. The MCP recognizes Flynn and uses a laser to suck the intruder into the game (see Figure 28). Inside the game, Flynn, a "user," interacts with programs piloted by users outside the network before the MCP seized them and forced them to participate in gladiator-style games. With Alan's TRON program and a second program called Ram, Flynn escapes the game field. Tron/Alan meets Yori/Lora, and they sneak to the input/output communication tower where TRON communicates with Alan the user, receiving data with which the trio of Flynn, TRON, and Yori defeat the MCP. The MCP vanquished, Flynn returns to the "real" world outside the computer with the files necessary to prove that he authored *Space Paranoids*. The film concludes with Flynn, now an ENCOM executive, arriving at work via helicopter (see Figure 29).

Throughout the film, *TRON* lingers over displays of technology, from the lab space Lora works in to Dillinger's futuristic desk interface to the crowded interior of Flynn's arcade. While the computer animation in *TRON* is used sparingly (see Figure 30 for an example), the film works to remind viewers of the presence and importance of computer technologies to the narrative. The effects-drenched, live-action footage that makes up the bulk of Flynn's adventure inside the ENCOM computer system and the lighted suits worn (see Figure 31) both by Flynn in these scenes and by the programs he encounters imply

FIGURE 28. Flynn is pulled into the digital world by the Master Control Program in *TRON*.

FIGURE 29. Near the end of *TRON*, Flynn is greeted on the roof of ENCOM by his friends as he arrives at work by company helicopter.

FIGURE 30. The "light cycle" race in *TRON* is one of only a few computer-animated scenes in the film.

FIGURE 31. The light suits worn by programs in *TRON* are part of the film's distinctive aesthetic.

computer technology even when they do not rely on it. *TRON* is, ultimately, a fantasy of computer technology, more frequently showing spectacular landscapes of what coming computer advances might look like rather than lingering over current technological realities.

While computer animation inspired *TRON* and the possibilities presented by the medium drive the film, the minimal use of computer animation is part of *TRON*'s distinctive aesthetic—an aesthetic associated most strongly with the nondigital special effects that make up the imagined computerized world. These aesthetic choices also mean that while the physical space covered by the film's action is relatively small, the narrative is able to operate in a much larger imagined landscape inside the machines. The possibilities are tantalizing and present viewers with an imagined, alien environment marked in equal parts by technological beauty and danger.

WARGAMES SYNOPSIS

While the action of TRON occurs within the relatively small world of the ENCOM mainframe, WarGames is a caper on a much grander scale, taking characters to locations across the West Coast. WarGames opens on a missile command exercise where a missile commander refuses to turn his key to enable an attack, worrying that the attack is a false alarm and that he will be facilitating the deaths of thousands of innocent people. At headquarters, military officers and government agents assess how to improve the missile command response rate, noting that 22 percent of the missile commanders had failed to launch. McKittrick (Dabney Coleman) proposes taking the men out of the loop and relying on the judgment of the War Operation Plan Response (WOPR) computer. After a dispute in which General Berringer (Barry Corbin) is figured as a good ol' boy with a misplaced faith in his human missile commanders, a decision is made to turn control over the missile system to WOPR.

Meanwhile, in Seattle, David (Matthew Broderick) is playing *Galaga* at an arcade before rushing out to arrive late at his biology class, where he is sent to the principal's office for cracking a joke. High school heartthrob Jennifer (Ally Sheedy; Figure 32) offers David a ride home on her scooter, where he invites her upstairs to show her why he will not have to make up biology in summer school. He enters the school's network and changes his and Jennifer's grades using a password he saw while in the office. Jennifer demands that he change her grade back, which he does, only to raise the grade again after she leaves. The next day, Jennifer interrupts David while he is playing *Galaga*, asking him to change her grade again. At his house, he tells her that he had already reraised the grade, and she sees him making illegal long-distance calls (phreaking) to California using his

FIGURE 32. Ally Sheedy *(right)* at a *WarGames*-inspired
promotional event at Video Invasion arcade in Toronto in
1983 with the arcade owners Wayne Fromm and Genia
Fromm. Reprinted with permission of *Play Meter* magazine.

computer system. He explains that he is trying to obtain information
on a game he read about in a magazine. He finds an unidentified
computer and, believing it to be related to the game, attempts to log
in. When his log-in fails, he asks the system for help. The system says
help is not available, but responds to "help games" with the message
"Games refers to models, simulations, and games that have tactical
and strategic applications" and a list of games running from *Falken's
Maze* to *Global Thermonuclear War*. David visits some hacker friends
(see Figure 33), who advise him to look for the system's backdoor,
which they suspect is related to the *Falken's Maze* game.

To locate the game's backdoor, David begins researching Falken. At the library, David discovers Stephen W. Falken, a game and computer expert who died in 1973 after the deaths of his wife and son, Joshua, whose name turns out to be the log-in for the system. David logs in and launches a game of *Global Thermonuclear War*. The "game" David is playing triggers a flurry of activity back at the military control center, where officials believe the Russians are attacking. The next day, David is arrested by FBI agents outside a 7-11. He surreptitiously logs into the system while in custody and realizes that the system Falken named Joshua does not know the difference between reality and a game. David escapes and goes to Oregon with Jenny to find Falken, who he has learned is living under an assumed name. Falken initially refuses to help but eventually acquiesces, and the three return to headquarters to attempt to prevent World War III. David logs in and sets Joshua to tic-tac-toe. The game ends in a tie. He then sets Joshua to play himself, and Joshua plays again and again, ending in a draw each time and sucking power from the rest of the system. Joshua, realizing that there are no possible winning versions of the game, then runs iterations of global thermonuclear war and decides that the only winning move is not to play. The movie ends with the crisis averted and the drawling general's judgment revealed as superior to McKittrick's.

FIGURE 33. David *(right)* visits two hacker friends who advise him on how to access the secured computer system in *WarGames*.

FIGURE 34. In the lower half of the poster for *WarGames*, David and Jenny launch a game of *Global Thermonuclear War*, unaware of its connection to the war-room show in the top half of the poster.

Compared with the fantastical special effects and groundbreaking computer animation that mark *TRON* visually, *WarGames* is cinematically straightforward. While David is shown using his computer (as on the poster in Figure 34) and accessing networks, we see little of the technology's working other than what is obvious from a few feet away. The military facility that houses WOPR is visually overwhelming, marked by enormous screens and seemingly endless control panels, and WOPR itself is a massive presence. But the physical evidence of technology is rarely the primary focus, as the camera trains instead on the human characters and their struggle to contain the actions of the computer system. Even in scenes where David is actively communicating with Joshua, the camera reveals Joshua's screen output only briefly, choosing to focus instead on the way that David, Jennifer, Falken, and other characters are responding to Joshua. These choices, combined with the film's familiar use of establishing shots and text overlays to communicate location, and a score that would easily fit in a host of military or action films, locate *WarGames* in a cinematic tradition removed from science fiction despite the film's story line.

RECEPTION

Both *TRON* and *WarGames* faced significant problems during production and initial release. Disney had not ventured into computer animation prior to *TRON*, and although the movie remains a landmark of technological innovation in filmmaking, its initial reception was lukewarm. The release triggered a significant drop in the price of Disney's stock;[12] this response may have been unavoidable, as the film's flop came amid significant changes to the company, including the opening of the grossly overbudget EPCOT Center, the launch of the Disney Channel and Touchstone Pictures, and the ousting of CEO Ron W. Miller.[13]

Although Miller's projects ultimately proved lucrative, stockholders were still skittish about the changes, and, additionally, Disney's live-action studio had long been floundering; at the time of *TRON*'s release, the studio's most recent hit was in 1968, with *The Love Bug.* Underwhelming publicity efforts did the film no favors; while other studios spent up to $10 million per picture in publicity and advertising, E. Cardon Walker, Disney's advertising and public relations manager, refused to raise even minuscule budgets for promotional efforts, citing Disney's conviction "that the only publicity worth the money was free."[14] Eventually, *TRON* attained moderate success, grossing $33 million for a production cost of roughly $17 million.[15] *WarGames* likewise faced problems before its release, with the director John Badham replacing Martin Brest over differences between Brest and the producers.[16] However, *WarGames* was a blockbuster success for MGM, grossing over $79 million in the United States alone on a budget of just $12 million, making it the fifth-highest-grossing film in the United States for 1983.[17]

Both films gained some critical approval. *TRON* received Oscar nominations for costume design and sound,[18] and *WarGames* garnered nominations for cinematography, sound, and writing. Reviewing *TRON* in 1982, Roger Ebert awarded four stars to the "technological sound-and-light show that is sensational and brainy, stylish, and fun."[19] He had similarly high praise for *WarGames* in 1983, calling the movie "a scary and intelligent new thriller that is one of the best films so far this year," and awarding it the same star rating.[20] Ebert's positive reaction to *TRON* was not widely shared, however. *Variety* found the plot underwhelming: "Screenwriter-director Steven Lisberger has adequately marshalled a huge force of technicians to deliver the dazzle, but even kids (and specifically computer game freaks) will have a difficult time getting hooked on the situations."[21] The *New York Times* perhaps best summarized the negative critical responses to the film, saying simply, "It is beautiful—spectacularly so, at times—but dumb."[22] The plot of *TRON* manages to be both convoluted and facile, resulting in reviews that offered conflicting accounts of what exactly had happened but agreed that what had happened was not particularly interesting.

WarGames fared better with critics and made a strong showing at the Cannes Film Festival.[23] Solid reviews extended to outlets including *Variety,* which credited the film's director with much of its success: "Although the script has more than its share of short circuits, director John Badham solders the pieces into a terrifically exciting story charged by an irresistible idea."[24] Some critics were less enamored; the *New York Times* reviewer Vincent Canby dismissed the film as "an entertaining movie that, like a video game once played, tends to disappear from one's memory bank as soon as it's finished."[25] The film's continuing popularity, however, contradicts this assessment.

Both films have fared well in the long run because of substantial cult followings and retain a high level of cultural visibility decades later. This persistent attention has carried through multiple VHS and DVD releases and contributed to the push to produce sequels of both, including *WarGames 2:The Dead Code* (2008) and *TRON 2.0* (2011).[26] Less-sanctioned celebrations of the films, particularly *TRON*, persist as well: *TRON* fan and computer consultant Jay Maynard made a name for himself as "The Tron guy," appearing at public events in a true-to-film *TRON* suit that he designed and constructed.[27] The afterlife of these films speaks to their continuing salience; whether or not they are "good" in the sense of attaining critical or financial success, they have retained significance for audience members, including those who first viewed the films as children and have now grown up to become part of the technological and cultural elite.

LONG-TERM RECEPTION

The ongoing popularity of *TRON* and *WarGames* owes not only to the nostalgia of computer aficionados such as Maynard but also to the persistent cultural relevance of the narrative elements and character types set out in the films. The protagonists of both films draw on character types emergent in the late 1970s and 1980s and have been subsequently enshrined as part of the stock narratives of the computer age. This narrative is one in which computer technologies are closely associated with violence and masculinity. David and Flynn, operating under a similar moral code and sharing intellectual and cultural habits, are among the earliest examples of a character type further developed and entrenched in films such as *Sneakers* (1992), *Hackers* (1995), and *Takedown* (2000). The narratives around these fictional characters are also echoed in popular discourse surrounding both computer industry superstars such as Bill Gates[28] and Steve Jobs,[29] and high-profile hackers including Kevin Mitnick (a speaker and security consultant formerly considered the most-wanted computer criminal in the United States), Jonathan Joseph James (a.k.a. c0mrade, the first juvenile convicted and incarcerated for cybercrimes in the United States), and Robert Tappan Morris (who created the Morris Worm and became the first person prosecuted under the 1986 Computer Fraud and Abuse Act).[30]

Although Flynn and David were written into existence during the lifetimes of several of the people mentioned here, their national notoriety came near the beginning of the rise of the computer culture that made celebrities of Gates, Jobs, and others. Many viewers of *WarGames* and *TRON* would have been peering into computer culture as outsiders who lacked not only immediate familiarity with but even second-degree knowledge of the culture depicted on-screen. The films circulated nationally in areas far removed from the industry's hubs, reaching relatively rural areas where the computerization of work and education was usually proceeding slowly. These films thus served in some ways as introductory cultural texts, particularly for young viewers.

The Flynn and David characters earned their iconic status partly because of the work done by the screenwriters. By talking with computer enthusiasts, the screenwriters for *WarGames* developed their plot and characters, enabling them to create a film with great appeal for technologists despite a lack of technological know-how and the minimal tech savvy evidenced in the film. *WarGames* evolved from a 1979 script titled *The Genius,* in which a dying scientist must pass his knowledge on to a smart-alecky teenager.

The script's writers, Walter F. Parkes and Lawrence Lasker, met Stanford Research Institute–associated futurist Peter Schwartz, who told them about the developing youth hacker culture. The teenage smart aleck with a solid head for technology, that unlikely heir to the throne of scientific achievement in the original script, was in fact a rough summarization of the young men finding their way into the computer industry by hook or by crook. The connections that Schwartz saw between "youth, computers, gaming, and the military" sparked the changes to the script of *The Genius* that resulted in *WarGames.* According to Schwartz:

> There was a new subculture of extremely bright kids developing into what would become known as hackers. SRI was in Palo Alto, and all the computer nerds were around: Xerox PARC, Apple just starting—it was all happening right there. SRI was node number two of the Internet. We talked about the fact that the kinds of

computer games that were being played were blow-up-the-world games. Space war games. Military simulations. Things like Global Thermonuclear War. SRI was one of the main players in this.[31]

The writers also interviewed real-life hacker David Scott Lewis, the basis for the David Lightman character.[32]

The success of *WarGames* reflects the careful negotiations made between technological knowledge and mass appeal. The writers represent hacking and phreaking in a way that actual hackers and phreaks found accurate at a cultural level without burdening the film with details that would have overwhelmed less technologically savvy viewers. They also retain the connection among youth, computers, gaming, and the military that caught Schwartz's attention. This distillation of identifying characteristics frames a distinct type of masculinity. The film's roots in the experience of real hackers contribute to the film's resonance and imbue the film's hero with characteristics valued in this emergent subculture. The movie, in turn, helped abstract and solidify those valued characteristics.

Using a different set of tactics, the developers of *TRON* aspired to make a computer-focused narrative that would be accessible to a wide audience. Steve Lisberger and his business partner Donald Kushner had a previous success with *Animalympics* (1980), an animated television special spoofing the Olympics. Lisberger saw a sample reel of computer-generated imagery from MAGI (Mathematical Applications Group, Inc.) in 1976, shortly before encountering *Pong*. Lisberger and Kushner initially conceived of an entirely animated film set in a computer world and took the idea to several studios, but none expressed interest.

The pair found an unlikely home for their project at Disney, a company with little history of accepting projects from outside producers. The animators reconceived the film as a mix of animation and live action, which likely disappointed Lisberger, who was an early convert to computerized effects, claiming in 1982 that computer graphics would eventually replace all visual effects.[33] As a film, *TRON* serves as a vehicle for the then cutting-edge visual effects. Although only a few minutes of the film were completed as computer animation, the distinctive style still proved eye-catching. The film's visual aesthetic (showcased on the film's poster; Figure 35) is the work of a trio of influential artists including the French comic book artist Moebius; Syd Mead, an industrial designer who had worked on *Blade Runner* (1982) and would later work on *Aliens* (1986); and the commercial artist Peter Lloyd.

While *WarGames* seduced audiences through its depiction of an emergent youth subculture, *TRON* relied instead on the novelty of its visual content. Critics who found fault in *TRON* often focused on the seeming vapidity of the film's aesthetic obsessions. Although the plot and characters of *TRON* are largely subsidiary to the film's imagery, they carry a set of implications about computer technologies, masculinity, violence, and intellectual prowess echoed in *WarGames*. Both films hinge on a slippage between reality and virtuality, and address anxieties about the risks of computerization; their creation near the pinnacle of the arcade craze and release just months before the U.S. video game industry crashed is hardly coincidental. Yet the most compelling reason for reading these films in tandem emanates from connections made explicit in *WarGames*—that among youths, computers, gaming, masculinity, and the military.

The domination of humans by machines has proved to be one of the most persistent plots in narratives addressing human uneasiness with smart machines. Although *TRON* is less explicitly militarized than *WarGames,* the MCP's stated goal is domination of the human world, an imagined global takeover not too far removed from the enslavement or eradication of humanity conceived in *The Terminator* and *The Matrix*. In both *TRON* and *WarGames* the computer is figured as sentient: the personified computer system Joshua in *WarGames* demonstrates a capacity not only to experience ludological pleasure but also to learn; *TRON*'s MCP has a maniacal desire to control the human world, believing itself a more capable manager than the flawed users who currently boss around most programs.

These monster computers or computer programs tend to fall into two general categories: machines similar to Joshua, which make poor judgment calls based on a fundamental inability to understand complex situations, or machines like the MCP, which desire to control or harm humans for their own gain. In certain related narratives, the focus is on what makes characters human in the first place, asking viewers to consider whether the story's artificially intelligent character deserves some of the same empathy afforded human characters.

FIGURE 35. The *TRON* (1982) poster showcases the film's futuristic aesthetic.

Famously, in *Blade Runner,* different edits of the film provide different answers to the question of whether the film's titular character, the blade runner Rick Deckard (Harrison Ford), is himself a replicant; furthermore, the last of the two replicants Deckard is tasked with retiring are, themselves, unnervingly human, carrying out a romance and trying to escape the forced menial labor and artificially finite life span that is the lot of all replicants. Neither *TRON* nor *WarGames* ventures into this murky territory. Joshua may be rather personable in its presentation through voice, but exists only as a computer program, not as an embodied humanoid character; the MCP is sentient, but so power hungry and malicious as to seem completely unhuman. While Joshua and the MCP differ in the reasoning for their actions, both constitute a significant threat to humans, and both have to be stopped by the protagonists.

TRON and *WarGames* both bear the fingerprints of late Cold War politics. The officials at Missile Command in *WarGames* mistakenly believe that the Russians are attacking, in what is perhaps a not-too-subtle reference to *Dr. Strangelove.* The FBI agents handling David treat him as a communist agent, with one character noting, "He fits the profile perfectly. He's intelligent but an underachiever, alienated from his parents, has few friends, a classic case for recruitment by the Soviets." This description of David, of course, parallels the negative traits associated with video gamers both during the time of the film's production and release and in the present.

TRON's corporate setting less directly addresses global politics, but the MCP's treatment of the lesser programs he lords over echoes the actions of a tyrannical dictator. The MCP and his agent Sark demand that the programs sent to the game grid renounce the belief in "users," and they threaten those who refuse to make such a renouncement with lesser training for the gladiatorial games they will be forced to play. In this context, Flynn as a user from outside the system fulfills the role of a wisecracking digital Christ, not only validating the beliefs of the faithful, but also enabling them to overthrow their tormentor and restore freedom. In this way, the plot incorporates themes from anticommunist propaganda distributed in the United States during the decades-long Cold War, which represented communists as "godless" and warned that communist takeover would result in the suppression of Christian faith.

TRON and *WarGames* are not the only popular films to engage with these kinds of issues. The early 1980s saw a spate of Hollywood films that more than flirted with anticommunism as a key plot point. In *Red Dawn* (dir. John Milius; 1984) a band of teenagers defend themselves against the invading forces, using guerrilla tactics and calling themselves "Wolverines" after their high school mascot; in *Invasion U.S.A.* (dir. Joseph Zito; 1985), Matt Hunter (Chuck Norris) forms a one-man defense against Latin American communist guerrillas led by a Soviet operative; and in *Rocky IV* (dir. Sylvester Stallone; 1985), Rocky Balboa (Stallone) challenges the Soviet boxer Ivan Drago (Dolph Lundgren) after the brutish Drago pummels Apollo Creed (Carl Weathers) to death in the ring. The engagement with Cold War policies may now serve to date these films but would have, at the point of their release, anchored them to contemporary concerns that were common film fare in the mid-1980s.

Flynn and David both embody a set of cultural and political values that emerged with video gaming and computerization in the 1970s and 1980s. Characterized by youthfulness, a high level of technological knowledge and intelligence, fierce competitiveness and independence, and a willingness to disregard rules and standards, these boyish early adopters survive and excel by showing themselves particularly adept at playing by the emergent standards of a society in flux. They distinguish themselves as exceptional embodiments of the technomasculine. This form of masculinity, first evolving in the 1970s and 1980s, has proved particularly salient in both fictional and documentary narratives about the development and diffusion of computer technologies, in which the accomplishments of individual entrepreneurs are fetishized and the names of successful individuals are often as well known as the products of the corporations they found or helm. Technomasculinity is not simply geek masculinity by another name, although it certainly draws on it, nor is it a masculinity aligned with or regimented by sports, even if it will occasionally appropriate sports rhetoric. It is a masculinity marked by technicity, by consumption of computer technologies and particular cultural products, by youthfulness, and a willingness to bend or break rules where convenient or efficient. It is a masculinity that rests not too uneasily with hegemony; its adherents can easily be imagined as inhabitants of Michael Kimmel's "guyland" or of the increasingly lengthy and powerful boyhood available to gamers as identified by Derek Burrill.[34]

Flynn is markedly older than David, but Flynn is figured as juvenile, a gamer king in jeans and sneakers who holds court over the arcade he owns and draws significant audiences to his record-breaking bouts of play; at one point, Lora reacts to one of Flynn's wisecracks by saying, "Now you can see why all his friends are fourteen years old." This comment, intended as a dig, may actually flatter Flynn, who seems to see his own boyishness as a particularly valuable personality trait. Alan serves as a sober, bespectacled foil to Flynn, which further underscores the latter's boyishness. Even while Lora may have chosen Alan over Flynn, there is a clear implication that Flynn is cooler and smarter than either. David's young age is highlighted throughout *WarGames,* and his youth alarms the military and governmental experts who try to handle him; notably, Falken, himself a gifted computer scientist and researcher, seems less shocked.

In *Die Tryin': Video Games, Masculinity, and Culture,* Derrick Burrill argues that the proliferation of gaming has facilitated the expansion of boyhood, which now exists not only as a premature form of manhood but also as a gendered identity accessible to adult men at any point.[35] While Burrill suggests that this use of boyhood may enable regressive, immature behavior, the narratives of gamer identity in both *TRON* and *WarGames* suggest boyhood is essential to success in the digital landscape. These boyish technoheroes in some ways complicate modernist ideals of hegemonic masculinity and in fact offer their geek credentials not as a social or professional limitation but as their most valuable asset. They are neither organization men nor men in gray flannel suits; age-wise, or at least interest-wise, they are barely men at all, and they are detached from many institutional sources of male power even as their gender is presented as integral to their achievements.[36]

The type of boyishness embodied by the teenage David and the adult Flynn allows both to exercise their intelligence in unorthodox ways, enabling them to take risks with little concern for potential pitfalls. They are reckless in a youthful way, but that very recklessness is what makes them so brilliant. Neither shows much concern for the consequences of their actions, assuming that they will be protected by their own abilities and privilege or—as suggested explicitly by

David when he tells Jennifer that he cannot go to jail for making illegal long-distance phone calls because he is not yet eighteen—by their youth.

The films articulate widely circulated assumptions about the identity, values, and cultural practices of gamers—who are, in these films, synonymous with hackers. These assumptions had taken shape over the previous decade in coverage of the coin-operated video game craze and the young players, figured simultaneously both as brilliant techno-wizards and as potential social deviants in need of careful attention from moral guardians. *TRON* and *WarGames* thus reclaim the boy genius gamer/hacker as desirable, a potentially powerful fighter in the Cold War race of arms and ideas. As the films lead viewers to conclude, the boyishness of the two protagonists is an asset that does not necessarily separate them from adulthood but instead allows them to enact adulthood differently. When, for example, David saves the day, McKittrick ruffles David's hair—an infantilizing gesture that David responds to in kind, ruffling the middle-aged bureaucrat's hair (Figure 36).

Although their youthful behavior may alienate them from more conventional concepts of manhood, boyishness allows them to solve

FIGURE 36. In *WarGames*, David responds in kind when McKittrick ruffles his hair in an infantilizing congratulatory gesture.

problems and confront potential enemies in innovative ways. The same tendencies that enable both protagonists to break rules and laws with bravado also enable them to take novel approaches to resolving broader conflicts. They are positioned as potentially powerful, if unconventional, assets both in military and in governmental defense strategies, and in capitalist corporate endeavors.

The skills that Flynn and David apply to the conflicts in the films are related to a deep understanding of games and gameplay and, by extension, of computerized systems and computer security. The games that both David and Flynn excel at are violent, and the situations that the two encounter because of their interest in these games are even more violent; there is in this a subtle suggestion that the violence of the games may prepare them to address violent situations outside the games—a potential that the military has long been interested in, funding the development of games for both training and recruiting purposes, a fact that doubtless helped inspire *The Last Starfighter.*[37] Both Flynn and David are competitive gamers, Flynn at *Space Paranoids* and David at the intergalactic shoot 'em up *Galaga,* and both are hackers of some kind.

David manipulates the grades that he and Jennifer have received in their biology class; he makes illegal phone calls via his terminal; and he first encounters Joshua via an unidentified computer in California, which he accesses in an attempt to uncover information about an unreleased game. Although Flynn's objective ostensibly stems from a more adult concern over having his intellectual property claimed by Dillinger, his strategies are removed only by degrees from David's. The two characters' hacking activities display a similar disregard for rules and regulations and an easy willingness to transgress established boundaries—legal and social—to locate information, demonstrate technological skill, or correct some perceived wrong. While much of what Flynn and David do is purposeful, the two gamer/hackers also work from an innate and seemingly insatiable curiosity.

Youthfulness in *TRON* and *WarGames* is posited as a form of masculinity unique to the computer age. The bright, capable, mischievous tech-savvy boy has a long history in U.S. popular culture that traces at least to coverage of early modern technologies like the light bulb and radio. But earlier boy geniuses were to grow up to be good organization men who contributed to American corporations and institutions, while the gamer/hacker is presented as a rogue operator. Even at the end of *TRON*, when Flynn has ascended to take Dillinger's place, the character flies solo, arriving at work via helicopter where he is met by his ex-girlfriend/employee Lora and Alan. Alan is not only Lora's current boyfriend but, like Lora, Flynn's underling. Whether Lora's and Alan's roles in the destruction of the MCP and the uncovering of Dillinger's treachery has been rewarded is unclear, but it is obvious that Flynn has received the greatest benefit for his role in their shared exploits.

David is exonerated at the end of *WarGames* through the "expert" McKittrick's loss of status. Teenage, mischievous David—not the overly confident technological evangelist McKittrick or the disenchanted AI expert Falken—best understands how to outthink Joshua and save the day. David, in saving the world from nuclear war, effectively erases his earlier misdeeds, removing himself from suspicion and proving himself not a communist agent but, in fact, a good all-American boy.

Similarly, Flynn, by working with Alan and Lora to expose Dillinger, proves himself not to be a security threat or substandard employee but the best software engineer that ENCOM has ever seen—a title he had apparently held prior to his dismissal by the corrupt Dillinger. Both Flynn and David are revealed as the rightful heroes of their stories—not to the viewers, who have been led to identify with the characters throughout their respective films, but to the other characters in their narrative. In both films, audience members are privy to information, such as David's relatively benign intentions or Flynn's unfair firing, which is either misunderstood or suppressed in the world of the film. In this way, the films put audience members in the position of participating vicariously in the exoneration and celebration of Flynn and David, as they, like the heroes, knew better all along than the institutionalized experts.

CONCLUSION

TRON and *WarGames* are key texts of computer culture, emerging as computers were first becoming prevalent in day-to-day U.S. life and contributing to what has become a dominant cultural narrative of the uses and abuses of computers in the digital age. The characterization of the gamer/hacker computer whiz presented in these films has re-tained its significance and continues to evolve in films like *Sneakers* (dir. Phil Alden Robinson; 1992), *Hackers* (dir. Iain Softely; 1995), *Office Space* (dir. Mike Judge; 1999), and *The Social Network* (dir. David Fincher; 2011).[38] In disseminating a cohesive, broadly accessible narrative of computer technology tied to violence, youth, and mas-culinity, *TRON* and *WarGames* established a blueprint for meaning making in the emerging realm of the digital. Drawing heavily from observations of emerging hacker culture and engaging, intentionally or otherwise, with popular press coverage of the video gaming phe-nomenon, these films helped reify gamer identity.

Based on the exploits of some of the earliest computer-literate youth, David and Flynn brought narratives of hacking, gaming, and technological wizardry to millions of viewers across the United States and beyond, expanding and reinforcing the masculine identity already emerging with the new computer technologies. They are prototypes not only for fictional characters in more recent texts but also for real-life tech entrepreneurs who present themselves and are presented through mediated narratives as embodiments of a simi-lar values system. Although the protagonists reclaim good guy status by the films' ends, similar narratives of tech-savvy whiz kids with a willingness to bend the rules cropped up in less celebratory coverage of hacking and phreaking; ultimately, however, even these activi-ties gained a certain veneer of righteousness based on their heroic predecessors. *TRON* and *WarGames* did much to establish the arche-type of the gamer boy genius and effectively broadcast this identity nationally and internationally to an audience largely composed of children; they thus molded and guided the early participants of the era of computerization.

By consolidating ties among computer technologies, youths, vio-lence, and the military, *TRON* and *WarGames* helped establish the emerging digital landscape in the popular imagination as a dangerous proving ground for young men coming of age in the era of comput-erization. As R. W. Connell, Kimmel, and Michael Messner have all argued, American masculinity has long depended on these kinds of trials and tests.[39] Not only did the films valorize their characters' exploits, they helped reinforce the presumed maleness of computer technologies including video games and echoed moral guardians' worries about the social effects of computerization and video game violence. In depicting the emergent computer society, Hollywood narratives conceived of a culture in which the virtual and the real converged at messy borders, with potentially catastrophic effects for inhabitants on both sides of the divide—a threat barely contained by the efforts of young men willing to play against previously established rules. As computer technologies have neared ubiquity, narratives like those presented in *TRON* and *WarGames* remain salient, influencing public perception not only of computer technologies but more importantly of technologists, from teenage gamers to middle-aged tech industry entrepreneurs to potentially threatening hackers.

Despite normalization, computer technologies retain a powerful mystique, as demonstrated in the recent film *The Social Network,* a dramatic retelling—and fictionalization—of how Mark Zuckerberg (Jesse Eisenberg) founded Facebook. The cinematic Zuckerberg displays a willingness to break rules; he hacks into school systems, insults his ex-girlfriend on the Internet, and maintains a wardrobe of jeans and hooded sweatshirts. But this boy genius narrative borders on condemnation, unfolding through legal proceedings about allegations that Zuckerberg ripped off the idea for Facebook from other students at Harvard and deliberately bilked his friend and cofounder out of his share of the company's earnings. The Zuckerberg revealed in the narrative is joyless, bitter, and lonely. He has a chip on his shoulder about the privileges enjoyed by wealthier and better-connected students, enduring the legal proceedings that provide the film's narrative structure with slumped shoulders and snide commentary. His social ostracization is presented as both the cause and the effect of his success; when his girlfriend breaks up with him, she assures him that

> you are probably going to be a very successful computer person. But you're going to go through life thinking that girls don't like you because you're a nerd. And I want you to know, from the bottom of my heart, that that won't be true. It'll be because you're an asshole.

His willingness to break rules has so poisoned his own social life that he is shown as incapable of connecting with other people in meaningful ways.

The film ends with the statement that Zuckerberg is the world's youngest billionaire, an achievement undercut by the final scene showing him obsessing over whether to send a Facebook "friend request" to the ex-girlfriend who dumped him; even his pining seems too self-serving to be pitiable. The Zuckerberg of the film is portrayed throughout as emotionally stunted and jealous—a far cry from the charming and brilliant characters at the center of *TRON* and *WarGames*.

If David and Flynn embody the most socially and culturally desirable gamer/hackers, the fictionalized Zuckerberg falls on the other end of the spectrum. His boyishness and willingness to break the rules may bring him financial success, but they also make him socially unpalatable to the point that his *Citizen Kane*–style loneliness seems well deserved. *The Social Network* gained wide critical acclaim and numerous Academy Award nominations, including the coveted Best Picture and Best Director nods, and won Best Film Editing, Best Screenplay Adaptation, and Best Original Score. The popularity of the quasi-biography may point to significant shifts in how young male technologists are viewed in the popular imagination. While David and Flynn save the world, Zuckerberg's development of a highly successful social networking site alienates everyone in his real-life social network. Enhanced by the presumed "real"-ness of the character, the brilliant boy gamer complete with the proverbial heart of gold seems to have been displaced by the blindly ambitious and socially stunted young entrepreneur.

To understand the rise, diffusion, and cultural effects of computing requires a critical understanding of early mass narratives of these technologies and the culture surrounding them. The vision of computerization in *TRON* and *WarGames* is one that has, in many ways, both come to pass and persisted, finding real-world expression in attempts to characterize successful entrepreneurs and technologists. In contemporary cinema, the character types imagined in *TRON* and *WarGames* have diverged into the more harshly depicted figures in *The Social Network*, who explore the world of boyish tech experts while eschewing the fantasy of happy-ever-after, and the characters in films such as *Death Race* (dir. Paul W. S. Anderson; 2008, a remake of the 1975 *Death Race 2000*) and *Gamer* (dir. Mark Neveldine;

2009), who take the consolidation of gaming, masculinity, violence, and youth to horrifying and bloody extremes. Although computer and video gaming technologies have become everyday reality, they retain an air of novelty and a tinge of potential terror, a terror often countered with idealized visions of what masculinity might mean in an era of computerization.

6

THE ARCADE IS DEAD, LONG LIVE THE ARCADE

NOSTALGIA
IN AN ERA OF
UBIQUITOUS COMPUTING

BARCADE: BROOKLYN

In the fall of 2010, during a research trip, I stop overnight in New York to visit a friend who lives in Brooklyn. During a night out, we land at Barcade, a combination bar–arcade, which is billed as "celebrating American craft beer and classic arcade games."[1] Vintage video game machines line the walls of Barcade; classics like *Tetris* (Atari, 1988), *Frogger* (Konami, 1981), and *Ms. Pac-Man* (Midway, 1981) are mixed with more obscure games and machines of a recent vintage. Drinks, including a wide selection of local and regional beers for those with more epicurean tastes, are available at the bar, which is nearly as packed as the machines. Patrons trying to attract the bartenders' attention hold up crumpled bills in their hands. Those waiting their turn to play video games line up their quarters on the cabinets, a practice that has long held as an arcade standard for queuing up.

The patrons at Barcade that night are, for the most part, younger than my friend and I are. When my friend says that he remembers a game from childhood, the player behind us in line asks how old he is, only to respond with visible surprise to my friend's admission that he is thirty. To say that the crowd is young is almost an understatement;

many of them are college students just old enough to drink. At least one young woman tells me confidentially that she has a fake ID. The average age of a Barcade customer is likely younger than the average age of a Barcade game. Yet the customers appear to have strong feelings about particular machines.

Those machines with the longest lines are usually the older, most famous games. *Ms. Pac-Man,* for example, is surrounded. Perhaps these hit games deserved their success, and their popularity in this neo-arcade reflects only their superior design. Or perhaps the arcade, too, has developed its canon, and customers simply gravitate to those games they have heard of before entering the bar. The truth is probably somewhere in between, with a game's popularity resulting both from exceptionally good design and from a few decades of notoriety. Barcade is a children's play space reimagined as an adult entertainment venue. It is also a place where the history of the video game machine folds back into itself—here, the video game returns to its origins as a bar amusement.

DAVE & BUSTER'S: AUSTIN

At Dave & Buster's outlets across the United States, the arcade is reborn as a multi-attraction entertainment center. It is a bar and a grill, an arcade, a midway. Or maybe it is whatever makes money. Friday nights at the D&B's in Austin attracts an assortment of patrons, from working-class families to teenagers to groups of twentysomethings dressed in their finest club attire. On a Friday night in January 2012, I drag a group of friends with me for fieldwork. The arcade tokens have been replaced with plastic cards—called "Power Cards"—and every machine is outfitted with a card reader.[2] Game credits are purchased and then stored electronically in customer accounts; the tickets dispensed as prizes by the machines can also be turned in at the prize counter to be stored electronically, accessible by card. Arcade currency has gone digital. We purchase cards and load them up at kiosks, feeding the machines paper money or swiping our debit and credit cards and then selecting an amount. A couple watches me reload my card, one explaining to the other how the machine works. "She's not from America," he tells me. I smile and say the machine hardly makes sense to me, either.

The chain's branding calls the arcade a "Million-Dollar Midway," but the space's arcade roots are showing. Shoot-'em-up and racing games are mixed with Skee-Ball machines and quarter pushers—the machines with the sliding shelves of quarters, always threatening to spill into the hopper if you drop yours in at just the right moment. Machines spew tickets, and the trade-in counter—really more of a trade-in room at this particular location—does a brisk business in stuffed animals, novelty grills (for teeth), knickknacks, and even blenders and other small appliances. On the arcade floor, I hit the jackpot on Big Bass Wheel, a spin-the-wheel-type game I had just been informed is surely rigged, and then spend way too much time trying to top myself at Skee-Ball. There are midway-style games— basketball shooting games, a game that you operate by jumping as hard as you can on a platform, a horse race game where players compete by rolling balls up a ramp to move their numbered horses forward.

I wander the floor after blowing all my credits and notice a college student with a fancy camera and tripod shooting his friends playing various brightly lit games for a class project. Eventually, I stumble across a veritable *Dance Revolution* (Konami, 2009) virtuoso.[3] As he plays on and on, a crowd gathers. He falls into backbends to hit the machine's sensors with his hands before popping back on his feet. In a place where so many of the gamers are either very young or very drunk on neon cocktails, to see someone so exceptionally skilled is a treat. I watch for a while, but can determine only that he seems young—his hair hangs in his face, his T-shirt is oversized, and his jeans are faded. When the game ends, he slouches off, nothing in his movements to suggest the fleet-footed performance he has just given. I do not have the opportunity to speak to him, but I am pretty sure I know his name; the teenagers at the youth center where I volunteer have told me in awed tones about some guy named Kevin—"kinda shy, but pretty nice" who is a total rock star at *DDR*. As he disappears into the crowd, I realize that I have just seen a rare bird—an arcade legend in his natural habitat.

THE ARCADE IN PRESENT TENSE

From the 1970s to the present, much has changed, both in the video game industry and in the arcade game's cultural position. The industry crash of 1983 remapped video gaming. At its peak, Atari was an industrial giant, controlling 80 percent of the U.S. videogame market before shortfalls in profits and poorly received games took a toll both on Atari and on parent company Warner Media.[4] In 1983 Atari lost more than $356 million, laid off 30 percent of its ten thousand employees, and moved all manufacturing to Hong Kong and Taiwan. While Atari was the most influential of the video game companies operating at the time, other industry leaders were flailing as well. In 1983 Mattel's electronics division ran at a deficit of $201 million and laid off more than one-third of its staff. Activision lost somewhere between $3 million and $5 million during a three-month period, and profits at Bally sank precipitously.[5] Nervous about the market crash, Coleco sought to diversify, releasing the Adam Computer and venturing into the toy business by licensing Xavier Roberts's dolls as Cabbage Patch Kids; the dolls' success was not enough to keep the company from filing for bankruptcy in 1988.[6]

The crash cleared the field of some key competitors. Even as the industry rose from its ashes, it rose in different forms. The growth of home computing greatly increased the popularity of computer games, and many gaming startups focused on these in the wake of the 1983 crash. The crash also cleared the way for companies like Sega and Nintendo to make further inroads into the U.S. market and, in the case of Nintendo, to dominate the home console market.[7] Changes to the video game industry allowed the industry to recover and thrive over time, but the once-booming U.S. coin-op video game market was radically reduced. During the crash and in its immediate aftermath, many arcade owners shuttered their businesses and many coin-op game manufacturers shifted away from video games or closed, with few of the video game–focused coin-op manufacturers surviving the decade. But even after the decline in the number of arcades and the slowing flow of new arcade games, the arcade persists.

Dave & Buster's and Barcade represent two contemporary versions of the video game arcade. While Barcade in Brooklyn (shown in Figure 37) uses video games as an advertised attraction and a way to distinguish itself from other bars in the neighborhood, many other bars use video games (both classic and new) as on-site amusement options. For Barcade, the strategy has been so successful that the company has expanded, with locations in New York, Jersey City, and Philadelphia, and has inspired similar businesses like Emporium Arcade Bar in Chicago. Barcade's CEO and managing director, Paul Kermizian, says that the success of the business has depended on maintaining a balance in focus:

> I think the balance between both is key. We try to not make one seem more important than the other. We are dedicated to our craft beer selection and we are dedicated to our classic video games. We put an equal amount of care and work into curating and maintaining both. Hopefully that shows.

That balance is hard won, given the difficulties in maintaining a fleet of old arcade games. According to Kermizian, "They break all the time," and employees have to pay attention to customers' treatment of the games to try to protect them.[8] The challenge seems worth it, though, as it has helped Barcade remain busy in a neighborhood increasingly crowded with entertainment options.

FIGURE 37. Brooklyn's Barcade (opened in 2004) boasts banks of vintage coin-op video games and an impressive collection of craft beer. Photograph reprinted with permission of Barcade.

As during the heyday of the video game arcade, many of the machines standing singly or in small groups in neighborhood bars are owned by route operators, some of whom have been in business for not just years but generations. In other cases, the games are bought outright by the business owners, who use the machines to lure and hold the attention of their paying customers and as a secondary way to generate income. Dave & Buster's has its roots in the video game arcade—one of the chain's founders started in the business by operating an arcade.

Despite the 1983 crash, arcades did not die out, and today they occupy a different, diminished, but still visible part of the entertainment and amusement business. Many of the largest arcade companies persist to the present day, either as chains or as exceptionally large individual arcades. For example, the arcade chain that fought all the way to the U.S. Supreme Court for its right to operate an arcade in Mesquite, Texas, has undergone buyouts and spinoffs but is now part of a large chain of arcades. Aladdin's Castle, Inc. separated from its parent corporation in 1989 and operated independently until 1993, when it was purchased by Namco Limited. Namco Limited merged Aladdin's Castle with Namco Operations to form Namco Cybertainment, which remains the largest arcade operator in North America, with twenty thousand machines in over one thousand locations.[9]

The Dave & Buster's chain of entertainment centers, intended to appeal to both youths and adults, uses the slogan "Escape into Play" and advertises itself as "the only place with a restaurant serving everything from wings to New York Strips, a bar with the best happy hour and a Million-Dollar Midway filled with the latest interactive and video games."[10] The first Dave & Buster's opened in Dallas in 1982, the brainchild of two men from Little Rock, Arkansas, one who ran a restaurant/bar and the other who ran an arcade and games joint next door. The two business owners developed the idea for a combination restaurant/bar and arcade after noticing the overlap in their clientele. Today, more than fifty Dave & Buster's locations are scattered across the United States.

While Dave & Buster's advertises itself as a family-friendly place, the company's website clearly features pictures of adults, many of whom appear to be dressed for a postwork happy hour, with ties askew and shirt sleeves rolled up. The explicit appeal to adults, even

FIGURE 38. In this advertisement from 2008, a bored commuter is transported from his dull drive to an exciting driving game at Dave & Buster's.

if it is masked by claims of providing "family fun," is one strategy that has distinguished Dave & Buster's from competitors and likely helped the business to expand even as other arcades were closing. Further, the chain's multiple offerings (food, drink, and entertainment), and its courting of corporate parties and events has helped ensure that the business has multiple moneymaking strategies. The arcade at Dave & Buster's may be an integral part of the business, but it is not the only source of revenue.

Television advertisements for Dave & Buster's demonstrate this reliance on multiple revenue streams. In a 2008 advertisement, a man bored by his daily commute is transported to Dave & Buster's, where he plays a racing game in front of a small crowd (Figure 38). According to the ad, there is now "even more to come back for" at Dave & Buster's; the patrons shown are respectable young adults. A 2010 advertisement using the chain's "Escape into Play" slogan features adults in business casual attire, including high heels and suit-style skirts on women and shirts and ties on men, playing in the arcade. These scenes of play are intercut with footage lingering over the

FIGURE 39. The American Classic Arcade Museum, located inside Funspot, features an impressive collection of video game uprights alongside other items from the period. Courtesy Aaron McGaffey.

preparation of "one of eight incredible entrees." The advertised "Eat & Play combo" includes one entrée and a $10 game card for $15.99. The outfits featured in the spot clearly suggest that the "Eat & Play combo" is an appropriate postwork activity for young professionals.[11]

The company's advertisements also, at times, place Dave & Buster's in the history of the video game arcade. Notably, a campaign launched late in 2011 uses 8-bit-style audio including recognizable bits of the original *Pac-Man* (Namco, 1980) soundtrack along with 1980s-style typefaces to advertise the launch of *Pac-Man Battle Royale* (Namco, 2011) at Dave & Buster's. *Pac-Man Battle Royale* is a four-person game using the franchise's original visual and audio style. Dave & Buster's has proved forward-looking in its efforts to maintain a diversified business and to attract adult consumers, both through advertising and through its bar-and-grill–style restaurant. But in this backward-looking advertisement, the chain relies on stereotypes of the arcade. Despite the gender inclusivity evidenced by many of the company's advertisements, this one, which deliberately references the classic arcade era in its aesthetic, features only three people, all young men.[12]

While Dave & Buster's has benefited from efforts to expand the audience for the arcade and diversify revenues, other arcades depend on their historic roots and their old-fashioned games. Arcades in tourist areas, like the Casino Arcade at the Santa Cruz Beach Boardwalk and the Playland Arcade at the Santa Monica Pier, predated the popularity of video games and survived the crash, partly because they benefit from a steady stream of vacationing customers. Further, the long history of these tourist-trap arcades means that they had an established presence that predated the fad for video games and often retained a diverse spread of machines. Video games may have taken up prime real estate during the height of the craze, but they did not completely displace older moneymakers like the claw machines that never quite manage to scoop up the stuffed animals packed inside or the pinball machines and other mechanical games. Some of the more famous arcades, like the Funspot Family Fun Center (shown in Figure 39) in Weirs Beach in Laconia, New Hampshire, which originally opened in 1952, have become tourist destinations in and of themselves. Funspot houses the American Classic Arcade Museum, which features 180 classic games from the 1970s and 1980s at any time; it is also home to the Annual International Classic Video Game and Pinball Tournament. In 2008 Guinness World Records named Funspot "The Largest Arcade in the World."[13] The annual tournament has helped Funspot gain notoriety and has built a loyal following among classic gaming devotees.

There are also newer arcades in the United States, which include both "Japanese style" arcades and arcades intended specifically to appeal to retro and classic gamers. The arcades that bill themselves as Japanese style tend to focus on the shoot-'em-up and fighting game genres, and on newer rather than vintage or classic games. Japan's popular "game centers," which are part of everyday life for many Japanese people, have become an object of fascination for Americans fixated on Japanese culture.[14] Other new arcades focus on classic machines from the video game era and earlier. For example, the Pinballz Arcade in Austin has a variety of games but focuses on pinball, housing more than eighty machines, including a few dozen video game uprights, and also offering machine sales and game repair on arcade amusements.[15]

REMEMBERING THE ARCADE

The arcades that have survived and thrived have done so by tapping into the intense nostalgia with which many Americans remember the arcade. Nostalgia, as I use it here, refers to a longing for the past, which cannot be recovered. The nostalgic past is irrecoverable partly because it is idealized, and this idealized form of the past often points not to the superiority of the past but to the shortcomings and disappointments of the present. That is, nostalgia often expresses a displaced desire for a better present.[16] Arcade nostalgia is a product of the digital age and is postmodern; while nostalgia for the 1950s expresses a longing for the promises of modernity made good, the nostalgia for the arcade seems to express a longing for a more pleasant postmodern era.

Arcade nostalgia manifests itself not only in the attachment to the arcade as a place, or as an environment, but also in the attachment to specific games directly associated with the arcade. Adults old enough to have their own families now take their children to arcades to experience something they themselves remember fondly from childhood; others continue to use the arcade as an amusement space for themselves and their peers. Younger players visit arcades for some of the same reasons that youths visited those original video game arcades in the 1970s and 1980s, but their attraction to older "classic" games is doubtless shaped by the historical and cultural notoriety of these games. Even arcades that specialize in newer games often rely on golden era ideas of what an arcade should be; the campaigns evident in *RePlay* to make arcades neat, orderly, well supervised, and family friendly have certainly left a legacy, as evidenced by chains like Main Event Entertainment, based in Dallas, which combines arcade games, billiards, bowling, laser tag, glow-in-the-dark mini golf, rock climbing, and other amusements into sprawling "family fun centers."[17]

The arcade industry has performed admirably given reports of its death, which, to paraphrase Mark Twain, may have been greatly exaggerated. Certainly the arcade is no longer a mainstay of every small town and shopping mall in America. The form of the video game arcade has changed, and the popularity has declined from the time when video gaming made *Life*'s "Year in Pictures" as a hot new trend.

But as computer technologies and video games have both become more broadly diffused and familiar, the arcade has been recognized as a keystone to the history of digital culture. The arcade as it is remembered has become a symbol of a bygone era and a site ripe for cultural and historical nostalgia. Nostalgia has been a significant factor in shaping both the contemporary arcade and our cultural memory of the historical video game arcade. Not only has nostalgia affected how we imagine and reimagine the arcade as contemporary physical site, but it has affected how we conceive of the historical arcade. The rehabilitation of the video game arcade has become a major project. The arcade, once a cultural fad, has now become a privileged cultural site in need of protection; particularly successful games have become part of the arcade's canon. The classic arcade is presented as a kind of living time capsule that consumers can visit and play in, and even newer arcades are often presented as part of a proud cultural tradition.

Outside the arcade, consumers are invited to revisit the arcade as cultural site through consumer products from sweatshirts and T-shirts to toys and games, and through media products including not only adaptations and rereleases of now-historic games but major film and television releases. These products, while they suggest a kind of preservation or celebration of the arcade, are themselves part of a process of editing and revision. Much has been written about the way that documentary efforts bear the fingerprints of their creators, reflecting the editorial decisions, interests, and even biases of those performing the labor of documentary production; documentaries addressing the history of video gaming are no exception to this set of issues.

Even novelty items like candies packed in *Pac-Man*-themed tins participate in this editorializing of the past, as certain games such as *Pac-Man* and *Donkey Kong* are reiterated over and over again in a marketplace of licensed merchandise. This process may reflect individual companies' willingness to license their games' characters—and the persistence of these companies, as many out-of-print titles belong to companies that have long folded. But, as pointed out by Matthew Thomas Payne in his critique of plug-and-play systems, it also reinforces and amplifies the significance of certain games, limiting the canon of video gaming.[18] While *Pac-Man* and *Donkey Kong* are important, their perceived importance obfuscates the diversity of games on the market during the same historical period. The historical canon of the video game arcade machine, like all canons, is a limited one.

The arcade is reconstructed through memory as is the field of gaming and the gamers themselves. Popular depictions of gaming both during the peak of arcade culture and in the aftermath have focused on specific types of gaming and certain kinds of gamers. The celebration of competitive gaming, in particular, has determined the conceptualization of what gamers looked like, how they played, and why. Just as the average runner is probably not an Olympic athlete or even a marathoner, the average arcade gamer likely was not a world record holder or similarly competitive gamer. Pinning down just how prominent highly competitive gamers were in the average arcade is difficult, and certainly there was some variance as some arcades, particularly those that made a habit of hosting tournaments, likely had a more prominent community of competitive gamers.

After the fact, however, the presence of competitive gamers has increased as the narratives of competitive game play have become more prominent than narratives of casual or social gameplay. Just as the content of arcades and the diversity of games played has narrowed in memory, so has the diversity of players and ways of playing been narrowed by a focus on the most notable players. Both factors have altered how the arcade is remembered after the fact, and so has personal nostalgia and the shifting of memory among gamers, arcade owners, industry insiders, and others who experienced and helped shape the culture of the video game arcade.

ARCADE AS PRESERVATION PROJECT

Despite their persistence and the warm nostalgia with which many patrons seem to view independent arcades, these businesses frequently face difficulties in surviving. The popular narrative of the arcade for at least the past decade has been one of endangerment, of something in need of saving. Arcades have been beleaguered businesses since their outset; unfavorable zoning ordinances, licensing and registration requirements, and other civic codes often placed a financial burden on arcades and placed them in opposition to other local businesses. Moral crusades against the arcade itself or against specific arcade games further isolated arcades from local business communities.

While the U.S. Supreme Court ruling in *City of Mesquite v. Aladdin's Castle, Inc.* dampened efforts to regulate arcades, arcade owners in many cities had to negotiate appealing to young customers while placating parents and other moral guardians. The 1983 film *Joysticks* is based on the struggles of a group of teens to "save" their local arcade from a wealthy businessman's efforts to have the joint shut down. While the film is a *Porky's*-style romp complete with bikini-clad co-eds and subculture stock characters, the idea that a narrative of an arcade under attack might particularly resonate with teens is not farfetched. The arcade in *Joysticks* is cartoonish, and the farce is certainly not invested in depicting a "real" arcade, yet the movie conveys a genuine affection for the arcade, a set of feelings perhaps already amplified and altered by nostalgia, as the arcade's golden age was already reaching its ending. The film's anti-arcade faction is given the face of an uptight fat cat, but the idea that established business owners might not welcome an arcade as part of the local business community, again, may reflect, as through a funhouse mirror, the experience of arcade owners and patrons struggling to maintain respectability.

So in many places, the arcade may have needed saving even during the heyday of coin-operated video gaming. Even before the industry crash of 1983, measures aimed at limiting youth access to arcades and the spread of arcades shaped the work that arcade owners had to do to stay in business. After the crash, the situation became untenable for many arcade owners, and waves of closures rocked the industry further.[19] Not all arcades closed, but many did, and many dedicated arcade-goers found themselves without a local arcade. For them, the closure of a beloved neighborhood or town arcade seemed to signal the closing of an era. Those arcades that still persist have come to be seen as holdouts; the ones that have retained a commitment to stocking now-vintage machines have become informal historical landmarks in their own right, living museums of a bygone era of gaming.

Because the arcade is so established as the fertile soil from which all video gaming grew, the arcade is a privileged site not only for those gamers who grew up going to arcades but for those who grew up without them as well. In this way, preserving the arcade has become a cultural preservation effort much like efforts to preserve beloved record stores or movie theaters. This is not to suggest that the arcade is the sole point of origin for video gaming more broadly, given the integral role played by PC-based computer games and the home console market; it is, however, to suggest that the public nature of video game arcades granted them an especially high profile partly because it meant that they appealed to journalists and other media makers and attracted the attention of moral guardians.

The nostalgia for the arcade is often expressed through and coincides with nostalgia for specific games. The surprisingly ephemeral nature of arcade machines meant that many gamers experienced the "loss" of beloved games even in places where there never were arcades or where the arcade survived the crash. Individual games installed in coin-op Laundromats, bowling alleys, convenience stores, and other nonarcade locations helped establish video games as part of everyday life; they also helped extend exposure to arcade machines far beyond the confines of the arcade. The nostalgia for the arcade as a space and the nostalgia for the arcade as represented by individual arcade games are not mutually exclusive, and many people who feel nostalgia for one likely have nostalgia for the other.

Because the history of the video game arcades and the history of the games that occupied those arcades are so intimately intertwined, that this would be the case seems perfectly reasonable. It also means that efforts to "save the arcade" or to save individual games often serve similar ends even when they are ostensibly discrete projects. Arcade preservation efforts help create demand for vintage arcade machines, and interest in "classic" video gaming helps fuel the desire to preserve arcades. Preservation efforts take various forms and include commercial and nonprofit efforts from a wide range of organizations.

The methods of preservation and the specific aspect of the arcade deemed worth preserving vary greatly. The development of the Multiple Arcade Machine Emulator (MAME) platform (see Figure 40) beginning in 1997 and continuing to the present is perhaps one of the best-known efforts at preserving arcade hardware. The initial MAME release was made by the Italian software developer Nicola Salmoria; since then, the coordination of the project has passed through several people, with Angelo Salese serving as the current coordinator. MAME has helped preserve access to numerous classic arcade games, making them available for play on home computer systems.[20] However, as a project, MAME has the preservation of the hardware—the machines themselves—as its primary objective; enabling users to play the games is a secondary objective or side effect:

> MAME is strictly a non-profit project. Its main purpose is to be a reference to the inner workings of the emulated arcade machines. This is done both for educational purposes and for preservation purposes, in order to prevent many historical games from disappearing forever once the hardware they run on stops working. Of course, in order to preserve the games and demonstrate that the emulated behavior matches the original, you must also be able to actually play the games. This is considered a nice side effect, and is not MAME's primary focus.[21]

In focusing on preservation, the MAME development team has signaled a dedication not to arcade *games* but to arcade *machines* as significant cultural artifacts.

FIGURE 40. The MAME website outlines the project, provides updates, and links to current downloads.

By focusing on "the inner workings of the emulated arcade machines," MAME's developers have committed themselves to the hardware that enabled classic games. Arcade machines relied on diverse hardware types, and the ROM formats used varied from circuit boards to laser discs to magnetic tape, many of which are difficult to preserve or to copy. This commitment to the hardware means that the project is one explicitly of *technical* preservation rather than *cultural* preservation. Obviously, these two areas overlap, but the focus on the technologies that enable the games distinguishes MAME from most preservation efforts.

While MAME explicitly states that the ability to play the games is "a nice side effect," the project has yielded more than two thousand playable games. MAME users are incredibly dedicated to replicating the experience of arcade play, building or modifying cabinets to accommodate computer systems so that the MAME interface more closely resembles the physical interface of an arcade game, or purchasing ready-made "MAME cabinets" from makers such as X-Arcade.[22] MAME's goal may be to preserve hardware systems and interfaces, but the "side effect" of playable games has attracted the loyalty of many gamers. The playable game ROMs allow older gamers to play games from their childhood and enable younger gamers to play games unavailable in public places. The sheer number of games accessible through MAME has made the project one of the most comprehensive efforts at preserving classic games, even while the project's purpose remains the emulation of arcade hardware.

The interest in game archiving sparked by MAME has helped drive interest in ephemera related to video games, as MAME gamers went looking for graphics relevant to their MAME experience. The Arcade Flyer Archive (TAFA), an online archive of numerous video game, pinball, and arcade game flyers, developed from personal collections. TAFA resulted from the merging of the MAME Flyer/Poster Archive, founded by Gerard Maathuis to provide Flyer Packs for MAME, and Arcade Nostalgia, founded by Eric Jacobson. Today, TAFA is overseen by Jacobson and Dan Hower, a serious collector who has contributed roughly half of the flyers accessible through TAFA. Using the slogan "Remember the games. Feel the nostalgia" since the launch of its current site design in 2005, the site is positioned as a nostalgic enterprise and clearly has gamers/fans as its intended audience.

While TAFA is not a professionalized archive, it holds one of the most extensive catalogs of arcade flyers in the world. Further, the archive positions itself as a tool for preservation efforts, including MAME, and as a useful cultural history resource:

> The Arcade Flyer Archive (TAFA) is a digital repository for advertisement flyers that are used by the coin-operated amusement industry to promote the sales of its games. Over time flyers represent much more than a marketing brochure. They capture a unique blend of the industry's history, graphic design trends and advertising campaigns. Most importantly, they bring out the nostalgia of countless people who have grown up with the culture of video games, pinball machines and arcade games. Unique cabinet designs, attractive artwork and real screen shots—all of which represent the visual language of coin-operated games, make flyers sought after items for collectors and effective tools for restoring games to their original factory specifications.[23]

While both TAFA and MAME engage in preservation efforts, MAME is framed as a technical, rather than a cultural, enterprise. TAFA, while explicit in its cultural preservation efforts, is not a professional archive, in the sense that the people engaged in curating and preserving the flyers are not trained archivists.

At present, TAFA has more than six thousand video game flyers, thirteen hundred pinball game flyers, and seventeen hundred arcade game flyers.[24] The collection continues to grow as individuals are encouraged to share their collections by scanning and uploading the images. While enabling trips down an arcade-focused memory lane is presented as a core motivation for continuing TAFA, the archive is simultaneously framed as a rich resource for historians interested in the video game industry, graphic design, and advertising. (I can attest that TAFA's holdings have proved incredibly useful for my own research into arcade history.) Further, the flyers are presented as a valuable resource for helping with game restorations and other preservation activities.

While TAFA is fundamentally a volunteer or amateur effort at archiving arcade culture, it serves as a bridge between fannish collecting and professionalized archiving. TAFA and similar projects fuel interest in the cultural history of video gaming and help demonstrate the interest in and necessity of preserving video gaming culture. Although Rochelle Slovin mounted *Hot Circuits,* the first retrospective of the video game, at the Museum of the Moving Image in 1989, sustained interest in the arcade as historical topic has taken hold at academic institutions only more recently, with several significant archival efforts being mounted in the past decade.

The International Center for the History of Electronic Games, part of the Strong National Museum of Play, holds over twenty thousand items related to the history of electronic gaming, the largest collection in the world.[25] Since its founding in 2008, the UT Video Game Archive, housed at the Dolph Briscoe Center for American History at the University of Texas, "seeks to preserve and protect the work of videogame developers, publishers and artists for use by a wide array of researchers."[26] In the UK the National Media Museum and Nottingham Trent University announced the National Videogame Archive, a joint project intended "to preserve, analyse and display the products of the global videogame industry by placing games in their historical, social, political and cultural contexts."[27] In all the examples cited here, these professional archives are affixed to existing institutions.

These recent heavily institutionalized efforts at video game preservation are matched by the dedicated work of less conventional preservationists—the owners, for example, of Funspot, who have maintained a large collection of arcade games and have begun presenting at least part of their collection in the context of a second-floor "museum" that includes informational chat labels on games and other things; or of Twin Galaxies, which for years documented, in exacting detail, the top score records for hundreds of games while also documenting the organization's own history.[28] The preservation of the arcade, like much of cultural preservation, is not a solely academic pursuit; indeed, much preservation work is led by individual gamers and industry members who engage in their own preservation and documentary efforts or who contribute to larger projects by donating materials or helping publicize broader projects.

The vogue for preserving video game history is not isolated and seems to be linked with the vogue for geek chic arcade history, which I define here as the glamorization of arcade culture by celebrating and propagating arcade games themselves and affiliated cultural artifacts through consumer goods, artworks, and popular media. While most professional preservationists may cringe to hear their work reduced to an act of nostalgia, I do not wish to do that; "nostalgia" may be one of the easiest ways to track public interest in a topic, so it makes sense that the professional preservation of arcade culture and games gains momentum at a time when nostalgia for the arcade is running particularly high.

Educational institutions and nonprofits are not the only organizations invested in the preservation of the "classic" gaming era. In 2009 Stride Gum launched a "Save the Arcades" promotion, which tapped into the idea of the arcade as an endangered cultural institution. Stride invited gamers to play *Zapatur* online and give their points to their favorite arcade; the arcade with the most points would win $25,000 to help keep its business afloat. The competition highlighted four arcades: Arcade UFO in Austin, Texas; Game Galaxy in Nashville, Tennessee; Starbase Arcade in San Rafael, California; and Star Worlds Arcade in DeKalb, Illinois. As part of the promotion,

FIGURE 41. With a bar for alcohol and snacks, Ground Kontrol is a two-story arcade featuring custom tile mosaics and retro-futuristic furniture. The Portland, Oregon, business is all-ages prior to 5 p.m., then caters exclusively to the twenty-one-and-over crowd after that, when alcohol is served. Photograph by the author.

Stride gave $10,000 to Challenge Arcade in Wyomissing, Pennsylvania, to help sustain the struggling arcade.[29] The winner of this first round, however, was not Challenge Arcade, which received its cash infusion as part of a public relations effort for the larger campaign. Arcade UFO won the first "Save the Arcades" campaign.[30] The promotion was so successful that Stride followed up the competition with "Save the Arcades 2" in 2010 with Ground Kontrol Classic Arcade in Portland, Oregon (shown in Figure 41), winning over Arcade Infinity in Rowland Heights, California, and Rocky's Replay in Winter Park, Florida.[31]

Although many of the arcades featured in both Save the Arcades and Save the Arcades 2 are relatively young, the language used to mobilize gamers to help, either by playing the relevant game and donating points or by helping publicize the campaign through social networking channels, is a language of endangerment and preservation.[32] The arcades, like bald eagles and giant pandas, need saving. The campaign presents itself as a direct appeal to gamers and is an effort by the chewing gum company to capture gamers as a consumer demographic. Those visiting the Save the Arcades website after the conclusion of the second campaign were greeted by a brief message summarizing the competition's results and then encouraging the audience, interpellated by the site as "gamers," to continue their preservation efforts: "Continue to keep classic gaming alive by hanging out at your neighborhood arcade."[33] The language here stresses the arcade's largely eclipsed role as neighborhood fixture and insists on gaming as a kind of community activity. While certainly the arcade has served that role at various historical points, the number of people who experience the arcade as a community gathering place in the present is finite; the number of neighborhoods that house a local arcade has dwindled to the point that the neighborhood arcade is an anomaly, a destination.

FRAMING AND INTERPRETING ARCADE NOSTALGIA

The nostalgic remaking and reimagining of the arcade results from and serves various social, cultural, and political purposes. There is no singular correct reading of arcade nostalgia, and the more widespread and salient the arcade becomes as nostalgic site, the truer this is. Bearing that in mind, I address the nostalgia for the video game arcade in a somewhat nonlinear, nonintegrated manner; there are many threads of meaning to pull on and interpret, and to untangle these threads in hopes of arriving at a singular analysis of what arcade nostalgia might mean is less helpful than to consider each one and see how they interact. Those nostalgic for the arcade as childhood pleasure zone may also be nostalgic for a feeling of mastery provided by gaming, for the arcade as elite gamer enclave, or even for the arcade as the embodiment of a moment of expansion and affluence in the tech industry. In looking back to the arcade as a model, or as a privileged site, cultural producers and consumers both use the arcade to stand in for specific values.

There are many primary examples of the forms that arcade nostalgia takes—from classic gaming championships to the co-option of early video game aesthetics in movies like *Wreck-It Ralph* (2012) and advertisements such as the Dave & Buster's "Pac-Man Battle Royale" launch advertisement discussed earlier. By critically examining how the arcade circulates in the present, I provide insight into the kinds of popular meanings the arcade has taken on and position the nostalgic arcade in its historical and cultural context. I use the term *nostalgic arcade* as a way to differentiate this contemporary imagined and somewhat abstract arcade from the historical arcade in which it is rooted and the arcades, both new and old, that are operating as businesses.

That is, the nostalgic arcade, while inspired by history, tells more about the present than it does about the past. As Fredric Jameson theorizes, this "nostalgia for the present"—a longing for a different present expressed as a desire for the past—shapes the way the past is remembered and revisited. Nostalgia is a deeply emotional perspective, and the nostalgic arcade is more an emotional site than a historic one. The resurrection of the arcade is not a documentary project, even when it takes the form of documentary film; it is instead an excavation and reinterpretation of the past that is contingent and partial.

THE ARCADE AS CHILDHOOD

Although both children and adults were patrons of early arcades, the most visible customers of these amusement halls were often teenagers and children. Arcades were meeting points for youths who were allowed to roam and meet with friends, or to attend events like birthday parties or other celebrations, and visits to the arcade may also have been a kind of reward or treat in some families. All of these helped cement the idea of the arcade as a happy or comfortable place and associate it with more positive aspects of childhood. For players who experienced the arcade unsupervised as teenagers, the arcade may also represent an opportunity to exercise early economic and social autonomy. The arcade, then, can be a stand-in for childhood more generally, and the nostalgic attachment to the arcade can be a nostalgic attachment to youth itself.

Related to the idea of the arcade as a stand-in for the pleasurable aspects of childhood or adolescence is the idea of the arcade, and in particular, of individual arcade games, as beloved toys; attachment to childhood toys in a consumer culture is a profound one. Toy manu-facturers at various price points work diligently to inspire the kind of intense connections that turn child owners into adult collectors and aficionados. The manipulation of adult nostalgia for childhood playthings has been an incredibly profitable marketing technique for companies like Mattel, which caters to adult collectors of their chil-dren's playthings and attempts to create demand for specific prod-ucts, both new and old, by manufacturing scarcity and keeping an eye on trends that affect not only children's Christmas wish lists but adult consumer desires.

For example, in 2010 Mattel launched an incredibly successful campaign that allowed consumers to vote on the next career for the Barbie "I Can Be" line; the winning Computer Engineer Barbie received attention both in the mainstream press and in tech-focused publications including *Wired, Gizmodo,* and *PC World* and helped in-crease sales of the line by 144 percent.[34] Mattel received half a million votes for the winning career, and the doll's accessories and design were chosen with input from professionals from the Society of Women Engineers and the National Academy of Engineering.[35] The voting process helped identify and build a likely consumer base of adults— including women who themselves work in computer engineering and related fields and of parents and others who want to encourage young girls to consider careers in those fields. Even more transparently, Mattel releases numerous dolls marketed to adult collectors, includ-ing an annual holiday Barbie line and reissues of classic Barbie dolls.

Walter Benjamin, who wrote several pieces on the importance of toys and was himself a toy collector, believed that the brutality of World War I had helped fuel a growing interest in old toys. In 1928 he wrote:

> When the urge to play overcomes an adult, this is not simply a regression to childhood. To be sure, play is always liberating. Surrounded by a world of giants, children use play to create a world appropriate to their size. But the adult, who finds himself threatened by the real world and can find no escape, removes its sting by playing with its image in reduced form. The desire to make light of an unbearable life has been a major factor in the growing interest in children's games and children's books since the end of the war.[36]

According to Benjamin, the kind of nostalgia that draws adults to toys—both older or antique toys and newer children's playthings—is much more complex than a simple longing for childhood. With a nod to Benjamin, I would argue that even when the nostalgic arcade becomes a key site for revisiting childhood, the notion of childhood is one that needs to be considered carefully; to end the analysis at "childhood" is reductive. Childhood is not a monolithic category or experience, and individuals' attachments to specific artifacts of childhood draw on complex emotional sources. Further, Benjamin's notion that nostalgia can be driven by historical circumstances that make life more difficult in meaningful ways is an important one.

The specificity of individual people's nostalgic attachments is something well illustrated by individual narratives. In addition to informing corporate marketing and manufacturing decisions, the longing for childhood as embodied in childhood playthings has served as a narrative trope in cultural works such as Citizen Kane (1941) and in gamer novels like Lucky Wander Boy and Ready Player One.[37] In Orson Welles's famous film, a reporter explores the mysterious dying word of the newspaper magnate Charles Foster Kane; Rosebud turns out to be the name of Kane's beloved childhood sled, a stand-in, in the film, for the window of Kane's childhood during which he was actually happy. Similarly, in D. B. Weiss's novel, the main character, Adam Pennyman, works in a cubicle farm at a dot-com entertainment company while completing The Catalogue of Obsolete Entertainments. The eccentric catalog of video games is a personal project that ultimately consumes Pennyman entirely as he obsesses over his favorite game, *Lucky Wander Boy.*

The book is peppered with Pennyman's encyclopedia entries, which include intense analysis of the games' cultural—and presumably personal—meanings. As Pennyman delves into game after game, it becomes apparent that he is trying to make sense of his own life, of his transience, his lack of connection, and his profound boredom. The titular *Lucky Wander Boy* has been an obsession of Pennyman's since high school, when he spent hours playing the game only to have it unplugged and carted off just as he was about to enter the game's mysterious third level. Pennyman's longed-for game is, of course, rare, leading him to spend much of the novel trying to track down a working arcade machine. At the same time, the game's creator seems almost accessible, as the company Pennyman works for has inexplicably purchased the movie rights for a game that failed so abysmally that most cabinets were destroyed. Pennyman eventually grows so disgusted with his employer that he vandalizes the work site and gives the company's servers and computer equipment away to a group of day laborers. What happens next is somewhat ambiguous.

Weiss offers several possible endings for the narrative, each labeled "replay." The book's structure here takes pointers from video games that offer multiple possible endings depending on player action, much like the ludic "Choose Your Own Adventure" book series, an "interactive" style of book first published in the late 1970s. The books, aimed at young readers and still published by the Choose Your Own Adventure Company, allow readers to make choices about how characters should behave; these choices then shape the unfolding of the narrative and the story's conclusion.[38] In *Lucky Wander Boy,* the varied endings are presented with no warning or choice. The notion of a "replay" suggests that each of these outcomes is possible and may, as in a video game, exist in the text simultaneously.

In the ending in which Pennyman manages to meet the game's designer, Pennyman travels to Kyoto only to find that she has no interest in preserving the integrity of a game design she sees as fundamentally poor, and that she has sold the options to the game to fund her current venture, Super Lucky Spank, a spanking parlor catering to Japanese businessmen. Araki Itachi tells Pennyman that the future is not in video games: "I am the future. The future is not in silicon or fiber optic cable or in a million polygons a second. The future is infantile. The future is humiliation. The future is punishment. For me, the future is money. We do extremely well."[39] In another ending, Pennyman does not go to Kyoto, choosing instead to reconcile with his girlfriend, Clio, who has supported his encyclopedia project and whom he has neglected as a result of his obsession with *Lucky Wander Boy*; in this version, the couple moves to Chicago, and Pennyman does not think of the game much until he is on his deathbed. In all versions of the narrative, however, Pennyman's obsession with seeing the game's third level is clearly mirrored to a desire to figure out some grand life secret; he believes that the enigmatic, surreal game is a puzzle to be solved and that the solution will somehow enable him to be fundamentally *better.*[40]

In this way, the game is not only a return to his own childhood obsessions but a porthole or an opportunity to reframe his life, as if the failure to reach level three has triggered a longer chain of shortcomings and failures. What Pennyman is grasping at is not the game itself but happiness, or at least his own nostalgic idea of what happiness might look like—a game level he never saw and therefore believes capable of imparting some meaningful and transformative intellectual and emotional experience. The game designer herself rejects this kind of role, ridiculing the idea that the game means anything or reflects the future. Her insistence that the spanking parlor she currently runs is not only more lucrative but in many ways more meaningful is a tremendous disappointment to Pennyman; it is also an interesting twist as Pennyman had himself become sexually fixated on the game's developer.

Lucky Wander Boy is part of a narrative tradition that dates at least to *Citizen Kane,* but it is also part of a more recent legacy created by books that detail the lives of pop culture obsessives. One example that gained unusual popularity, and later infamy owing to the author's flamboyant personal life, is Frederick Exley's novel *A Fan's Notes*; it is the "fictional memoir" of a man who fixates on professional sports and in particular the career of NFL star Frank Gifford.[41] More recently, the British author Nick Hornby has made a career writing about pop culture–obsessed men. In perhaps his best-known work, *High Fidelity,* a record store owner comes of age by realizing that people should be judged not by what they like but what they are like, a realization he has partly because he is confronted with the deplorable record collection of a nice couple he has just met.[42] In *Juliet Naked*, a woman winds up meeting and becoming involved with the obscure American songwriter her boyfriend has obsessively followed for years.[43] That *Lucky Wander Boy* has its own cult following, and that the novel has gone out of print and itself become a collectible object, is worth noting. At one point, new copies of the paperback sold for upward of fifty dollars on Amazon.com's used book marketplace.[44]

In both *Citizen Kane* and *Lucky Wander Boy*, the toy or game in question represents something outside itself, and this is surely the case with other collectable toys and games; the most obvious connection may be childhood or youth, but toys can also stand in for more specific emotional states or even for more abstract values associated with youth, such as "innocence" or "ambition." Arcade games are particularly ripe for this kind of emotional attachment, as they were so rarely owned by the children and teens who most enjoyed playing them. They were objects to be visited at arcades and other sites and, for young fans, may have seemed to simply disappear at the point they were removed from locations. That arcade games existed in public places made them appear more permanent even as it meant that they were fundamentally transient. The owners and operators of the machines often lacked sentimental attachment to them, viewing them as money-making investments. Machines lagging in popularity were often removed from locations, sold, or made over using conversion kits, their cabinet graphics painted or otherwise covered and their boards ripped out and unceremoniously replaced. The fact that individuals rarely owned the arcade machines they loved means that the sense of loss may be particularly profound, as the machines may have seemed particularly stable in existing in a set place.

While individual games can trigger loyalty and fervor, this dedication often also extends to the arcade itself. The arcade as physical, real-world space was an important landmark for many teens and children during its heyday. Although I have argued that the arcade served numerous purposes, in particular to train young gamers to engage in specific cultural and economic practices, the video game arcade had leisure as its primary purpose. The arcade was a place to play. The longing for the arcade, particularly among those who work in tech fields characterized by extraordinarily demanding work schedules, may represent a longing for play as privileged pursuit.[45]

Again, the connection to childhood is significant, as many may recall childhood as a time during which they had leisure as their primary occupation.[46] This concept is intimately bound with broader conceptions of youth or of play. The longing for leisure sites also has more adult examples, such as when people develop intense emotional attachments to vacation homes or even to destinations that served as the site of particularly memorable leisure trips. In either case, the arcade's function as a playscape is important.

This function is important for youth and for those who came to the arcade as adults, and is one that has some resonance even for younger gamers who never had access to a "classic arcade" before the arcades began struggling. Nearly every person whom I have interviewed about their experience in the video game arcade suggested that the arcade was a social space; they went with friends, met friends there, or befriended other patrons who enjoyed similar games. In this way, the arcade may have served a similar function to a neighborhood bar, providing an easy social meeting space. Nostalgia for the arcade is nostalgia both for an idealized past childhood and for an idealized present adulthood. The emotional tie to the arcade would be strengthened by the emotional bond to friendships associated with the arcade. As much of gaming has moved online and fewer adults join organizations like bowling leagues, the arcade's decline may be linked to memories of routine social interaction with a closely networked community.[47]

Persistent social ties around the childhood experience of the arcade can also help fuel interest in preservation efforts. In several interviews touching on the history of the Twin Galaxies Arcade, players mentioned the time spent in the arcade as a significant social outlet. Indeed, the lasting friendships among gamers have helped drive efforts to establish a Video Gaming Hall of Fame and Museum in Ottumwa, Iowa. Josh Gettings, who played at Twin Galaxies during his childhood and who now owns a bike shop in the town, became involved in the project through his friendship with Tim McVey:

> Tim McVey had his—there was a documentary being filmed of, of him recently and I was interviewed as part of that and during the in-

terview they asked me what my plans were for the twenty-fifth anniversary of Tim's billion point score, and I hadn't really thought of it and I told them I would probably have a quiet moment of reflection. And, they said maybe you could crack open a beer during that quiet moment of reflection, and I said yeah, that could happen and maybe I'd get a couple friends together and we'd do that and they were like yeah, now we're going somewhere with this. So, Mark and Tim and I decided for this 25th anniversary we were going to get together and recognize Tim's achievement and so we did.[48]

After celebrating the anniversary of his record, McVey e-mailed Walter Day to thank him for his support over the years. McVey copied Gettings, who is active in community revitalization efforts, on the message. Gettings contacted Day to ask his opinion on how he would suggest Ottumwa recognize its role in video gaming history. Day wrote back to suggest building a hall of fame and museum, an idea he had originally had in the 1980s. Much of the energy behind the push to build the International Video Game Hall of Fame has come from McVey, Gettings, and their peers, people who, as children, frequented Twin Galaxies and who, as adults, have retained their social ties to each other and their interest in gaming.

ORIGINAL GAMERS

There is a running, somewhat cheap, joke that if every aging rock and roll fan who responds "I was there, man" to stories about Woodstock had actually been there, the concert would have been several times its size. In the case of Woodstock, these claims attempt to establish authenticity with regard to music and participation in the attendant subculture; the arcade can serve a similar authenticating function. Events like the Classic Gaming Expo (CGE), "the world's first and largest event paying tribute to the people, systems, and games of yesteryear," allow thousands of people to converge and share their interest in classic games.

As geek chic has risen, so likely have the number of people who claim to have been dedicated habitués of the video game arcade— CGE began in 1999 and has steadily grown in scope and attendance since then.[49] Claims of youthful arcade obsession serve the dual function of authenticating a specific kind of gamer identity and of demonstrating some kind of long-running investment in electronic gaming and related technologies. In this way, the nostalgia for the arcade is expressed via an often competitive effort to authenticate membership in arcade gaming's original insider elite by proving themselves the most authoritative sources of gaming lore or skill.

This particular subset of arcade nostalgia finds clear articulation in arguments about how older arcade games were "better" despite their relative lack of technical sophistication. Justifications of this ranking of classic games over contemporary games include the claim that the games were more challenging or more engaging, or that the games required a higher level of skill to play. These kinds of claims, again, are a routine part of nostalgia, particularly among adults who want to impress upon younger folks that while they may have had things harder than today's kids, they were better for their additional efforts. For adults who were exceptional gamers as children, the arcade may stand in for youthful feelings of accomplishment, mastery, or competence.

In the documentary *The King of Kong: Fistful of Quarters* (dir. Seth Gordon; 2007), Steve Wiebe is framed as a protagonist as he decides to pursue the world record in *Donkey Kong* after being laid off from his job as a software testing engineer. Wiebe had played video games before but had not previously been a competitive gamer. Throughout the film, Wiebe's decision to pursue the world record is presented as an attempt to ameliorate insecurities brought on by unemployment. Wiebe's wife notes that he was a gifted musician, but none of his musical projects ever quite took off, and that he was a standout high school athlete, but did not pursue sports past graduation—claims that are backed up by footage of Wiebe playing drums and piano and pictures of him in high school baseball and basketball uniforms. The editorial choice to contrast Wiebe's youthful ambitions and current unemployment is likely intended to win over audience sympathies, making him seem like a nice guy underdog in need of some kind of victory.

Wiebe is contrasted with Billy Mitchell, one of the young men featured in the photograph taken by *Life* in Ottumwa, Iowa. Mitchell is a small business owner and remains active in competitive gaming and, throughout the film, is portrayed as an accomplished insider with a monumental ego. I do not want to comment on the accuracy or inaccuracy of the portrayals of these two men but on how these portrayals bolster the notion that gaming is achievement oriented and that kind of achievement is satisfying and desirable for both children and adults. Both Wiebe and Mitchell have a string of youthful accomplishments to look back to, and in the context of the film, classic arcade gaming is a way to either access or reinscribe those boyhood and adolescent accomplishments.

ARCADE AS MASCULINE ENCLAVE AND PROVING GROUND

The arcade of history was certainly frequented by more men than women, but the nostalgic arcade seems to be an exclusive male enclave. In *King of Kong,* for example, the focus is on two male gamers, and the images of the arcade shown throughout the movie (including the *Life* photograph from the 1982 "Year in Pictures") show the arcade as a male-exclusive space. While there is historical evidence to suggest that the arcade attracted more male consumers, there is little to suggest that it was a particularly exclusive environment (see, e.g., the images captured by Ira Nowinski of women players, such as Figures 42 and 43). Evidence, like Nolan Bushnell's claim that 40 percent of the income from *Pong* machines came from women players, suggests that arcades had a small but significant female consumer base. Further, women worked in the game industry in various capacities, including public relations, graphics, and game design. The question of why the arcade exists in cultural memory as a male domain raises interesting issues about gender socialization for youth and the conditions under which adult men are allowed to wax nostalgic about their own childhoods.

In one way, the nostalgic arcade seems to express a longing for an adolescent homosocial space and transposes it onto the arcade. Examples of such environments are easy to find, given the sex-segregated nature of youth activities; many of these activities, like scouting and sports, are directly tied to notions of socializing boys and "making men."[50] And, indeed, the ease with which many individuals seem to remember the arcade as a particularly male place may, in fact, reflect more the memories of people who tended to socialize in sex-segregated ways as children; men reflecting on the arcade visits of

FIGURE 42. In photographing arcades in the Bay Area in 1981 and 1982, Ira Nowinski frequently caught businesspeople on their lunch hour or after work. Here a woman takes a break from playing at a bank of *Pac-Man* machines at Pier 39 in San Francisco. Courtesy of Department of Special Collections and University Archives, Stanford University Libraries.

their youth may remember the arcade as a particularly male place because they simply did not notice, or at least did not significantly interact with, the girls who were in the arcade. Their experience of the arcade may have been of the arcade as a homosocial environment even while the actual arcade population had a significant number of women in its ranks.

The popular press coverage of the arcade often focused exclusively on the young, male gamers or on top scoring players, helping establish the arcade as a kind of technoplayground for boys; films and other popular depictions of the arcade further reinforced this perception. Thus the nostalgic perception of the arcade may reflect just how effectively the arcade was shaped by media representations and how consistent popular representations of the arcade were.

These representations establish the arcade as a kind of natural habitat for the technomasculine. Even cursory research into the arcade or a brief viewing of one of the several recent documentaries about classic arcade gaming provides evidence to support this inter-pretation of the arcade. Those men remembering the arcade would likely remember their own experience of the arcade as being one of boyish camaraderie, and this impression would be strongly rein-forced by popular representations of the arcade both during the pe-riod and after the fact. The *Life* photograph may be one particularly famous example of this, but numerous examples of similar coverage at a smaller scale are available from local and regional media outlets and have continued to the present, as evidenced by films like *TRON* and *WarGames* and by the extensive newspaper coverage of Twin Galaxies events.

A more subtle reason that nostalgia may have rendered the ar-cade so explicitly male may reflect the social and cultural limitations placed on sentimentality for men. Cultural stereotypes of appropri-ate masculine behavior not only shape the different ways boys and girls experience childhood but create significant differences in the

FIGURE 43. Ira Nowinski caught this image of two young women engrossed in a game in Berkeley, California, in his series of photographs of arcades taken in 1981 and 1982. Courtesy of Department of Special Collections and University Archives, Stanford University Libraries.

way adult men and women speak about their childhoods. Under pressure to "be a man," many men may find it risky or uncomfortable to verbalize general nostalgia for childhood. But if the arcade is rendered a particularly masculine place, a place where boys proved themselves skilled and disciplined, then it, like high school football teams and youthful pranks, may serve as a safe topic for men who wish to express a sentimental longing for their youth. To long for a hypermasculinized, hypercompetitive environment would minimize men's potential for gender transgression when engaging in nostalgia. The masculinization of the arcade in cultural memory may have to do with the desire to have a childhood site that is a safe subject of nostalgia for men.

Indeed, in discussing the closeness he feels to other competitive gamers with whom he grew up with, Tim McVey (Figure 44), who gained fame as a champion *Nibbler* (Rock-Ola, 1982) player, explicitly ties video gaming to the most privileged kind of buddy story, the war story:

> This is going to sound goofy, but the way I could put it I guess is maybe somebody that was in Vietnam with somebody. You— Video games aren't a war, and I don't want to downplay it and make it like that. I don't mean it that way at all. I just mean unless you were there and knew what was, what that was about, it's kind of hard to relate maybe on some level so I, I've seen where Vietnam vets can talk to other Vietnam vets because they know what each one went through. They've got a really good understanding. Well, you know you were there years ago with these people from Twin Galaxies and you talk about the old days and they're like yeah, I remember that and I was there and Tim was there and everybody remembers it so it's kind of a camaraderie, and uh the nostalgia and uh just the competition. . . . the best want to play the best, and ah that's what I think has kept a lot of us together.[51]

While McVey indicates some hesitation in drawing too close a parallel between the bonding opportunity provided by the arcade and the kind of bonding that occurs in war zones, his choice of analogy drives home the way that the masculinization of arcade stories may reflect men's desire to express nostalgia or social intimacy while retaining masculine credibility.

McVey, who has remained a noteworthy gamer and who is the subject of a forthcoming documentary, grew up in Ottumwa, Iowa, so he has had a special closeness with the competitive gaming community. Twin Galaxies was his local arcade during the peak of its visibility, and he remembers playing against top gamers during summer vacations when many would come to town. McVey's personal attachment to gaming is unique, both because of his own exceptional skill as a gamer and because of his long-running friendship with many classic competitive gamers. His sense of gaming as a community-based activity and his sense of the arcade as a particularly treasured community space, however, reflects a more broadly held sentiment.

In his oral history interview, McVey estimated that roughly one-third of the arcade's customers were women, but suggests that they played different games. Articles in *Play Meter* and *RePlay* from the time also suggest that this was the case. Even so, McVey's closest arcade gaming friendships have been with men, and he expresses those relationships in particularly masculine terms.[52] For McVey and

FIGURE 44. Tim McVey, who has played video games competitively since childhood, poses with his home *Nibbler* cabinet in 2009. Photograph by the author.

for many other gamers who frequented arcades in their youth, the arcade was a male environment despite the presence of girls; for those who have come to know the arcade after the fact, the historical record has provided ample evidence that the arcade belonged to men and boys. The historical and contemporary focus on *competitive* gaming in so much coverage of gaming further entrenches the notion of the arcade, and of gaming, as a masculine enclave and a place where boys might prove themselves.

ARCADE AS TECHNOLOGICAL BOOM

The video game arcade developed largely because of the high commercial success of video games. During their first few years on the market, video game uprights displaced longtime moneymakers like cigarette machines, pool tables, and pinball machines as the top earners for route operators. The earnings potential of individual games helped fuel their further distribution, and the lure of creating a hit game helped draw old-line coin-op makers into the video game market and inspired startup companies like Exidy. Video games were some of the first computers many people encountered, and they were one of the first places where computers became culture. Similarly, the video game arcade, with quarters pouring out of change machines and into coin-op games, became one of the most visible signs of a boom in the technology and coin-op sectors. The late 1990s marked the rise of another boom in the technology sector, with significant growth in e-commerce and other online businesses.[53] For many professionals, this period was one of unprecedented success and prosperity.

The arcade nostalgia that emerged during this boom has persisted and expanded in the wake of the dot-com bubble burst of 2000. The NASDAQ peaked on March 10, 2000, at 5132.52, roughly doubling its value a year earlier. From March 2000 to October 2002, however, the stock market entered a crash that resulted in the loss of $5 trillion in companies' market value.[54] Companies failed, and even those that managed to stay open for business often implemented significant layoffs. For many who worked in the tech and dot-com industries, the halcyon days of the boom were over.

Nostalgia for the arcade rose with the boom of the 1990s and continued through the crash. Many adult technologists of the period had developed an early interest in computers through youthful exposure to video games played either in the arcade or on home systems. As the economic promise of computing careers seemed increasingly unreliable, video games became a symbol of precrash computing; that the specific games which seem to be so at the heart of this nostalgia are those that predate the industrial crash of 1983 is unsurprising. In the wake of the post-1990s crash, the appeal of the precrash, pre-1983 arcade with its promise of a future of technological progress, and individual success, makes sense. That is, at the moment when these promises are proved to ring hollow, those most affected by exaggerations of economic and professional potential turn back to moments when those promises seemed not to be exaggerated and when possibilities seemed more reliably accessible.

The arcade embodied ideas about technology, about money, and about success that teens and young men carried with them into adulthood. In the wake of an industrial crash that demonstrated just how untenable those ideas might be in the real world, the arcade may have seemed an especially idyllic environment, a treasured part of childhood, a place that embodied the kind of youthful ambition and confidence that had fueled so much of the dot-com boom. Again, however, this is a kind of nostalgia for the present—the arcade comes to stand in for the way that people *wish* the present felt. The history of the arcade itself is submerged as it is reduced to a cultural style, something perceived and circulated as fundamentally *better* than the present.

The nostalgic arcade as imagined in the present represents the late 1970s and early 1980s just as, say, the television series *Happy Days* might represent the actual 1950s.[55] The nostalgic arcade is not imaginary in the sense of being fabricated. After giving and expanding on a list of cultural markers included in a 1959 Philip K. Dick novel, Jameson notes: "The list is not a list of facts or historical realities (although its items are not invented and are in some sense 'authentic'); but rather a list of stereotypes, of ideas of facts and historical realities."[56] The nostalgic arcade exists in this way, as a constellation of stereotypes, of fragments of facts and historical realities mixed seamlessly with the values and desires of the present.

Like most nostalgias, this postmodern nostalgia for the arcade is fundamentally conservative, expressing a longing for an eclipsed era. It is also nostalgic in glamorizing specific aspects of arcade culture that are proscribed by class, race, and gender. While the arcade as it existed was likely a stopping-off point for many youths and adults, the arcade of nostalgic representations, including those in documentary films like *Chasing Ghosts* and *The King of Kong,* is one populated almost exclusively by young white men with both the time and the money to play video games as much as they wanted—a desire that drove many of these young gamers to become competitive at the national and international level. The longing for the arcade of memory is a longing not only for the arcade's aesthetic properties but for a glamorized technoculture where young white men were dominant—as gamers in the arcade and as professional technologists in the public sector.

The conclusion suggested in chapter 2, that we are still in the arcade, holds here; the boy genius is still fetishized, and the idea of brilliant male tech geeks remaking the economic and cultural landscape should not seem too outlandish to anyone who has picked up an issue of *Wired* magazine or who saw any of the media coverage of the death of Apple CEO and cofounder Steve Jobs.[57] The celebration of Jobs as a visionary and the public outpouring of grief at news of his passing show how enthusiastically technological advances are heralded and demonstrate the extent to which technomasculine ideals are celebrated and accepted as models of success. Even as the arcade itself has become an endangered cultural site, the social, political, and cultural ideologies learned, tested, and taught in the arcade have become prevalent modes. The values of the arcade have gone mainstream, and even when their moral rightness is questioned, the political, social and monetary rewards available to those who embrace them are significant.

7

THE FUTURE IS NOW

CHANGES
IN GAMING
CULTURE

IN MAY 2012 Anita Sarkeesian, a media critic and the producer of *Feminist Frequency,* launched a Kickstarter campaign seeking $6,000 to fund a series of videos addressing sexism in video games. The Internet exploded. Sarkeesian far exceeded her fund-raising goal, with more than $158,000, but she also became the subject of an aggressive campaign of harassment.[1] The harassment, which has now lasted years, included denial of service attacks on her website, efforts to expose her personal information online, the repeated vandalism of her Wikipedia page with racist and misogynistic language and pornographic images, hateful comments on her YouTube video, and even a video game called *Beat Up Anita Sarkeesian,* inviting players to virtually punch Sarkeesian in her face, which became increasingly bruised and disfigured as the game progressed.[2] While much of the harassment eventually tapered off, the sheer vitriol of the response drew extensive media attention. In reporting on the ongoing smear campaign nearly a year later, the *Daily Dot* called Sarkeesian "the great male-gamer bogeyman."[3]

Sarkeesian and her work continue to provoke a knee-jerk

response in some circles, but I bring her up here not to defend the validity of her work but to simply say that if a fund-raising campaign seeking voluntary donations to make a simple video series on sexism in gaming can provoke this kind of rage, then something somewhere in contemporary gaming culture has gone rancid. Sarkeesian's experience is extreme, but it is not isolated. Women who participate in gaming culture—as gamers, as critics, and even as industry professionals—face significant harassment.

Jenny Haniver, an artist and gamer, has expanded a college art project on her experiences playing *Call of Duty* as a woman into a blog chronicling her in-game interactions. The blog includes dozens of recordings and transcriptions of in-game harassment. Rape threats and comments on Haniver's appearance are common—the latter even though no images of Haniver are readily available.[4] *Fat, Ugly, or Slutty* is another blog addressing the in-game harassment of women. The organizers behind the blog post user-submitted documentation including screen captures and recordings. The blog's title references the frequency with which women playing video games are derided as fat, ugly, or slutty.[5] It is easy for me to believe these experiences, both because they are widely documented and because I have had them myself.

And, of course, as of writing, it is difficult to discuss gaming at all without mentioning GamerGate, which is, at best, a leaderless consumer movement launched in 2014 to fight against perceived corruption in gaming journalism. At worst, it is a disorderly and dangerous mob dedicated to purging gaming culture of perceived interlopers—of women critics like Sarkeesian and of women indie game developers like Brianna Wu and Zoe Quinn, all three of whom were forced to leave their homes after receiving death and rape threats that included their home addresses and other personal details. While Quinn, Wu, and Sarkeesian—stripped of their names and referred to as "Literally Who 1," "Literally Who 2," and "Literally Who 3," by at least some active in GamerGate—have made headlines in mainstream news outlets, the harassment they have faced is not isolated but reflects broader issues.

Video gaming is a major cultural form, but it is a major cultural form with an almost overwhelming gender problem. My research here grew out of a desire to understand that problem at its point of origin. The common assumption that gaming is and rightly should be for boys and men even in the face of empirical evidence that women make up a large percentage of gamers is neither natural nor logical. It is the product of a long-standing historical and cultural construction of video gaming and video gamers begun during the golden era of the video game arcade. To make sense of contemporary gaming culture, we must understand its past. This understanding is also essential to making meaningful interventions in the present.

Throughout this book, I have posited that the video game arcade became a point of articulation for anxieties over economic, cultural, and technological changes. Early coverage of video gaming in trade journals, newspapers, popular magazines, and even Hollywood films worked to soothe these concerns by presenting gamers and gaming as representative as an emergent ideal of masculinity—one associated with youthfulness, technological competency, intellectual abilities, creativity, boyishness, and a particular type of militarism, which I have termed the technomasculine. Gaming also functions as a homosocial space, a cultural enclave for young men who came to view video gaming as a place where they could cultivate and display skill and prove their own prowess and competence.

When gamers are presented positively, such presentations frequently invoke some of the same attributes that popular and trade press used to defend and advocate for video gaming as a youth pastime in the 1970s and 1980s. Consider, for example, the story of Johnathan Wendel's rise to fame as a full-time professional gamer. In 1999 a teenage Wendel spent $500 to travel to Dallas, Texas, and compete in a *Quake* (id Software, 1996–) series video game tournament. Placing third in the tournament, Wendel won $4,000. The prize impressed Wendel's father and encouraged Wendel to pursue competitive video gaming as a career.[6] Since then, Wendel, known as Fatal1ty, has won over $500,000 in tournament prizes and become one of the best-known professional gamers in the world. He holds twelve world titles in five separate games and has attracted media attention outside the limited confines of gaming sites and magazines, covered by publications like *Forbes* and *Business Week,* and featured on *60 Minutes* and MTV's *True Life.*[7]

Wendel's success on the professional gaming circuit has garnered him lucrative licensing deals and helped drive his own entrepreneurial efforts. At present, the Fatality brand sells computer gaming hardware like sound cards, headsets, motherboards, custom computers, and other components.[8] While the $125,000 prize purses available in contemporary game tournaments far exceed the spoils available to young competitive gamers in the late 1970s and early 1980s, the language through which competitive gaming is defended and celebrated today demonstrates continuity for its focus on competitive gamers' discipline and technological skill, their intelligence, and their similarities to athletes.[9]

Wendel is often called the first professional gamer. That is debatable, but he is the most famous at present, and his competitive record is impressive. I bring him up here not to celebrate him as a pinnacle of gaming achievement but to highlight how his career demonstrates the continued importance of the historic period of video gaming I have considered throughout this book. Wendel's rise to prominence as a professional game player, as a world champion with endorsement deals and branded merchandise and media interviews, has clear ties to video gaming's early world record culture. The language through which Wendel is celebrated, and through which Wendel himself expresses both his gaming achievements and his personal interests, echoes early defenses of video gamers from advocates like Walter Day.

Day worked hard to position gamers as mischievous but fundamentally talented and exceptional young men, and he did so partly by celebrating gaming achievements through terms and imagery often used to describe athletes. Special events like the Olympic Arcade Tricathlon further highlighted this connection to sports. At least one tournament invited players to compete against a professional athlete. The 1983 *Super Pac-Man* Tournament in Denver, Colorado, pitted gamers against Billy McKinney of the Denver Nuggets. The tournament included hundreds of players at fourteen arcades across the city, with five hundred participants receiving NBA tickets to watch the top two participants compete as part of half-time entertainment.[10]

While Day and other video game boosters defended young gamers as being similar to athletes, e-sports today, as T. L. Taylor has explored at length, is increasingly a global business with its own circuit of competitions, and its own stars and fans.[11] Legitimized by the visible professionalization of these competitions, today's gamers sometimes claim they are athletes. Wendel is quick to point out that in addition to training eight hours a day on games, he runs daily, claiming that his physical fitness contributes to his gaming excellence. He also frequently references his own background with sports, having played tennis and golf during his youth and adolescence.[12]

Further, Wendel's company and brand celebrate Wendel as an "E-Sportsman" and note that his training regimen resembles that of any other athlete. While the lucrative licensing and endorsement deals available to Wendel may reflect a recent expansion of video gaming as a market sector, his interest in entrepreneurship and his framing as an entrepreneur again reflect the celebration of young male gamers as bright and innovative, and as particularly well suited to the challenges and opportunities provided by a technologically advanced, service-based economy. The nongame achievements of competitive gamers continue to be used to justify or defend their gaming, the implication being that the skills and habits learned from gaming have helped these people to cultivate desirable qualities.

The role of violence and competition as integral values of video gaming find clear expression in contemporary tournament culture as well. The heralding of individual achievement through video game competition is at the very heart of tournament culture. Further, tournaments tend to privilege certain violent game genres. Wendel has made his name as a champion with first-person-shooter game franchises like *Doom* (1993), *Quake*, and *Painkiller* (2004); while tournaments and records exist for a diversity of games, the largest cash prizes, the greatest level of visibility, and the most fame go to those who distinguish themselves through games like these: first-person-shooter games that are often war themed. Game companies often directly sponsor the large prize purses offered in video game tournaments, which ensures that the tournament will draw wide participation and generate publicity. It also helps ensure that the most competitive, and by extension, highest-profile, gamers will choose to play a particular game. The overrepresentation of first-person-shooter games in competitive play likely reflects several factors. First-person-shooter games remain dependable top sellers, and the investment represented by a tournament purse helps distinguish titles and highlight specific games. Further, the significance of first-person shooters in tournament play is self-perpetuating, as games similar to those already played at high-level tournaments seem ripe for tournament play. After all, game companies and tournament organizers could assume that a cohort of champions interested in *Doom,* for example, might be expected to show an interest in playing freshly released games in the same genre.

Finally, even as video gaming has spread, the cost of gaming continues to influence who games and how. Wendel's success narrative involves him clearing out the $500 in his bank account to compete in his first tournament, and the cost of gaming remains significant, particularly with regard to computer games that require sophisticated graphic cards and other specialized equipment to operate properly. Just as young gamers in the 1970s relied on disposable income to play arcade games enough to advance their skill, today's gamers require adequate resources to obtain high-end computers that meet the required specifications of certain games. As games feature more sophisticated graphics and require faster operating speeds, adequate computer equipment for gaming is a shifting target, requiring steady upgrades. While console systems are generally less costly than computers, games for both of these systems frequently cost in excess of $50 at release. Historically, as now, not all competitive gamers are wealthy, but most live at a comfortable enough level that the cost of gaming—both the financial cost and the cost in terms of leisure time—is not a barrier to entry.

While I have focused throughout this book on representations of video gamers, specifically competitive arcade gamers, during video gaming's early commercial history, I conclude by pointing to Wendel as a way to demonstrate how salient codes of representation developed in coverage of early gamers remain even in the face of radically diversified gaming practice. Throughout, I have argued that popular narratives of arcade gaming consolidated ties between digital media technologies, masculinity, youth, capitalism, and violence. This consolidation remains at the very heart of popular ideas of gamers and gaming. Wendel's Fatal1ty brand bears the fingerprints of this constellation of ideas. Wendel, the "cyber athlete" or "E-Sportsman," is enabled by computer technologies that he also sells; his youth is highlighted in popular and in official profiles; and the games he plays revel in violence both militarized and otherwise. Further investigation of how these ideas have shaped and limited gaming bear careful consideration. Even as arcade culture has narrowed to serve as a niche entertainment, video gaming has expanded greatly through the console and computer markets, as well as through phone-based mobile games and other platforms. In this expansion, video gaming has diversified, but many of the ideologies embedded in early game practice persist and have troubling implications for issues of representation, inclusivity, and access.

Changes to the video gaming landscape have not erased the gaming culture that developed with the arcades in the 1970s and 1980s, and much has persisted. Continuities in gamer identity—the extension of athletic competition as metaphor for gaming, the insistence on gamers' intelligence and entrepreneurialism, the focus on violent games as representative of the medium—stem from an existing distillation of ideas and identities cultivated in and around the video game arcade. The public careers of contemporary professional gamers like Wendel demonstrate the ongoing resonance of gamer identities forged during the earliest years of public video gaming. Further, they demonstrate the extent to which gaming culture at the highest levels of competitive play reflect inequities of access and participation. Even as the video game industry has shifted and the audience for video gaming has expanded to include Americans across demographic categories, narrower notions of what gaming can and should look like continue to shape popular narratives of gaming and sustain a gaming culture that is limited and exclusionary.

That this narrowness of gaming at a cultural level has continued despite a broadening of gaming practice and an expansion of access to gaming is particularly troubling and highlights the extent to which video gaming as a culture can reflect significant prejudices. Current statistics suggest that the majority of people play video games, with 51 percent of American households owning a dedicated gaming console and 59 percent of Americans playing video games.[13] Additionally, the average gamer is thirty-one years old, and adult women make up 48 percent of gamers.[14] The spread of gaming from young male obsession to a nationalized experience of media culture has coincided with changes in the industry, including an increase in affordable video game consoles, the proliferation of home computers, and the rise of social media games played through platforms like Facebook.

Yet these shifts have not eliminated the common perception of the gamer as a young white man with a penchant for technology and an impulse for entrepreneurial pursuits, nor have they unseated violent video games from their position as the most visible of popular games. This remains true despite evidence suggesting that boys under seventeen make up just 17 percent of contemporary gamers.[15]

The overt celebration of young male achievement and the elevation of violent games as "hardcore" in the face of this diversification in gameplay and in gamer identity may be an instance of retrenchment, an attempt to protect some part of gaming as an elite male enclave as this status is increasingly challenged. For young men who have come to view gaming as a place to prove themselves and their masculinity, the increased visibility of women as gamers, and even competitive gamers, presents as threat. I am careful to point out, however, that this set of issues is not inherent to video gaming itself; to assume otherwise is not only technologically deterministic but flies in the face of significant evidence that cultural factors—within the gaming industry at the level of production, in the gaming community at the consumer end, and in a broader culture that too often associates particular digital technologies with areas of male expertise—overtly shape video gaming participation and practice and alienate women, even as they make up an increasingly large percentage of the industry's consumer base.

Much has changed in the gaming industry over the decades from the industry crash of 1983 to the present, but the ongoing significance of notions of gaming culture first deployed prior to the crash warrant careful consideration. The assumed maleness and youth of gamers has had profound implications for public discourse around the medium. This limiting discourse has helped bolster sexist and ageist assumptions about gaming and gamers, and has served to justify exclusionary practices in gaming communities and the industry. These practices are sufficiently prevalent to be a source of tension among gamers and have sparked creative responses from some community members.

Amber Yust, for example, developed Commentless Kotaku, a browser extension that blocks the user from viewing comments on popular gaming site Kotaku, which are known to frequently descend into sexism and homophobia.[16] Haniver's *Not in the Kitchen Anymore,* mentioned earlier, directly confronts the types of stereotypes employed in in-game chatter:

> It's a stereotype that all female gamers are: fat, ugly, lonely, bad at video games, and should be in the kitchen, making a sandwich. And that's essentially the focus of my blog—the dated, hostile, and sometimes downright weird reactions men, and occasionally even other women, have to interacting with females in an anonymous setting that is considered to be male dominated (online video games, specifically first person shooters). . . . By exposing this type of behavior, I'm hoping to raise awareness—and possibly push people to remember that it's a real live person on the other side of that microphone.[17]

To Kotaku's credit, the site has since significantly beefed up its comments moderation policy in hopes of making the site friendlier and more inclusive.[18]

But players in a variety of gaming environments and forums continue to sling and collect abuse, much of it heavily gendered. In one particularly well-documented incident, one of the stars of a Capcom-sponsored fighting-game reality show defended sexual harassment as an important part of the culture:

> The sexual harassment is part of the culture. If you remove that from the fighting game community, it's not the fighting game community . . . it doesn't make sense to have that attitude. These things have been established for years.

He later went so far as to claim efforts to cultivate a less misogynistic atmosphere among competitive fighting-game players was "ethically wrong."[19]

The overt focus on violent games as the most competitive and difficult of games, even as they make up a fraction of the games available on the market, has provided fodder to critics who reiterate C. Everett Koop's early assertion that there is "nothing positive in video games."[20] Critics who focus on violence in video gaming can rightly be accused of myopia in dismissing an entire media form, particularly given that as of 2013, the vast majority of video games rated by the Entertainment Software Review Board—91 percent—were deemed appropriate for all ages. The industry's disproportionate promotions effort for violent games like the first-person-shooter franchises favored by many high-profile professional tournaments provides significant justification for this perception, as do the sales figures for these games, which frequently rank among annual top sellers.

Increasingly, statistics about video game players and video game sales bear out the notion that gendered and age-based perceptions of video gaming represent cultural biases more than they reflect who is actually participating in gaming as day-to-day practice. Further, these biases have roots in the earliest years of industrial history and find clear expression in coverage of early video games and in popular narrative representations of early gamers. Their persistence drives home the importance of considering the historical context that generated these limited ideas of who games and what video gaming represents. We are still confronted with notions of masculinity, technology, computer culture, and video gaming that find clear expression in early video gaming culture. These ideas remain integral to video gaming culture and, as I argue, have become widely embedded throughout culture as computerization, digital media, and video gaming have reached wide dispersal.

Yet while the values of the video game arcade have become widely deployed across contemporary culture, they are also readily recognizable in a video game industry, and in gaming media, that celebrates a particularly narrow idea of what competitive gaming means and what competitive gamers look like. These ideas and values remain concentrated in video gaming culture. That Johnathan Wendel has become a posterboy for competitive gaming is far from surprising; as a young man with viable claims to athleticism, tech savvy, and intelligence, he is a clear successor to gamers like those celebrated in *Life* magazine's 1982 "Year in Pictures" issue.

Given how widespread gaming has become across gender and age, perhaps the line of succession should not be so clear. Further, given the recent history of instability and overspeculation in the technology sector, perhaps the celebration of technological savvy and entrepreneurial impulses should be less enthusiastic. While films like *The Social Network* point to anxieties about the social desirability of the skills and characteristics that enable success in the tech sector, these criticisms are countered by the tales of financial success often included in the same narratives. The outpouring of public grief and admiration expressed at the 2011 death of Apple cofounder Steve Jobs certainly speaks to the continued significance and admiration heaped on technologists of a certain stripe. In the case of Jobs, a notorious record of verbally abusing employees and willfully allowing the exploitation of workers at the factories contracted to manufacture Apple products did little to dampen enthusiasm.[21]

While gaming has evolved, popular narratives of gaming continue to focus on and celebrate the achievements of certain types of gamers and to value certain types of games. The valuing of first-person-shooter games as "hardcore" is fueled by industrial intervention through advertising and public relations efforts. Further, these types of games, while often costly to produce because of their technical demands, also hold the highest promise of financial return. In 2010 five of the ten top-selling games (*Call of Duty: Black Ops, Halo: Reach, Red Dead Redemption, Call of Duty: Modern Warfare 2, Assassin's Creed: Brotherhood*) carried a mature rating, largely for violence; while the industry is quick to note that violent games make up just a fraction of the games on the market, these games tend to sell disproportionately well.[22] And, as in the case of *Death Race*, the controversy generated by violent games often helps drive sales.

If almost 60 percent of people play games, then the gaming landscape should reflect some of that diversity at least in terms of the gender, race, and age of notable gamers. But diversity remains a nettlesome and troubling topic in gaming at several levels. Writing about sexism in game design, the cultural critic Latoya Peterson notes that contemporary video gaming offers only four playable black female characters.[23] While white women may be more broadly represented on-screen, the hypersexualization of these women characters presents its own set of issues. On-screen gender inequities are echoed and possibly fueled by a dearth of women working in both the game design industry and as gaming critics. A 2005 survey conducted by the International Game Developers Association found that just 11.5 percent of respondents were women, and there is little to indicate significant improvement since.[24]

Representations of competitive gaming have helped sustain and propagate images of gaming as young male enclave even in the face of overwhelming statistical evidence demonstrating the significant number of women participating in gaming culture. While the early video game arcade was a visible embodiment of emergent cultural values, the persistence of the video game arcade as privileged cultural site demonstrates an ongoing commitment to these values. Video game arcades continue to offer a highly visible arena for public gaming, but *Guitar Hero* tournaments in bars, Wii sports sessions in retirement community rec rooms, and even Facebook wall posts updating friends and family of individuals' activities in games like *Candy Crush Saga* demonstrate the ongoing role that gaming has in public media practice and contribute to the ubiquity of video and computer gaming.

Despite these shifts in gaming practices and the diversification of gamers, media representations continue to draw attention to the rarified world of competitive gaming and continue to celebrate the achievements of young, white men, deploying a language of success and competence cultivated in the early years of the industry. And women who dare criticize that culture, like Anita Sarkeesian, often find themselves targets for sustained abuse. To make sense of the contemporary culture of video gaming requires careful consideration of the historical trajectory that has so bound gaming to a now naturalized set of values and practices.

From 1972 to the present, much has changed in video gaming. The reshaping of the industry hastened by the 1983 market crash significantly shifted the development of gaming, and increasingly sophisticated media technologies have allowed for more cinematic gaming experiences in arcades and on home consoles and for the spread of gaming to mobile media platforms like cellular phones and tablet computers. Gaming has also become increasingly widespread, aided by the ongoing involvement of early adapters who continue to play classic games or who have followed emerging trends and furthered by deliberate efforts by the industry to expand markets. The proliferation of high-speed Internet access has also affected gaming, allowing for advances in massive-multiplayer-online-role-playing games like Blizzard's highly successful *World of Warcraft* (1994–), which has over ten million subscribers.[25]

Yet, even in the face of these changes to the landscape of video gaming, much of the medium's history persists and affects gaming at the level of production and day-to-day practice. In excavating the origins of popular notions of gamer identity and investigating the cultural, economic, and political values embedded in it, my research works to historicize and unsettle narratives that too frequently assume that the maleness of gaming is somehow innate. In asking what the values of the video game arcade were and are and pointing to how these values are still deployed, this project also points to the significance that arcade video gaming—often remembered as a moment in pop culture history—has had for the development not only of video gaming but of digital culture more broadly.

The rise of video gaming as mass medium from the early 1970s to the present coincides with and has been shaped by significant upheavals in cultural and economic values; during this same period, video gaming functioned as an early training course in these emergent values and in the technical skills prized in the new service-based economy. Video gaming's early history is inextricably bound to these changes, and popular coverage of video gaming became a point of articulation for emergent values and for anxieties about the same. To consider the video game arcade is not only to consider an important stage in the history of video gaming but also to consider the cultural history of key transitions in the United States. The arcade persists, but so do its values, at play in contemporary video gaming and at work through the structuring of labor and market.

∩OTE5

INTRODUCTION

1. Cassell and Jenkins, "Chess for Girls?," 11.
2. Entertainment Software Association, "Industry Facts."
3. Watters, "Player."
4. Guins, *Game After.*
5. Caraher et al., "Why We Dug Atari."

1. THE MICROCOSMIC ARCADE

1. Yi, "They Got Game."
2. Aladdin's Castle in Wichita Falls operated in Sikes Senter Mall. The location closed in the late 1990s. There is currently an arcade called Tilt operating a few doors down from the former Aladdin's location.
3. The initial MIDI standard was developed in 1982. MIDI specifications allow pieces of electronic music to be played across synthesizers, so that a piece of music composed on one synthesizer may be played back with consistent fidelity on other types of synthesizers. See Pisano, "MIDI Standards."
4. Connell, *Masculinities,* 55.
5. Kimmel, *Manhood in America,* 267.

204 NOTES TO CHAPTER 1

6. Kirsh, *Children, Adolescents, and Media Violence*; Kutner and Olson, *Grand Theft Childhood*.
7. Poole, *Trigger Happy*, 236–37.
8. Chapter 3 addresses the history of gaming's earliest moral panic, which was triggered by *Death Race*, a game inspired by the 1975 film of the same name.
9. Juul, *Half-Real*, 56.
10. "Slot Machines and Pinball Games," 62–70.
11. Slovin, "Hot Circuits," 139.
12. Kasson, *Amusing the Million*, 98–100; Rosenzweig, *Eight Hours*, 192–203.
13. "Bernstein Report," 92.
14. Watters, "Player."
15. "Starcade"; Kiesler, Sproull, and Eccles, "Pool Halls, Chips, and War Games," 451–62.
16. Gallup, "Gallup Youth Survey," 100.
17. Tim McVey, interview by author, June 17, 2011; Cindy Toopes, interview by author, June 16, 2011.
18. Kimmel, *Manhood in America*, 7–8, 26; Messner, *Power at Play*, 14–15.
19. "Lucrative Business."
20. Josh Gettings, interview by author, June 17, 2009; Mark Hoffman, interview by author, June 18, 2009; Tim McVey, interview by author, June 17, 2009.
21. Hoffman, interview.
22. Mann, "Court Delays Ruling."
23. Abramson, "Game Parlors Face Curbs."
24. Kasson, *Amusing the Million*, 98–100; Peiss, *Cheap Amusements*, 180–81; Rosenzweig, *Eight Hours*, 192, 203.
25. *City of Mesquite v. Aladdin's Castle, Inc.*, 455 U.S. 283 (1982).
26. Subsequent court cases had similar results; in 2011 the U.S. Supreme Court ruled against a California ban on the sale or rental of "violent" games to minors. The ruling in *Brown, Governor of California, et al. v. Entertainment Merchants Association et al.* deployed some of the same rhetoric as the ruling in previous cases, but also explicitly protected the right of youths to access "violent" materials. There is, to date, no legal precedent in the United States for restricting youth access to violent materials, only for restricting access to sexually explicit, pornographic materials; *Brown v. EMA*, 564 U.S. (2011).
27. *Roth v. United States*, 354 U.S. 476 (1957); Cohen, "Many Meanings," 1–54.
28. Biven, *Jimmy Carter's Economy*, 155.
29. Towle, *Democracy and Peacemaking*, 179.
30. Frum, *How We Got Here*, 290–302.
31. Harvey, *Condition of Postmodernity*, 285.
32. Mandel, *Late Capitalism*.
33. McCraw, *Prophets of Regulation*, 237.
34. Lichtenstein, *State of the Union*, 213.

35. Kimmel, *Guyland*, 17–18.

36. Jameson, *Postmodernism*, xx–xxi. In *The Origins of Postmodernity*, Perry Anderson provides a broader historicization of postmodernity as a concept and its deployment. Anderson points out that the term dates at least to the 1930s, but he, too, places the rise of postmodernity as a lived cultural and economic reality to the 1950s and later. Indeed, the uses of the term he cites through the 1950s are negative, marketing things that are less than modern, and postmodernity as a deliberate intellectual and aesthetic practice is placed as emerging through the 1970s (4–24).

37. Lichtenstein, *State of the Union*, 99.

38. Harvey, *Condition of Postmodernity*, 125–29.

39. Hinc, *Rise and Fall of the American Teenager*, 141, 225.

40. Sharp, "Peep-boxes to Pixels," 278–85.

41. Susman, *Culture as History*, 197.

42. Juul, *Half-Real*, 56.

43. Harpold, "Screw the Grue," 96–97.

44. Walter Day, interview by author, June 17, 2009.

45. *City of Mesquite v. Aladdin's Castle, Inc.*, 455 U.S. 283 (1982).

46. Gee and Hayes, *Women and Gaming*; Taylor, "Becoming a Player," 51–66.

2. GAMING'S GOLD MEDALISTS

1. Day, "Chapter Four."

2. "Video Game V.I.P.S.," 72–73.

3. Ibid.

4. Butler, "Athletic Genders."

5. Messner, *Power at Play*, 31.

6. Ibid., 19.

7. Taylor, *Raising the Stakes*, 114–16.

8. Day, "Chapter Four."

9. Ibid.

10. Day, interview, June 17, 2009.

11. Ibid.

12. Day, "Our Unique History."

13. Day, "Chapter Three"; Day, "Chapter Four."

14. Day, interview, June 17, 2009.

15. Slovin, "Hot Circuits," 137–53; Turkle, *Life on the Screen*.

16. Zuboff, *In the Age of the Smart Machine*, 7.

17. West, "Wooing Women Gamers."

18. Cassell and Jenkins, "Chess for Girls?," 11.

19. Lenhart et al., "Who's Not Online."

20. Walter Day, interview by author, June 18, 2009.

21. "Starcade Contestants."
22. Douglas, *Inventing American Broadcasting,* 189.
23. Mintz, *Huck's Raft,* 284–87.
24. Hendershot, "Atomic Scientist, Science Fiction Films, and Paranoia," 31–41.
25. Launius, "Heroes in a Vacuum."
26. Jenkins, "'Complete Freedom of Movement,'" 274–76.
27. Day, "Chapter Four."
28. Day, interview, June 17, 2009.
29. Breen, "Steve Jobs."
30. *Oxford English Dictionary,* s.v. "mischief."
31. Taylor, *Playing for Keeps,* 4.
32. "Coke Picks Arcade Set," 13.
33. "Olympic Tricathlon Slated," 65.
34. "Jumper Wins Olympic Arcade Tricathlon," 15.
35. Morris, "Video Games Push for Olympic Recognition."
36. Putney, *Muscular Christianity.*
37. Green, *Fit for America,* 203.
38. "Editorial: Where Are the Powerful Voices?," 3.
39. Beley, "Fighting City Hall," 34.
40. "Interestingly, the new machines do not seem to have aroused the curiosity of the Mafia, once a big operator of coin machines in New York and Chicago. 'That all seems to have been cleared up,' says Edward Joyce deputy chief of the Organized Crime and Racketeering Section of the U.S. Department of Justice" (Range, "Space Age Pinball Machine").
41. Boasberg, "TV Video Games," 20–21.
42. Karlen et al., "How Many Missing Kids," 30; Best, "Rhetoric in Claims-Making," 101–21; Finkelhor, Hotaling, and Sedlak, "Children Abducted by Family Members," 805–17.
43. Kao, "Carpal Tunnel Syndrome."
44. Collins, "Children's Video Games."
45. Klemersud, "'Bang! Boing! Ping!'"
46. Kent, "Super Mario Nation," 35–48.
47. *King of Kong.*
48. Gilbert, *Cycle of Outrage,* 11.

3. ADAPTING VIOLENCE

1. *Brown* refers to California governor Jerry Brown; the case was previously known as *Schwarzenegger v. EMA,* in reference to then governor Arnold Schwarzenegger. The EMA is the Electronic Merchants Association and is the international trade association of the home entertainment industry, primarily video gaming.
2. The video game industry took a page from the film industry's Motion

Picture Association of America ratings system with the establishment of the Entertainment Software Review Board in 1994 as a self-regulatory measure in an effort to placate demands for external regulation; today, nearly all games sold through retail outlets are rated.

3. *Brown v. EMA,* 564 U.S. (2011).

4. Connell, *Masculinities,* 55; Kimmel, *Guyland,* 16–18.

5. Van Gelder, " 'Death Race 2000' Is Short on Satire."

6. Ebert, "Death Race 2000."

7. Thomas, "Movie Review: Barbarism in Big Brother Era."

8. *Schlock! The Secret History of American Movies* (dir. Ray Greene; 2001).

9. "Death Race 2000 (1975)."

10. Ramao, "Engines of Transformation," 45.

11. Note that Motion Picture Association of America ratings are industry standards and do not carry the force of law. While theaters may choose to enforce age restrictions for certain films, there are no legal penalties for refusing or failing to do so.

12. *Memoirs v. Massachusetts,* 383 U.S. 413 (1966).

13. *Miller v. California,* 413 U.S. 15 (1973).

14. Advertisements indicate screenings of the film in January 1978, February 1978, March 1978 (when the film was showing in at least four venues), as well as November 1979 and February 1980. See, for example, "Movie Guide," 19; "Movie Guide," 28; "Movie Guide," 16; "Movie Guide," 93; "Movie Guide," 82; all in NewsBank/Readex, Database; America's Historical Newspapers.

15. Atari, *Gotcha;* "Gotcha."

16. Chase and crash games available in 1976 would have included *Demolition Derby* (Chicago Coin, 1975), *Destruction Derby* (Exidy, 1975), and *Crash 'N' Score* (Atari, 1975).

17. "Exidy Introduces," 29. Note: I am considering *Death Race 98* and *Death Race* as the same game. The company appears to use the names somewhat interchangeably, with the only difference between the two being the inclusion of the "98" on the cabinet graphics.

18. Exidy continued to advertise *Destruction Derby* in the same issue of *RePlay* to include the first advertisement for *Death Race 98*. The market for coin-op machines was such that particular games would continue to be strong sellers for several years, and companies would usually continue to offer them as long as there was a reliable market for new machines.

19. "Death Race from Exidy," 22.

20. "STEP ASIDE!," 15.

21. "New! Death Race by Exidy," 9.

22. Exidy, "Death Race Exidy Service Manual."

23. "New! Death Race by Exidy," 9.

24. Kent, *Ultimate History of Video Games.*

25. Campbell, "Just Less Than Total War," 183–200.
26. "Replay Route Analysis," 38.
27. Blumenthal, " 'Death Race' Game Gains Favor."
28. Ibid.
29. Harvey, "Postscript."
30. Brainard, "Exidy," 93–99, 100–102.
31. Ibid.
32. "Death Race Rerun," 32.
33. *Death Race 98* was first advertised in *RePlay* in March 1976, and *Death Race* was first advertised in the April 1976 issue. Given the proximity of these ads to each other and to other coverage of the game *Death Race*, with no mention of *Death Race 98*, they appear to have been part of the same publicity campaign. The evidence offered by industry coverage from the time suggests, as I believe, that the manufacturer treated them interchangeably.
34. Brainard, "Exidy," 93–99, 100–102.
35. Poole, *Trigger Happy.*
36. "Making of . . . Carmageddon."
37. Renaudin, "GTA 5 Doesn't Include Female Protagonist."
38. BradyGames, *Guinness World Records 2009 Gamer's Edition.*
39. "Suit: Video Game Sparked Police Shootings."
40. "Gamemaker Sued."
41. Narcisse, "Games Rated 'Mature.' "

4. ANARCHY IN THE ARCADE

1. Kerr, "Issue and Debate."
2. Collins, "Children's Video Games."
3. Lombardo, *Organized Crime in Chicago,* 95.
4. Ibid., 140.
5. Mesquite, Texas, Municipal Code 1353 (1977).
6. Shaw, "News," 58–59.
7. deWinter, "Midway in the Museum."
8. "Judges Denounce Pinball as Gambling."
9. "Pinballs as 'Racket' Fought by Mayor."
10. *Cossack v. City of Los Angeles,* 11 Cal.3d 726 (1974).
11. Porges, "Eleven Things You Didn't Know about Pinball History."
12. "PR Problems/PR Solutions," 130–32.
13. Connell, *Masculinities,* 54–56.
14. "President Reagan Makes Pro-Video Remarks," 16.
15. Kimmel, *Guyland,* 16–18.
16. "Region."
17. MacNeil, interview.
18. Feron, "Westchester Journal."

19. Abramson, "Game Parlors Face Curbs."
20. Associated Press, "Illinois, Massachusetts Towns Ban Video Games."
21. "Interestingly, the new machines do not seem to have aroused the curiosity of the Mafia, once a big operator of coin machines in New York and Chicago. 'That all seems to have been cleared up,' says Edward Joyce deputy chief of the Organized Crime and Racketeering Section of the U.S. Department of Justice" (Range, "Space Age Pinball Machine").
22. Kerr, "Issue and Debate."
23. Williams, "Video Game Makers Rap Surgeon General."
24. Licata, "Cleaning Up an Arcade," 46.
25. Kerr, "Issue and Debate."
26. *WNEK Vending v. Buffalo*, 107 Misc. 2d 353—NY: Supreme Court, Erie 1980.
27. *America's Best Family Showplace v. City of New York*, 536 F. Supp. 170—Dist. Court, ED New York.
28. *1001 Plays, Inc. v. Mayor of Boston*, 444 NE 2d 931—Mass.: Supreme Judicial Court 1983.
29. *Malden Amusement Co., Inc. v. City of Malden*, 582 F. Supp. 297—Dist. Court, D. Massachusetts 1983.
30. *Tommy & Tina v. DEPT*, 117 Misc. 2d 415—NY: Supreme Court 1983.
31. Clendinen, "Massachusetts Town Exiles Pac-Man."
32. *Marshfield Family Skateland, Inc. v. Marshfield*, 450 NE 2d 605—Mass.: Supreme Judicial Court 1983.
33. *Aladdin's Castle, Inc. v. City of Mesquite*, 630 F. 2d 1029—Court of Appeals, 5th Circuit 1980.
34. "Marshfield Voters Keep Longstanding Video Game Ban."
35. Baker, "After Thirty-Two Years."
36. Clendinen, "Massachusetts Town Exiles Pac-Man."

5. PLAY SAVES THE DAY

1. Slovin, "Hot Circuits," 137–54.
2. Many crime procedurals, including the series *Bones* (2005–), the *CSI* franchise (2000–), the series *Criminal Minds* (2005–), and the *Law & Order* (1990–) franchise, serve as examples of this tendency. Medical dramas like *Nip/Tuck* (2003–10), *House M.D.* (2004–2012), and *Nurse Jackie* (2009–2015), while ostensibly focused on the treatment of patients, frequently glory in the use of medical technologies.
3. Engelhardt, *End of Victory Culture*, 269.
4. Ibid., 272.
5. Huntemann, "Interview with Colonel Casey Wardynski," 178–88.
6. Engelhardt, *End of Victory Culture*, 271.
7. *The Terminator* franchise includes films from 1984, 1991, 2003, and 2009, and the 2008 television series *The Sarah Connor Chronicles*. The franchise has also

spawned a shockingly large number of video games, with the first officially licensed game being *The Terminator* DOS game released in 1990. To date, there are eighteen games based on *Terminator* films, and eight additional games based on *The Terminator* character and concepts but not directly on *Terminator* movies. These include, notably, *RoboCop versus The Terminator* (1992) based on both *The Terminator* and *Robocop* (1987, 1990, and 1993 films as well as television series, video games, and comics) franchises. *The Matrix* franchise includes the original film from 1999; the two sequels released in 2003; a collection of animated shorts in 2003; video games including *Enter the Matrix* (2003) and *The Matrix: The Path of Neo* (2005), and a MMORPG called *The Matrix Online*, which ran from 2005 to 2009; and *The Matrix Comics*, which ran from 1999 to 2004.

8. For a comprehensive definition of transmedia storytelling, see Jenkins, "Transmedia Storytelling."

9. Ryan and Kellner, *Camera Politica*, 228.

10. Carrigan, Connell, and Lee, "Toward a New Sociology of Masculinity," 551–604; Connell, *Masculinities*, 52–56; Taylor, *Raising the Stakes*, 112–16, 128–29.

11. Grimes, "Taking Swings at a Myth."

12. "'Tron' Hurts Disney Stock."

13. Stewart, *Disney War*, 45–48.

14. Ibid., 45.

15. The Internet Movie Database, "Box Office/Business for TRON (1982)."

16. "Badham Replaces Brest as 'War Games' Helmer," 7.

17. The Internet Movie Database, "Box Office/Business for WarGames (1983)"; The Internet Movie Database, "Box Office/Business for Star Wars Episode VI: Return of the Jedi (1983)"; Box Office Mojo, "1983 Domestic Grosses."

18. The Internet Movie Database, "Awards for TRON (1982)."

19. Ebert, "Tron."

20. Ebert, "WarGames."

21. "Tron."

22. Maslin, "Tron (1982)."

23. "Crowd Boos Bresson," 5–7.

24. "Wargames."

25. Canby, "'Wargames.'"

26. Interestingly, while the sequel to *WarGames* was a low-budget affair that went straight to DVD upon its release, *TRON 2.0* was a major studio release, given the full backing of Disney's now substantial publicity and promotional efforts and featuring Jeff Bridges, now an acclaimed actor, as a major character.

27. Maynard, "All about Jay Maynard."

28. The public image of Bill Gates is one dependent on his image as a young (or, as he ages—youthful) computer whiz with a sharp eye for business. The fact that Gates dropped out of Harvard has become part of this myth, allowing him to play the role of the boy genius and the self-made man even as his

greatest achievement seems to be the accrual of significant wealth. Gates is
an exemplary computer-age capitalist. John Steele Gordon and Michael
Maiello describe Gates as an opportunistic upstart and "one of the most serious
(and contentious) capitalists in the subculture of geeks who freely shared
new ideas in a group called the Homebrew Computer Club" ("Pioneers
Die Broke"). Giving a commencement speech at Harvard after receiving an
honorary degree from the university he had dropped out of in 1976, Gates
made light of his nonstandard career path, which has been a key part of his
public biography: "I want to thank Harvard for this honor. I'll be changing
my job next year, and it will be nice to finally have a college degree on my
resume. . . . For my part, I'm just happy that the Crimson called me 'Harvard's
most successful dropout.' I guess that makes me valedictorian of my own
special class. I did the best of everyone who failed. But I also want to be
recognized as the guy who got Steve Ballmer to drop out of business school.
I'm a bad influence. That's why I was invited to speak at your graduation.
If I had spoken at your orientation, fewer of you might be here today"
(Hughes, "Bill Gates Gets Degree").

29. Jobs's image, like that of Bill Gates, hinges partly on his dropping out of
college—in Jobs's case, the institution was Reed, not Harvard. Like Gates,
he also had early ties to the Homebrew Computer Club. His interest in
music culture is played up in many profiles and is further bolstered by the
market dominance of the iPod as the portable music player of choice. A
piece circulated by the AARP depicts Jobs as a music-obsessed iconoclast in
a turtleneck and jeans (Starr, "Never Settle!"). A profile in the *Guardian* quotes
Jobs as suggesting that Gates would "be a broader guy if he had dropped acid
once or gone off to an ashram when he was younger" (Campbell, "Guardian
Profile: Steve Jobs"). Profiles depicting Jobs as a bright and mischievous child
imply, not too lightly, that these characteristics remain key to his successes
as an adult (Andrews, "Steve Jobs").
30. "Ten Most Famous Hackers."
31. Brown, "*WarGames.*"
32. Takahashi, "Q&A That Is Twenty-Five Years Late."
33. Culhane, "Special Effects Are Revolutionizing Film."
34. Burrill, *Die Tryin'*; Carrigan, Connell, and Lee, "Toward a New Sociology
of Masculinity," 551–604; Kimmel, *Guyland.*
35. Burrill, *Die Tryin'.*
36. Whyte, *Organization Man*; Wilson, *Man in the Gray Flannel Suit.*
37. Deterding, "Living Room Wars," 21–38; Nichols, "Target Acquired," 39–52.
38. The representations of gender roles in these films, particularly with regard
to women characters' engagement with technology and male technologists,
are deeply fraught and worth further consideration. While some of these
films replicate the auxiliary roles filled by female characters in *TRON* and
WarGames, in others, particularly *Hackers,* women are presented not only

as expert technologists but as objects of intense sexual desire. Variances in female roles in these films is worth further consideration, as are more recent depictions of women as hackers, particularly on television with the character of Penelope Garcia on *Criminal Minds* (2005–).

39. Connell, *Masculinities,* 185–203; Kimmel, *Manhood in America,* 117–55; Messner, *Power at Play,* 11–23.

6. THE ARCADE IS DEAD, LONG LIVE THE ARCADE

1. Barcade, "About."
2. Dave & Buster's, "Power Cards."
3. *Dance Dance Revolution* has gone through several arcade releases. The release details provided here refer to the first of these. *Dance Dance Revolution* pioneered the rhythm and dance genre. Players compete by "dancing" on a platform or stage with colored arrows on it. Using their feet, players repeat sequences shown on the game's screen. This repetition of sequences has a predecessor in a popular 1978 electronic memory game, *Simon,* which was released by Milton Bradley. *Simon* was developed by the toy designer Howard J. Morrison in collaboration with Ralph H. Baer, who is known for several innovations in video gaming, including the first light gun (Walsh, *Timeless Toys,* 175).
4. Bison, "Atari," 52.
5. Kent, *Ultimate History of Video Games,* 239.
6. Ibid., 252–55.
7. Ibid., 278–89; Sheff, *Game Over;* Kohler, *Power-Up.*
8. Paul Kermizian, e-mail to author, August 12, 2014.
9. Namco Cybertainment, "Namco Cybertainment—About Us."
10. Dave & Buster's, "Dave & Buster's Restaurant, Bar, and Arcade."
11. "Dave & Buster's, "Dave and Buster's Escape."
12. Dave & Buster's, "Pac-Man Battle Royale."
13. "Funspot."
14. Kelts, *Japanamerica.*
15. Pinballz, "Pinballz Arcade."
16. Jameson, "Nostalgia for the Present," 517–37; Hutcheon, "Irony, Nostalgia, and the Postmodern," 189–207.
17. Boasberg, "TV Video Games," 20–21; "Where Are the Powerful Voices?," 3; Sharpe, "U.S. Arcades," 39–40; Main Event, "Main Event Entertainment."
18. Payne, "Playing the *Déjà*-New," 51–68.
19. Kent, *Ultimate History of Video Games,* 175–77.
20. "MAME | Project History."
21. "MAME | About MAME."
22. XGaming, "Arcade Machines."
23. "Arcade Flyer Archive—About Us."
24. "Arcade Flyer Archive."

25. "International Center for the History of Electronic Games."
26. UT Video Game Archive, "Mission." Note that the UT Video Game Archive also houses oral histories and photographs I collected in researching this project. Anyone interested in these materials should contact the archive to access them.
27. National Videogame Archive, "About."
28. "American Classic Arcade Museum at Funspot"; Twin Galaxies, "Twin Galaxies."
29. Buchanan, "Save the Arcades."
30. Gallaga, "Austin Arcade Wins $25K."
31. Stride Gum, "Help Save the Arcades 2."
32. Stride Gum, "Arcade Profiles."
33. Stride Gum, "Save the Arcades."
34. "Product Brand Development Campaign of the Year 2011."
35. Miller, "Barbie's Next Career?"
36. Benjamin, "Old Toys," 100.
37. Cline, *Ready Player One*; Weiss, *Lucky Wander Boy*.
38. "Choose Your Own Adventure."
39. Weiss, *Lucky Wander Boy*, 251.
40. Ibid., 251–88.
41. Frederick Exley worked in advertising, suffered from bouts of mental illness, and struggled with alcoholism. He was obsessed both with the football player Frank Gifford and with Ernest Hemingway. After the initial success of his writing career, he began using letterhead that featured a photograph of Exley looking similar to Hemingway. He also liked to be referred to as "Papa," a nickname often applied to Hemingway. Late in life, Exley became absorbed by conspiracy theories involving his brother and the CIA (Exley, *Fan's Notes*; Yardley, *Misfit*).
42. Hornby, *High Fidelity*.
43. Hornby, *Juliet Naked*.
44. Prices based on a search for "Lucky Wander Boy" in the "Books Department" on Amazon.com, April 5, 2011.
45. "In Britain and the United States children legitimately and regularly engage in what is called play, in contrast with the work punctuated by leisure pursuits which is said to typify adult life" (Hunt and Frankenberg, "It's a Small World," 119).
46. "In many cases, the activities of play carry nostalgic and class-informed notions of free time, leisure, and access" (Flanagan, *Critical Play*, 24).
47. Putnam, *Bowling Alone*.
48. Gettings, interview.
49. "Classic Gaming Expo."
50. Connell, *Masculinities*, 54–56; Kimmel, *Manhood in America*, 117–56; Messner, *Power at Play*, 9–23.

51. McVey, interview, June 17, 2009.
52. Ibid.
53. Abramson, *Digital Phoenix*; Lowenstein, *Origins of the Crash*.
54. Gaither and Chmielewski, "Fears of Dot-Com Crash."
55. Jameson, "Nostalgia for the Present," 517–37.
56. Ibid., 279.
57. Kane and Fowler, "Steven Paul Jobs"; Potter, Curry, and James, "Steve Jobs Dies."

7. THE FUTURE IS NOW

1. deWinter and Kocurek, "Rescuing Anita"; Sarkeesian, "Tropes vs. Women."
2. Marcotte, "Online Misogyny"; Lewis, "This Is What Online Harassment Looks Like"; Sarkeesian, "Harassment via Wikipedia Vandalism"; Totilo, "She's Not Hiding."
3. Morris, "Anita Sarkeesian Is Not Stealing Kickstarter Money."
4. Haniver, *Not in the Kitchen Anymore.*
5. *Fat, Ugly, or Slutty.*
6. "Playing Video Games."
7. Fatal1ty, "About"; "Game Boy"; Schorn, "Cyber Athlete 'Fatal1ty' "; "I'm a Gamer," *True Life*, MTV Productions, March 13, 2003.
8. Fatal1ty, "Products."
9. Note that these large purses are frequently funded by game development companies, ensuring that tournaments feature their games and effectively buying the game a great deal of publicity.
10. "Tournament News," 111.
11. Taylor, *Raising the Stakes.*
12. Fatal1ty, "About."
13. Entertainment Software Association, "Industry Facts."
14. Entertainment Software Association, "Industry Facts: Game Player Data."
15. Ibid.
16. "Commentless Kotaku."
17. Haniver, "About"; Narcisse, "One Female Gamer."
18. Totilo, "Note about 'Brutal' Comments."
19. Kuchera, "Sexual Harassment."
20. Entertainment Software Association, "Industry Facts."
21. "Steve Jobs"; Musgrove, "Sweatshop Conditions"; "You Are NOT Allowed to Commit Suicide."
22. Entertainment Software Association, "Essential Facts."
23. Peterson, "Tits Have It."
24. Wong, "Women Missing."
25. Cifaldi, "*World of Warcraft* Loses Another 800K Subs."

B I B L I O G R A P H Y

Abramson, Barry. "Game Parlors Face Curbs." *New York Times,* August 9,
    1981. www.nytimes.com/1981/08/09/nyregion/game-parlors-face
    -curbs.html.
Abramson, Bruce. *Digital Phoenix: Why the Information Economy Collapsed
    and How It Will Rise Again.* Cambridge, Mass.: MIT Press, 2005.
"American Classic Arcade Museum at Funspot." Accessed January 14,
    2012. www.classicarcademuseum.org/.
Anderson, Perry. *The Origins of Postmodernity.* New York: Verso, 1998.
Andrews, Amanda. "Steve Jobs, Apple's iGod: Profile." *Telegraph,*
    January 14, 2009. www.telegraph.co.uk/technology/apple/4242660
    /Steve-Jobs-Apples-iGod-Profile.html.
"The Arcade Flyer Archive." Accessed February 21, 2011. flyers.arcade
    -museum.com/.
"The Arcade Flyer Archive—About Us." Accessed February 21, 2011.
    flyers.arcade-museum.com/?page=about.
"Arcade Profiles." *Save the Arcades 2.* Accessed November 14, 2011.
    savethearcades.stridegum.com/arcadeprofiles.php#2?from=%2Findex
    .php.

215

Associated Press. "Illinois, Massachusetts Towns Ban Video Games for Youngsters." *Gadsen Times,* February 10, 1982. news.google.com /newspapers?id=KKUfAAAAIBAJ&sjid=Q9YEAAAAIBAJ&pg =2360%2C1399552.

Atari. *Gotcha.* www.arcade-museum.com/game_detail.php?game_id =7985.

"Atari Parts Are Dumped." *New York Times,* September 28, 1983.

"Badham Replaces Brest as 'War Games' Helmer; Cite Usual 'Differences.'" *Variety,* September 8, 1982, 7.

Baker, Billy. "After Thirty-Two Years, Video Games Return to Marshfield." *Boston Globe,* May 25, 2014. www.bostonglobe.com/metro /2014/05/24/marshfield-freed-from-ban-arcade-games/gA2Ds6z InxlObrnPcs8d9K/story.html.

Barcade. "About." Accessed January 14, 2012. barcadebrooklyn.com/.

Beley, Gene. "Fighting City Hall." *Play Meter* 2, no. 7 (1976): 34–37, 43–44.

Benjamin, Walter. "Old Toys." In *Walter Benjamin: Selected Writings Volume 2, Part 1, 1927–1930,* ed. Michael W. Jennings et al., 98–102. Cambridge, Mass.: Belknap Press of Harvard University Press, 1999.

"The Bernstein Report—New York Investment Firm Takes Close Look at the Video Industry." *RePlay,* April 1983, 92.

Best, Joel. "Rhetoric in Claims-Making: Constructing the Missing Children Problem." *Social Problems* 34, no. 2 (1987): 101–21.

Bison, Giselle. "Atari: From Starting Block to Auction Block." *InfoWorld,* August 6, 1984, 52.

Biven, Carl W. *Jimmy Carter's Economy: Policy in an Age of Limits.* Chapel Hill: University of North Carolina Press, 2002.

Blumenthal, Ralph. "'Death Race' Game Gains Favor, But Not with the Safety Council." *New York Times,* December 28, 1976. www.proquest .com.ezproxy.lib.utexas.edu/.

Boasberg, Louis. "TV Video Games and Respectability." *RePlay* (1976 Showbook): 20–21.

Box Office Mojo. "1983 Domestic Grosses." Accessed November 8, 2009. boxofficemojo.com/yearly/chart/?yr=1983&p=.htm.

BradyGames. *Guinness World Records 2009 Gamer's Edition.* New York: Time Home Entertainment, 2009.

Brainard, Kathy. "Exidy: Ten Years of Excellence in Dynamics." *RePlay* 9, no. 10 (1983): 93–99, 100–102.

Breen, Christopher. "Steve Jobs: Informed by His Era." *MacWorld*, October 7, 2011. www.macworld.com/article/162899/2011/10 /steve_jobs_informed_by_his_era.html.

Brown, Scott. "*WarGames*: A Look Back at the Film That Turned Geeks and Phreaks into Stars." *Wired*, July 21, 2008. www.wired.com/enter tainment/hollywood/magazine/16–08/ff_wargames?currentPage=all.

Buchanan, Levi. "Save the Arcades: Classic Arcades Are Dying. You Can Help." *Retro IGN*, August 11, 2009. retro.ign.com/articles/101 /1012795p1.html.

Burrill, Derrick A. *Die Tryin': Video Games, Masculinity, and Culture*. New York: Peter Lang, 2008.

Butler, Judith. "Athletic Genders: Hyperbolic Instance and/or the Overcoming of Sexual Binarism." *Stanford Humanities Review* 6 (1998): 2. www.stanford.edu/group/SHR/6–2/html/butler.html.

Campbell, Duncan. "The Guardian Profile: Steve Jobs." *Guardian*, June 18, 2004. arts.guardian.co.uk/features/story/0,11710,1241745,00.html.

Campbell, James. "Just Less Than Total War: Simulating World War II as Ludic Nostalgia." In *Playing the Past: History and Nostalgia in Video Games*, edited by Zach Whalen and Laurie N. Taylor, 183–200. Nashville, Tenn.: Vanderbilt University Press, 2008.

Canby, Vincent. "'Wargames,' a Computer Fantasy." *New York Times*, June 3, 1983. movies.nytimes.com/movie/review?res=9F0DE6D9103BF93 0A35755C0A965948260&scp=4&sq=wargames,%20movie&st=cse.

Caraher, William, Raiford Guins, Andrew Reinhard, Richard Rothaus, and Bret Weber. "Why We Dug Atari: 'Punk Archeologists' Explain That They Went Looking for More Than Just Video-Game Cartridges in a New Mexico Landfill." *Atlantic*, August 7, 2014. www.theatlantic .com/technology/archive/2014/08/why-we-dug-atari/375702/.

Carrigan, Tim, Bob Connell, and John Lee. "Toward a New Sociology of Masculinity." *Theory and Society* 14, no. 5 (1985): 551–604.

Cassell, Justine, and Henry Jenkins. "Chess for Girls? Feminism and Computer Games." In *From Barbie to Mortal Kombat: Gender and Computer Games*, edited by Justine Cassell and Henry Jenkins, 2–45. Cambridge, Mass.: MIT Press, 1998.

"Choose Your Own Adventure—30th Anniversary Timeline." 2008. www.cyoa.com/public/30thanniversary/index.html.

Cifaldi, Frank. "*World of Warcraft* Loses Another 800K Subs in Three Months." *Gamasutra*, November 8, 2011. www.gamasutra.com/view

/news/38460/World_of_Warcraft_Loses_Another_800K_Subs_In_
Three_Months.php.

Claiborn, Samuel. "The Dig: Atari E.T. Games Found in New Mexico Landfill." *IGN,* April 26, 2014. www.ign.com/articles/2014/04/26/the-dig-uncovering-the-atari-et-games-buried-in-new-mexico-desert.

"Classic Gaming Expo." 2010. www.cgexpo.com/index.htm.

Clendinen, Dudley. "Massachusetts Town Exiles Pac-Man and All That." *New York Times,* December 8, 1983. www.nytimes.com/1983/12/08/us/massachusetts-town-exiles-pac-man-and-all-that.html.

Cline, Ernest. *Ready Player One.* New York: Crown, 2011.

Cohen, Robert. "The Many Meanings of the FSM: In Lieu of an Introduction." In *The Free Speech Movement: Reflections on Berkeley in the 1960s,* ed. Robert Cohen and Reginald E. Zelnik, 1–54. Berkeley: University of California Press, 2002.

"Coke Picks Arcade Set for New TV Commercial." *RePlay,* May 1977, 13.

Collins, Glenn. "Children's Video Games: Who Wins (or Loses): No Great Demand for Help 'A Seductive World.'" *New York Times,* August 31, 1981. www.nytimes.com/1981/08/31/style/children-s-video-games-who-wins-or-loses.html.

"Commentless Kotaku." Accessed January 15, 2012. chrome.google.com/webstore/detail/kdknjinbdljpifdloehifdgmoaibhoof.

Connell, R. W. *Masculinities.* Berkeley: University of California Press, 2005.

"CPI Inflation Calculator." Bureau of Labor Statistics. Accessed October 10, 2011. www.bls.gov/data/inflation_calculator.htm.

"Crowd Boos Bresson at Cannes Prize Ceremony; 'WarGames' Plays Well." *Variety,* May 25, 1983, 5–7.

Culhane, John. "Special Effects Are Revolutionizing Film." *New York Times,* July 4, 1982. www.nytimes.com/1982/07/04/movies/special-effects-are-revolutionizing-film.html?sec=technology&spon=&pagewanted=all.

Dave & Buster's. "Dave & Buster's Escape into Play." Accessed January 14, 2012. youtu.be/VCdtS9Qu56w.

———. "Dave & Buster's Restaurant, Bar and Arcade for Family Fun, Parties, Meetings and More." Accessed January 1, 2011. www.daveandbusters.com/.

———. "Pac-Man Battle Royale at Dave and Buster's." Accessed January 14, 2012. youtu.be/3Sq6dkbw6uo.

————. "Power Cards." Accessed January 14, 2012. www.daveandbusters
.com/play/powercards.aspx.

Day, Walter. "Chapter Four: LIFE Magazine." Twin Galaxies. Last
modified February 8, 1998. Accessed February 2, 2008. oldtgi.twin
galaxies.net/index.aspx?c=17&id=616.

————. "Chapter Three: The Official Scoreboard." Twin Galaxies.
Last modified November 3, 2009. Accessed October 26, 2011. oldtgi
.twingalaxies.net/index.aspx?c=17&id=332.

————. "Our Unique History." Twin Galaxies. Last modified November
3, 2009. Accessed October 26, 2011. oldtgi.twingalaxies.net/index
.aspx?c=17&id=332.

"Death Race 2000 (1975)." Internet Movie Database. Accessed September
21, 2010. www.imdb.com/title/tt0072856/.

"Death Race from Exidy." RePlay 2, no. 7 (1976): 22.

"Death Race Rerun," Play Meter 2, no. 8 (1976): 31–32.

Deterding, Sebastian. "Living Room Wars: Remediation, Boardgames,
and the Early History of Video Wargaming." In Joystick Soldiers:
The Politics of Play in Military Video Games, edited by Nina B.
Huntemann and Matthew Thomas Payne, 21–38. London:
Routledge, 2009.

deWinter, Jennifer. "The Midway in the Museum: Arcades, Art, and
the Challenge of Displaying Play." Reconstruction 14, no. 1 (2014).
reconstruction.eserver.org/Issues/141/deWinter.shtml.

deWinter, Jennifer, and Carly Kocurek. "Rescuing Anita: Games,
Gamers, and the Battle of the Sexes." Flow 17, no. 3 (2012). flowtv
.org/2012/12/rescuing-anita/.

Douglas, Susan J. Inventing American Broadcasting, 1899–1922. Baltimore,
Md.: Johns Hopkins University Press, 1989.

Ebert, Roger. "Death Race 2000." Chicago Sun-Times, April 27, 1975.
rogerebert.suntimes.com/apps/pbcs.dll/article?AID=/19750427
/REVIEWS/808259998.

————. "Tron." Chicago Sun Times, January 1, 1982. rogerebert.suntimes
.com/apps/pbcs.dll/article?AID=/19820101/REVIEWS/201010350
/1023.

————. "WarGames." Chicago Sun Times, June 3, 1983. rogerebert.sun
times.com/apps/pbcs.dll/article?AID=/19830603/REVIEWS/3060
30301/1023.

"Editorial: Where Are the Powerful Voices?" RePlay, December 1976, 3.

Engelhardt, Tom. *The End of Victory Culture: Cold War America and the Disillusioning of a Generation.* New York: Basic Books, 1995.

Entertainment Software Association. "Essential Facts about the Computer and Video Game Industry." Accessed December 20, 2013. www.theesa.com/facts/.

———. "Industry Facts." Accessed November 5, 2013. www.theesa.com/facts/index.asp.

———. "Industry Facts." 2012. Accessed December 20, 2013. www.theesa.com/facts/.

———. "Industry Facts: Game Player Data." 2012. Accessed December 20, 2013. www.theesa.com/facts/gameplayer.asp.

Exidy. "Death Race Exidy Service Manual." ca. 1976. Accessed July 23, 2014. www.arcade-museum.com/manuals-videogames/D/DeathRace.pdf.

"Exidy Introduces: Death Race 98." *RePlay* 2, no. 3 (1976): 29.

Exley, Frederick. *A Fan's Notes.* New York: Vintage, 1988.

Fat, Ugly, or Slutty. 2013. fatuglyorslutty.com/.

Fatality. "About." Accessed December 5, 2011. www.fatality.com/about/.

———. "Products." Accessed December 5, 2011. www.fatality.com/index.php?option=com_content&view=article&id=130.

Feron, James. "Westchester Journal." *New York Times,* June 21, 1981. www.nytimes.com/1981/06/21/nyregion/westchester-journal-166113.html.

Finkelhor, David, Gerald Hotaling, and Andrea Sedlak. "Children Abducted by Family Members: A National Household Survey of Incidence and Episode Characteristics." *Journal of Marriage and Family* 53, no. 3 (1991): 805–17.

Flanagan, Mary. *Critical Play: Radical Game Design.* Cambridge, Mass.: MIT Press, 2009.

Frum, David. *How We Got Here: The 70's: The Decade That Brought You Modern Life—for Better or Worse.* New York: Basic Books, 2000.

"Funspot . . . The Spot for Fun!" Accessed February 4, 2011. www.funspotnh.com/.

Gaither, Chris, and Dawn C. Chmielewski. "Fears of Dot-Com Crash, Version 2.0." *Los Angeles Times,* July 16, 2006. articles.latimes.com/2006/jul/16/business/fi-overheat16.

Gallaga, Omar L. "Austin Arcade Wins $25K in 'Save the Arcades'

Contest." *Digital Savant,* October 9, 2009. mo.statesman.com/blogs /content/shared-gen/blogs/austin/digitalsavant/entries/2009/10/09 /austin_arcade_w.html.

Gallup, George. "The Gallup Youth Survey: Video Game Craze Sweeps Teenage America." *Play Meter* 8, no. 22 (1982): 100.

"Game Boy: Can Jonathan 'Fatal1ty' Wendel Win Credibility for Pro Gaming—and for Himself?" *Business Week,* October 10, 2005. www.businessweek.com/magazine/content/05_41/b3954113.htm.

"Gamemaker Sued over Highway Shootings." SFGate.com, October 23, 2003. articles.sfgate.com/2003–10–23/business/17515225_1_sony -computer-entertainment-america-punitive-damages-state-custody.

Gee, James Paul, and Elisabeth R. Hayes. *Women and Gaming: The Sims and Twenty-First Century Learning.* New York: Palgrave Macmillan, 2010.

Gilbert, Brian. *A Cycle of Outrage: America's Reaction to the Juvenile Delinquent in the 1950s.* New York: Oxford University Press, 1986.

Gordon, John Steele, and Michael Maiello. "Pioneers Die Broke." Forbes.com, December 23, 2002. www.forbes.com/forbes/2002 /1223/258_print.html.

"Gotcha." *The Killer List of Video Games.* Accessed April 27, 2011. www.arcade-museum.com/game_detail.php?game_id=7985.

Green, Harvey. *Fit for America: Health, Fitness, Sport and American Society.* Baltimore, Md.: Johns Hopkins University Press, 1986.

Grimes, William. "Taking Swings at a Myth, with John Henry the Man." *New York Times,* October 18, 2006. www.nytimes.com/2006/10/18 /books/18grim.html?_r=1&ex=1168750800&en=2c72dddaeac54265 &ei=5070.

Guins, Raiford. *Game After: A Cultural Study of Video Game Afterlife.* Cambridge, Mass.: MIT Press, 2014.

Haniver, Jenny. "About." *Not in the Kitchen Anymore.* Accessed January 15, 2012. www.notinthekitchenanymore.com/p/what-this-blog-is -about_27.html.

———. *Not in the Kitchen Anymore.* Accessed December 19, 2013. www.notinthekitchenanymore.com/.

Harpold, Terry. "Screw the Grue: Mediality, Metalepsis, Recapture." In *Playing the Past: History and Nostalgia in Video Games,* edited by Zach Whalen and Laurie N. Taylor, 96–97. Nashville, Tenn.: Vanderbilt University Press, 2008.

Harvey, David. *The Condition of Postmodernity: An Enquiry into the Origins of Cultural Change.* Cambridge: Blackwell, 1990.

Harvey, Steve. "Postscript: Controversial 'Death Race' Game Reaches 'Finish' Line." *Los Angeles Times,* August 10, 1977. www.proquest.com .ezproxy.lib.utexas.edu/.

Hendershot, Cyndy. "The Atomic Scientist, Science Fiction Films, and Paranoia: *The Day the Earth Stood Still, This Island Earth,* and *Killers from Space.*" *Journal of American Culture* 20, no. 1 (2004): 31–41.

Hine, Thomas. *The Rise and Fall of the American Teenager: A New History of the American Adolescent Experience.* New York: Perennial, 2000.

Hornby, Nick. *High Fidelity.* New York: Riverhead Trade, 1996.

———. *Juliet Naked.* New York: Riverhead Hardcover, 2009.

Hughes, Gina. "Bill Gates Gets Degree after Thirty Years." *The Techie Diva,* June 8, 2007. tech.yahoo.com/blog/hughes/13653.

Hunt, Pauline, and Ronald Frankenberg. "It's a Small World: Disneyland, the Family, and the Multiple Re-representations of the American Childhood." In *Constructing and Reconstructing Childhood: Contemporary Issues in the Sociological Study of Childhood,* edited by Allison James and Alan Prout, 105–22. Bristol: Falmer, 1997.

Huntemann, Nina B. "Interview with Colonel Casey Wardynski." In *Joystick Soldiers: The Politics of Play in Military Games,* edited by Matthew Thomas Payne and Nina B. Huntemann, 178–88. London: Routledge, 2009.

Hutcheon, Linda. "Irony, Nostalgia, and the Postmodern." *Methods for the Study of Literature as Cultural Memory, Studies in Comparative Literature* 30 (2000): 189–207.

"The International Center for the History of Electronic Games." Accessed November 16, 2011. www.icheg.org/.

The Internet Movie Database. "Awards for TRON (1982)." Accessed May 3, 2009. www.imdb.com/title/tt0084827/awards.

———. "Box Office/Business for Star Wars Episode VI: Return of the Jedi (1983)." Accessed January 13, 2011. www.imdb.com/title /tt0086190/business.

———. "Box Office/Business for TRON (1982)." May 2009. www.imdb .com/title/tt0086567/business.

———. "Box Office/Business for WarGames (1983)." Accessed May 3, 2009. www.imdb.com/title/tt0086567/business.

Jameson, Fredric. "Nostalgia for the Present." *South Atlantic Quarterly* 88, no. 2 (1989): 517–37.

———. *Postmodernism, or The Cultural Logic of Late Capitalism.* Durham, N.C.: Duke University Press, 2003.

Jenkins, Henry. "'Complete Freedom of Movement': Video Games as Gendered Play Spaces." In *From Barbie to Mortal Kombat: Gender and Computer Games,* edited by Justine Cassell and Henry Jenkins, 274–76. Cambridge, Mass.: MIT Press, 1998.

———. "Transmedia Storytelling." *Technology Review,* January 15, 2003. Accessed November 2, 2011. www.technologyreview.com/biomedi cine/13052/.

"Judges Denounce Pinball as Gambling, but Reserve Decision in Jersey Case." *New York Times,* October 9, 1941. query.nytimes.com/mem /archive/pdf?res=F40B12FD3B5C16738DDDA00894D8415B8188 F1D3.

"Jumper Wins Olympic Arcade Tricathlon." *RePlay,* March 1980, 15.

Juul, Jesper. *Half-Real: Video Games between Real Rules and Fictional Worlds.* Cambridge, Mass.: MIT Press, 2005.

Kane, Yukari Iwatani, and Geoffrey A. Fowler. "Steven Paul Jobs, 1955–2011." *Wall Street Journal,* October 6, 2011. online.wsj.com/article /SB10001424052702304447804576410753210811910.html.

Kao, Stephanie Y. "Carpal Tunnel Syndrome as an Occupational Disease." *Journal of the American Board of Family Practice* 16 (2003): 533–42. www.jabfm.org/cgi/content/full/16/6/533.

Karlen, Neal, Nikki Finke Greenberg, David L. Gonzalez, and Elisa Williams. "How Many Missing Kids." *Newsweek,* October 7, 1985, 30.

Kasson, John. *Amusing the Million: Coney Island at the Turn of the Century.* New York: Hill and Wang, 1978.

Kelts, Rol. *Japanamerica: How Japanese Pop Culture Has Invaded the U.S.* New York: Palgrave Macmillan, 2006.

Kent, Steven L. "Super Mario Nation." In *The Medium of the Video Game,* edited by Mark J. P. Wolfe, 35–48. Austin: University of Texas Press, 2001.

———. *The Ultimate History of Video Games: The Story behind the Craze That Touched Our Lives and Changed the World.* New York: Three Rivers, 2001.

Kerr, Peter. "Issue and Debate: Should Video Games Be Restricted by

Law." *New York Times,* July 3, 1982. www.nytimes.com/1982/06/03
/garden/issue-and-debate-should-video-games-be-restricted-by-law
.html?pagewanted=1.

Kiesler, Sara, Lee Sproull, and Jacquelynne S. Eccles. "Pool Halls, Chips,
and War Games: Women in the Culture of Computing." *Psychology
of Women Quarterly* 9 (1985): 451–62.

Kimmel, Michael. *Guyland: The Perilous World Where Boys Become Men,
Understanding the Critical Years between Sixteen and Twenty-Six.* New
York: Harper Collins, 2008.

———. *Manhood in America: A Cultural History.* New York: Free
Press, 1996.

Kirsh, Steven J. *Children, Adolescents, and Media Violence: A Critical Look at
the Research.* Thousand Oaks, Calif.: Sage, 2011.

Klemersud, Judy. " 'Bang! Boing! Ping! It's King Pong': 'A Sense of Control' Began in Amusement Park Prescription for Eye Ailments Balls
and Strikes." *New York Times,* April 23, 1978. ProQuest Historical
Newspapers The New York Times (1851–2007). (AAT 03624331).

Kohler, Chris. *Power-Up: How Japanese Video Games Gave the World an Extra
Life.* Indianapolis, Ind.: Brady Games, 2004.

Kuchera, Ben. "Sexual Harassment as Ethical Imperative: How Capcom's
Fighting Game Reality Show Turned Ugly." *The Penny Arcade Report,*
February 28, 2012. penny-arcade.com/report/article/sexual-harass
ment-as-ethical-imperative-the-ugly-side-of-fighting-games.

Kutner, Lawrence, and Cheryl K. Olson. *Grand Theft Childhood:
The Surprising Truth about Violent Video Games and What Parents Can
Do.* New York: Simon and Schuster, 2011.

Launius, Roger D. "Heroes in a Vacuum: The Apollo Astronaut as
Cultural Icon." *Forty-Third AIAA Aerospace Sciences Meeting and
Exhibit,* January 10–13, 2005, Reno, Nevada. klabs.org/history/roger
/launius_2005.pdf.

Lenhart, Amanda, et al. "Who's Not Online: 57% of Those without Internet Access Say They Do Not Plan to Log On." Pew Internet and
American Life Project, September 21, 2000. www.pewinternet.org
/~/media//Files/Reports/2000/Pew_Those_Not_Online_Report
.pdf.pdf.

Lewis, Helen. "This Is What Online Harassment Looks Like." *New States-
man,* July 6, 2012. www.newstatesman.com/blogs/internet/2012/07
/what-online-harassment-looks.

Licata, Tony. "Cleaning Up an Arcade: Out with the Hoods, In with the Families." *Play Meter* 6, no. 19 (1980): 46–47.

Lichtenstein, Nelson. *State of the Union: A Century of American Labor.* Princeton, N.J.: Princeton University Press, 2002.

Lombardo, Robert M. *Organized Crime in Chicago: Beyond the Mafia.* Champaign: University of Illinois Press, 2012.

Lowenstein, Roger. *Origins of the Crash: The Great Bubble and Its Undoing.* New York: Penguin Books, 2004.

"A Lucrative Business: Electronic Video Games in Best Places." *Dallas Morning News,* November 2, 1975. Ulrich (1553–846X).

MacNeil, Robert. Interview with Ronnie Lamm. *MacNeil/Lehrer News-Hour,* December 29, 1982.

Main Event. "Main Event Entertainment." Accessed January 25, 2011. www.maineventusa.com/.

"The Making of . . . Carmageddon." *Edge Magazine.* 2008. www.next-gen .biz/features/the-making-of%E2%80%A6-carmageddon?page=0%2C0.

"MAME | About MAME." Accessed January 27, 2011. mamedev.org /about.html.

"MAME | Project History." Accessed January 27, 2011. mamedev.org /history.html.

Mandel, Ernest. *Late Capitalism.* New York: Verso, 1978.

Mann, Jim. "Court Delays Ruling on Video Game Curbs." *Los Angeles Times,* February 24, 1982.

Marcotte, Amanda. "Online Misogyny: Can't Ignore It, Can't Not Ignore It." *Slate,* June 13, 2012. www.slate.com/blogs/xx_factor /2012/06/13/online_misogyny_reflects_women_s_realities_though _in_a_cruder_way_than_is_customary_offline_.html.

"Marshfield Voters Keep Longstanding Video Game Ban." *CBS Boston,* April 26, 2011. boston.cbslocal.com/2011/04/26/marshfield-voters -keep-long-standing-video-game-ban/.

Maslin, Janet. "Tron (1982)." *New York Times,* July 9, 1982. movies .nytimes.com/movie/review?res=9500E7DB103BF93AA35754 C0A964948260.

Maynard, Jay. "All about Jay Maynard, the TRON Guy." Accessed May 2, 2009. tronguy.net/.

McCraw, Thomas K. *Prophets of Regulation: Charles Francis Adams; Louis D. Brandeis; James M. Landis; Alfred E. Kahn.* Cambridge, Mass.: Belknap Press of Harvard University Press, 1984.

Messner, Michael A. *Power at Play: Sports and the Problem of Masculinity.*
Boston: Beacon, 1992.

Miller, Claire Cain. "Barbie's Next Career? Computer Engineer."
New York Times Online, February 12, 2010. bits.blogs.nytimes.
com/2010/02/12/barbies-next-career-computer-engineer/.

Mintz, Steven. *Huck's Raft: A History of American Childhood.* Cambridge,
Mass.: Belknap Press of Harvard University Press, 2004.

Morris, Chris. "Video Games Push for Olympic Recognition: Global
Gaming League Talking with China to Bring Competitive Gaming to
the Beijing 2008 Games." *CNNMoney,* May 31, 2006. money.cnn.com
/2006/05/31/commentary/game_over/column_gaming/index.htm.

Morris, Kevin. "Anita Sarkeesian Is Not Stealing Kickstarter Money to
Buy Gucci Shoes." *Daily Dot,* February 13, 2013. www.dailydot.com
/society/anita-sarkeesian-gamers-photoshop-shoe/.

Musgrove, Mike. "Sweatshop Conditions at iPod Factory Reported."
Washington Post, June 16, 2006. www.washingtonpost.com/wp-dyn
/content/article/2006/06/15/AR2006061501898.html.

"Namco Cybertainment—About Us." Accessed February 17, 2011.
www.namcoarcade.com/About.asp.

Narcisse, Evan. "Games Rated 'Mature' Are Made Less, Bought More."
Time, March 21, 2011. techland.time.com/2011/03/21/games-rated
-mature-are-made-less-bought-more/.

———. "One Female Gamer Records a Warfare in Words." *Kotaku,* November 8, 2011. kotaku.com/5857333/one-female-gamer-records
-a-warfare-in-words.

National Videogame Archive. "About." Accessed January 27, 2012.
nationalvideogamearchive.org/about.

"New! Death Race by Exidy." *RePlay* 2, no. 5 (1976): 9.

Nichols, Randy. "Target Acquired: *America's Army* and the Video Game
Industry." In *Joystick Soldiers: The Politics of Play in Military Video Games,*
edited by Nina B. Huntemann and Matthew Thomas Payne, 39–52.
London: Routledge, 2009.

"Olympic Tricathalon Slated." *Play Meter* 6, no. 1 (1980): 65.

Payne, Matthew Thomas. "Playing the *Déjà*-New: 'Plug It in and Play
TV Games' and the Cultural Politics of Classic Gaming." In *Playing
the Past: History and Nostalgia in Video Games,* edited by Zach Whalen
and Laurie N. Taylor, 51–68. Nashville, Tenn.: Vanderbilt University
Press, 2008.

Peiss, Kathy. *Cheap Amusements: Working Women and Leisure in Turn-of-the-Century New York*. Philadelphia: Temple University Press, 1986.

Peterson, Latoya. "The Tits Have It: Sexism, Character Design, and the Role of Women in Created Worlds." *Kotaku,* October 20, 2011. kotaku.com/5851800/the-tits-have-it-sexism-character-design-and-the-role-of-women-in-created-worlds?tag=opinion.

"Pinballs as 'Racket' Fought by Mayor; In Affidavit Opposing Suit for Injunction He Links Games with 'Criminality'; 5 Prosecutors Back Him, La Guardia Tells Court Metal of Machines Should Be Put to Wartime Uses." *New York Times,* January 29, 1942. query.nytimes.com/mem/archive/pdf?res=F70D1FFE3F5D167B93CBAB178AD85F468485F9.

Pinballz. "Pinballz Arcade." Accessed February 17, 2011. www.pinballz arcade.com/.

"Pioneers Die Broke." December 23, 2002. www.forbes.com/forbes/2002/1223/258_print.html.

Pisano, J. "MIDI Standards: A Brief History and Explanation." September 2006. mustech.net/2006/09/midi-standards-a-brief-history-and-explanation/.

"Playing Video Games for a Living." *Forbes Video,* May 26, 2006. www.youtube.com/watch?v=Q275Qh4ESao.

Poole, Steven. *Trigger Happy: Video Games and the Entertainment Revolution*. New York: Arcade, 2000.

Porges, Seth. "Eleven Things You Didn't Know about Pinball History: The Surprising History behind a Beloved American Pastime." *Popular Mechanics.* Accessed March 25, 2012. www.popularmechanics.com/technology/gadgets/toys/4328211-new-6#slide-1.

Potter, Ned, Colleen Curry, and Michael S. James. "Steve Jobs Dies: Apple Chief Made Early Personal Computer, Created iPad, iPod, iPhone." *ABC News,* October 5, 2011. abcnews.go.com/Technology/steve-jobs-dies-apple-chief-innovated-personal-computer/story?id=14383813#.TxHubPKJmSo.

"PR Problems/PR Solutions: What to Say When . . ." *Play Meter* 8, no. 22 (1982): 130–32.

"President Reagan Makes Pro-Video Remarks in Recent Florida Speech." *RePlay,* April 1983, 16.

"Product Brand Development Campaign of the Year 2011: Winner Ketchum West and Mattel/Barbie: After 125 Careers, Barbie Gets Her Geek On." *PR Week,* March 10, 2011. www.prweekus.com

/product-brand-development-campaign-of-the-year-2011
/article/197737/.

Putnam, Robert D. *Bowling Alone: The Collapse and Revival of American Community.* New York: Touchstone Books, 2001.

Putney, Clifford. *Muscular Christianity: Manhood and Sports in Protestant America, 1880–1920.* Cambridge, Mass.: Harvard University Press, 2001.

Ramao, Tico. "Engines of Transformation: An Analytical History of the 1970s Car Chase Cycle." *New Review of Film and Television Studies* 1, no. 1 (2003): 31–54.

Range, Peter Ross. "The Space Age Pinball Machine." *New York Times,* September 15, 1974. ProQuest Historical Newspapers The New York Times (1851–2007). (AAT 03624331).

"The Region; Irvington Board Acts on Video Machines." *New York Times,* June 16, 1981. www.nytimes.com/1981/06/16/nyregion/the-region -irvington-board-acts-on-video-machines.html.

Renaudin, Josh. "GTA 5 Doesn't Include Female Protagonist Because 'Being Masculine' Is Key to Story." *Gameranx,* September 10, 2013. www.gameranx.com/updates/id/17320/article/gta-5-doesn-t-include -female-protagonist-because-being-masculine-is-key-to-story/.

"Replay Route Analysis." *RePlay* 1, no. 1 (1975): 38.

Rosenzweig, Roy. *Eight Hours for What We Will: Workers and Leisure in an Industrial City, 1870–1920.* Cambridge: Cambridge University Press, 1983.

Ryan, Michael, and Douglas Kellner. *Camera Politica: The Politics and Ideology of Contemporary Hollywood Film.* Bloomington: Indiana University Press, 1988.

Sarkeesian, Anita. "Harassment via Wikipedia Vandalism." *Feminist Frequency,* June 10, 2012. www.feministfrequency.com/2012/06 /harassment-and-misogyny-via-wikipedia/.

———. "Tropes vs. Women in Video Games." *Kickstarter,* June 16, 2012. www.kickstarter.com/projects/566429325/tropes-vs-women-in -video-games.

Schorn, Daniel. "Cyber Athlete 'Fatal1ty.'" *60 Minutes,* January 22, 2006. www.cbsnews.com/stories/2006/01/19/60minutes/main1220146 .shtml.

Sharp, Phillip. "Peep-boxes to Pixels: An Alternative History of Video Game Space." In *Situated Play, Proceedings of DiGRA 2007 Conference.* Accessed February 12, 2009. www.digra.org/dl/db/07312.18290.pdf, 278–85.

Sharpe, Roger. "U.S. Arcades: Some Good, Some Bad, Some Ugly."
  RePlay, March 1977, 39–40.
Shaw, Mike. "News: Ban Author Critiques Industry." *Play Meter* 9,
  no. 13 (1983): 58–59.
Sheff, David. *Game Over: How Nintendo Zapped an American Industry,
  Captured Your Dollars, and Enslaved Your Children.* New York: Random
  House, 1993.
"Slot Machines and Pinball Games." *Annals of the American Academy of
  Political and Social Science* 269 (1950): 62–70.
Slovin, Rochelle. "Hot Circuits: Reflections on the 1989 Video Game
  Exhibition of the American Museum of the Moving Image." In
  The Medium of the Video Game, edited by Mark J. P. Wolf, 137–53.
  Austin: University of Texas Press, 2001.
"Starcade Contestants." *Starcade.* Accessed January 6, 2012. www.starcade
  .tv/starcade/contestantsframe.asp.
Starr, Alexandra. "Never Settle! Secrets of an Innovator: Apple CEO
  Steve Jobs Exemplifies Lifelong Learning and Creativity." *NRTA
  Live and Learn,* December 18, 2007. www.aarp.org/aarp/live_and
  _learn/Cover_Stories/articles/Never_Settle__Secrets_of_an
  _Innovator.html.
"STEP ASIDE!" *RePlay* 2, no. 4 (1976): 15.
"Steve Jobs: A Genius but a Bad, Mean Manager." *Inquirer,* October 25,
  2011. technology.inquirer.net/5713/steve-jobs-a-genius-but-a-bad
  -mean-manager/.
Stewart, James B. *Disney War.* New York: Simon and Schuster Paperbacks,
  2005.
Stride Gum. "Arcade Profiles." savethearcades.stridegum.com/arcade
  profiles.php#2?from=%2Findex.php.
———. "Help Save the Arcades 2 with Stride." Accessed January 25,
  2011. savethearcades.stridegum.com/.
———. "Save the Arcades." Accessed January 25, 2011. www.savethe
  arcades.com.
"Suit: Video Game Sparked Police Shootings." *ABC News,* February 15,
  2005. web.archive.org/web/20050307095559/http://abcnews.go.com
  /US/wireStory?id=502424.
Susman, Warren I. *Culture as History: The Transformation of American Society
  in the Twentieth Century.* Washington, D.C.: Smithsonian Institution
  Press, 2003.

Takahashi, Dean. "A Q&A That Is Twenty-Five Years Late: David Scott Lewis, the Mystery Hacker Who Inspired the Film 'War Games.'" *VentureBeat,* August 12, 2008. venturebeat.com/2008/08/12/a-qa-that -is-25-years-late-david-scott-lewis-the-inspiration-behind-the-film -war-games/.

Taylor, T. L. "Becoming a Player: Networks, Structure, and Imagined Futures." In *Beyond Barbie and Mortal Kombat: New Perspectives on Gender and Gaming,* edited by Yasmin B. Kafai et al., 51–66. Cambridge, Mass.: MIT Press, 2011.

———. *Raising the Stakes: E-Sports and the Professionalization of Computer Games.* Cambridge, Mass.: MIT Press, 2012.

"The Ten Most Famous Hackers of All Time." *IT Security,* April 15, 2007. www.itsecurity.com/features/top-10-famous-hackers-042407/.

Thomas, Kevin. "Movie Review: 'Barbarism in Big Brother Era' Review of Death Race 2000." *Los Angeles Times,* May 2, 1975. www.proquest .com.ezproxy.lib.utexas.edu/.

Totilo, Stephen. "A Note about 'Brutal' Comments and a Kotaku for Everyone." *Kotaku,* June 26, 2013. kotaku.com/a-note-about-brutal -comments-and-a-kotaku-for-everyon-589637991.

———. "She's Not Hiding from the Hate She's Getting for Examining Video Games. She's Exposing It." *Kotaku,* July 3, 2012. kotaku.com /5923224/rather-than-hide-from-the-hate-her-gaming+and+sexism -series-is-geting-online-anita-sarkeesian-wants-to-expose-it.

"Tournament News." *RePlay,* May 1983, 111.

Towle, Philip. *Democracy and Peacemaking: Negotiations and Debates, 1815– 1973.* London: Psychology Press, 2000.

"Tron." *Variety,* January 1, 1983. www.variety.com/review/VE1117795 896.html?categoryid=31&cs=1&p=0.

"'Tron' Hurts Disney Stock." *New York Times,* July 8, 1982.

Turkle, Sherry. *Life on the Screen: Identity in the Age of the Internet.* New York: Touchstone, 1995.

Twin Galaxies. "Twin Galaxies." Accessed January 14, 2012. www.twingalaxies.com/.

UT Video Game Archive. "Mission." Accessed January 27, 2011. www.cah.utexas.edu/projects/videogamearchive/mission.php.

Van Gelder, Lawrence. "'Death Race 2000' Is Short on Satire." *New York Times,* June 6, 1975. www.proquest.com.ezproxy.lib.utexas.edu/.

"Video Game V.I.P.S." *Life,* January 1983, 72–73.

Walsh, Tim. *Timeless Toys: Classic Toys and the Playmakers Who Created Them*. Kansas City, Mo.: Andrews McMeel, 2005.

"Wargames." *Variety*, January 1, 1983. www.variety.com/review/VE1111 7796199.html?categoryid=31&cs=1&p=0.

Watters, Ethan. "The Player." *Wired*, October 2005. www.wired.com /wired/archive/13.10/bushnell.html.

Weiss, D. B. *Lucky Wander Boy*. New York: Plume, 2003.

West, Matt. "Wooing Women Gamers—and Game Creators." CNN, June 20, 2008. www.cnn.com/2008/TECH/ptech/02/27/women .gamers/index.html.

"Where Are the Powerful Voices?" *RePlay*, December 1976, 3.

Whyte, William H. *The Organization Man*. Philadelphia: University of Pennsylvania Press, 2002.

Williams, Betty. "Video Game Makers Rap Surgeon General." *Kentucky New Era*, November 11, 1982. news.google.com/newspapers?id=3yAv AAAAIBAJ&sjid=ZtwFAAAAIBAJ&pg=2720%2C1376979.

Wilson, Sloan. *The Man in the Gray Flannel Suit*. New York: De Capo, 2002.

Wong, Wailin. "Women Missing from Video Game Development Work Force: Although Many Women Are Gamers, Few Think to Make a Career Out of Their Hobby." *Chicago Tribune*, August 5, 2010. articles.chicagotribune.com/2010–08–05/business/sc-biz-0806 -women-gamers-20100805_1_international-game-developers -association-game-development-gaming-world.

XGaming. "Arcade Machines." Accessed January 27, 2011. www.xgaming .com/store/category/arcade-machines/.

Yardley, Jonathan. *Misfit: The Strange Life of Frederick Exley*. New York: Random House, 1997.

Yi, Matthew. "They Got Game: Stacks of New Releases for Hungry Video Game Enthusiasts Mean It's Boom Time for an Industry Now Even Bigger Than Hollywood." SFGate, December 18, 2004. www.sfgate.com/cgi-bin/article.cgi?f=/chronicle/archive/2004 /12/18/MNGUOAE36I1.DTL.

"You Are NOT Allowed to Commit Suicide: Workers in Chinese iPad Factories Forced to Sign Pledges." *Daily Mail*, May 1, 2011. www.dailymail.co.uk/news/article-1382396/Workers-Chinese-Apple -factories-forced-sign-pledges-commit-suicide.html.

Zuboff, Shoshana. *In the Age of the Smart Machine: The Future of Work and Power*. New York: Basic Books, 1988.

I ∩ ◘ E X

advertising, xii, xiv–xv, xvii, 7, 15,
16, 34, 42, 43, 56, 76–81, 88,
108, 134, 154, 156, 157, 159,
167, 168, 172, 199
arcade: business structure, 5,
17–18, 156; emotion, 172,
176, 177, 178; era, xxii, 4, 38,
159, 161, 163, 191; historical
site, as, xvi, 6, 161, 164–65,
171–72, 188, 200; industry,
161; prizes, 110, 152, 173,
191–92, 193; sensory/physi-
cal experience, 3, 6–10, 12,
71, 111, 160–61, 166, 171,
177, 178, 182–83, 200. *See also*
arcade games/machines; arcade
preservation; arcade venues;
entertainment venues; fam-

ily fun centers; Japanese-style
arcade; nostalgia; regulation
and bans
Arcade Flyer Archive, The
(TAFA). *See under* arcade preservation
arcade games/machines, 3, 5,
8–10, 11, 15, 17–18, 20–21,
27, 30, 42, 48, 50, 59, 76, 80,
83, 86, 94, 100, 152, 159, 160,
162, 175
arcade preservation, xxv, xxvii,
29, 31, 162, 163–71, 178;
Arcade Flyer Archive, 167–68;
Arcade Nostalgia, 167; Atari
Dig, xxv–xxvii; International
Center for the History of Electronic Games, 168; Learning

63, 65, 68, 70, 80, 92, 99, 100,
101, 114, 115, 117, 123, 125,
138, 141, 143, 144, 146–47,
148, 177–78, 179–80, 182, 187,
188, 191, 192, 193, 194, 195–
96, 198. *See also* gender;
sports/athleticism
"games for girls" movement, xii–
xiii. *See also* gender
gaming, xii, xiii, xiv, xvi, xvii,
xviii–xix, xxi–xxii, xxv, 3, 33,
37, 38, 48, 49, 116, 121, 168,
190, 191, 195, 196, 198, 199.
See also competition/e-sports;
gaming behaviors
gaming behaviors, xviii, 22, 55,
92, 97, 101, 102, 109, 142, 165;
addiction/obsession, 31, 62,
195; game levels, xviii, 10, 14.
See also competition/e-sports;
gamer identity; gaming
gender, xii, xiii, xvi, xxii, xxiii,
12, 19, 20, 33, 38, 41, 50,
51, 53, 55, 56, 142, 159, 181,
184, 188, 190, 197, 198, 199;
boyhood/young manhood,
xiii, xiv, xx–xxi, 1, 13, 38,
41–42, 43, 52, 53, 56, 65, 93,
115, 142, 143, 144, 146, 147,
148, 181, 188; education,
52–53, 100; inequality/male
exclusivity, xiii, xvi, 41, 50–51,
181, 182, 188, 200; women/
girls, xii–xiii, xiv–xv, xxii,
xxiii, 19, 20, 28, 33, 42, 43,
50, 51, 52, 55, 56–57, 64, 65,
68, 85–86, 114, 122, 123, 126,
157, 173, 181–82, 183–84, 185,

186, 190, 191, 195, 196, 197,
199, 200
gendered play spaces, 53, 142, 197.
See also gender
gold standard, 24
Grand Theft Auto franchise, 80,
88–89, 90
graphics, xix, 68, 74, 76, 78,
80–81, 82, 85, 89, 137, 167,
168, 177, 181, 194; cabinet,
xix, 1, 4, 6, 49, 76, 78, 80, 82,
85, 86, 122, 151, 166, 167, 175,
177, 185; on-screen, xix, 8, 67,
80–81, 82, 136, 199
Greenland, Doug, 38, 39, 40, 65.
See also Life magazine's "Year
in Pictures"
Guinness Book of World Records. See
world record

hacking, 54, 115, 117, 136, 137,
143, 146, 147, 148. *See also*
phreaking
harassment against women, xxii,
xxiii, 189–91, 197. *See also*
gender
home computing, 17, 154, 165,
195
home console, xii, xvi, xxiii, 10,
17, 113, 194, 195, 200; market,
2–3, 154, 164, 195. *See also*
home console systems/com-
puters
home console systems/computers:
Atari 2600, xi, 10; Game Boy,
xi; Intellivision, 10
homosocial, 20, 181, 182, 191. *See
also* gender

CARLY A. KOCUREK is assistant professor of digital humanities and media studies and director of digital humanities at the Illinois Institute of Technology.